D0173201

# THE GREAT BOOK OF
# PHILADELPHIA
# SPORTS LISTS

**Glen Macnow** has been a host on 610 WIP sports talk radio for 11 years, following a career as a sportswriter for the *The Philadelphia Inquirer*. He has written more than 15 books, including two extremely popular volumes he co-authored on local sports–*The Great Philadelphia Fan Book* (with Anthony Gargano) and *The Great Philadelphia Sports Debate* (with Angelo Cataldi).

**Big Daddy Graham** has been with WIP for nine years. He is one of the most successful standup comics ever in Philadelphia, working more than 4,000 shows and appearing with stars such as Ray Charles and Smokey Robinson. He is a features reporter for FOX-29 TV in Philadelphia.

**Also by Big Daddy Graham:** *Last Call*

# THE GREAT BOOK OF

# PHILADELPHIA

# SPORTS LISTS

## GLEN MACNOW & BIG DADDY GRAHAM

### RUNNING PRESS

PHILADELPHIA · LONDON

© 2006 by Glen Macnow and Ed Gudonis
All rights reserved under the Pan-American and International
Copyright Conventions
Printed in the United States

*This book may not be reproduced in whole or in part, in any form or by any means, electronic or mechanical, including photocopying, recording, or by any information storage and retrieval system now known or hereafter invented, without written permission from the publisher.*

9  8  7  6  5  4  3
Digit on the right indicates the number of this printing

Library of Congress Control Number 2006904304

ISBN-13: 978-0-7624-2840-3
ISBN-10: 0-7624-2840-6

Cover and interior designed by Joshua McDonnell
Cover photo taken by Pier Nicola D'Amico
Edited by Greg Jones
Interior photo research by Susan Oyama
Typography: Boton and Helvetica

This book may be ordered by mail from the publisher.
Please include $2.50 for postage and handling.
**But try your bookstore first!**

Running Press Book Publishers
2300 Chestnut Street Suite 200
Philadelphia, PA 19103-4371

**Visit us on the web!**
**www.runningpress.com**

# Table of Contents

# Dedication

Dedicated to my mother, Joan Macnow, who taught me the value of making lists—even if I didn't always complete all the tasks on them.

—Glen Macnow

This book is dedicated to anyone I have ever had an argument with.

—Big Daddy Graham

# Acknowledgments

Many of our media colleagues contributed their expertise to this book. Special thanks go to Ray Didinger, Anthony San Filippo, Paul Jolovitz, Ruben Frank, J Russell Peltz, Tim Logue, Zack Hill, John Russell, Ace Caccioroti, Will Bunch, Peter Mucha, George Mallet, Jackie Scheuer, and Gregg Murphy.

Thanks to Greg Jones, for approving the project and shepherding it through completion.

We also relied on an informal panel of fans, whose memories added immeasurably to many chapters. They include Harry C. Blaker, Chris Bozzi, Bruce Brachman, Saul Clark-Braverman, Harvey Cohen, Cruz, Rick Seymour Cutler, Darren "Dutch" DeGaetano, Jay Florio, Robert A. Foster, Bill Fricker, Demond Gladden, Francine Green, Earl "Buzz" Griffin, Rick Hamilton, Bill Harkness, John Heiser, Michael S. Hunn, Kevin Johnson, Mary Ann Kalnin, Steve Kennedy, Sheldon Kilby, Tony Locobianco, Paul McGovern, "No Wait" Mike, Eric J. Miller, Jon Moss, Spins Nitely, Jerome O'Neill, "Mount Airy" Phil, Craig Rittase, Geoff Robinson, Mike Romano, Joe Sharp, Drew Singer, "Movie Irv" Slifkin, Delorah K. Sullivan, Al Thompson, Neil Tobin, and John Troncellitti.

In a book full of names, theirs deserve to be listed.

# Introduction

What famous Philadelphia athlete made his screen debut starring as John Wayne's adopted Cherokee son?

What future Hall of Famer was traded away for two players whose combined age was 73?

What two local players dated *Sports Illustrated* swimsuit models? Hint: Both were past their primes when they arrived in town. (The athletes, not the models).

Those questions and thousands more are answered in this book. From the substantive (best-ever rookie season by a Philadelphia player), to the silly (dumbest local mascot), *The Great Book of Philadelphia Sports Lists* compiles the greatest, funniest, most exciting and most heartbreaking moments in our local history.

We've even tossed in some off-sports topics to add grist to the mill. Because, let's face it, when guys aren't debating sports, they're probably debating movies, music, food, and women—most often women.

And we asked some friends—about 50 or so—to lend their expert opinions. So you'll read Billy Cunningham's biggest coaching challenges, John Chaney's favorite eateries, Bob Saget's top Philly sports memories, Bernard Hopkins's all-time great Philly fighters, and much, much more.

The lists are designed—in some cases—to be definitive. And—in other cases—we hope they'll serve to start debate. Heck, the two main authors couldn't agree often enough that we faced off in a few point-counterpoint arguments.

We also realize, even as we write this book, that sports is constantly changing. So coaches we laud may get fired tomorrow, records we cite may eventually be broken, et cetera. That's okay. Feel free to write your own revisions in the margins.

So enjoy this book at the beach, by your bed stand, or—dare we say—in the bathroom. Just be sure not to walk into your favorite Philadelphia sports bar (that's a chapter as well) without it.

And if you're a bartender, you better not even *think* of not having a copy behind the bar, because it'll be sure to start many a great conversation—and resolve many a bet.

Big Daddy grew up in Southwest Philadelphia; I have lived in the Pennsylvania suburbs for more than two decades. So, we started a debate: Which area spawns more great athletes?

Of course, Big Daddy stood up for his hometown. I lobbied for the sticks. And we even involved a third party, who argues that the pre-eminent stars come from South Jersey.

Here are our lists. Let's start with mine, since it's the most impressive. But you be the judge.

**Honorable Mentions:** Jim Furyk, Brendan Hansen, Kevin Jones, Joe Klecko, Jameer Nelson, Lisa Raymond, Jay Sigel, Mickey Vernon.

**10. Billy "White Shoes" Johnson.** A flamboyant 170-pound water bug out of Chichester High and Widener, he's also the choreographer of the best touchdown dance in history. Johnson made the NFL's 75th anniversary team as a punt returner. Hmmm, Big Daddy, I don't see any Philly natives on that all-time team.

**9. Rip Hamilton.** Yeah, I hate that goalie mask, too. But all the kid out of Coatesville has done is average nearly 18 points per game in the regular season over a career, and raise that to 21 points per game in the playoffs. A true clutch player—just how we raise them in the 'burbs.

**8. Herb Pennock.** I'm going old school here with this Kennett Square legend. Pennock pitched 22 seasons in the majors (1912–34) and twice finished in the top four in MVP voting. He finished with 240 wins and a spot in the Hall of Fame. The top all-time winner from Philly? Bucky Walters with a mere 198 Ws.

**7. Leroy Burrell.** As a high school kid from Lansdowne, Burrell long jumped more than 24 feet and once scored more points in the state track finals than every member of the second-place team combined. Burrell set the world record for the 100-meter dash in 1991, and then re-set it in 1994. (On a side note, is there any title cooler than to be known as the "world's fastest human?")

**6. Emlen Tunnell.** Raised in Radnor, that famed breeding ground of football talent. Tunnell played 14 seasons (1948–61), mostly for the Giants, and was referred to as "Offense on Defense." He retired as the NFL's all-time interception leader. The first African-American inducted into the Pro Football Hall of Fame.

**5. Eddie George.** An amazing athlete out of Abington who won the Heisman Trophy in 1995 by rushing for 1,927 yards and 24 touchdowns at Ohio State. He went on to rush for more than 10,000 yards in the NFL. A shame he never played for the Eagles. By my count, there are four Heisman winners from the area—George, Ron Dayne of Berlin, N.J., Mike Rozier of Camden, and John Cappelletti of Upper Darby. You got any from the city, Big Daddy?

**4. Mike Richter**. This isn't really a fair debate here, since you city guys only know how to play hockey on sneakers and with those orange Mylec balls. Richter, born in Abington and raised in Flourtown, won more than 300 games with the New York Rangers. He was a three-time All-Star and the MVP of the 1996 World Cup, in which he led the United States to the championship.

**3. Mike Piazza.** "The Pride of Norristown," as Don Tollefson invariably refers to him. We always thought he was from Phoenixville. Piazza began as a 62nd round draft pick, chosen mostly as a favor to his dad. He'll finish his career as the best offensive catcher in Major League history. There was a period from 1995–97 when Piazza was second only to Frank Thomas as the most dangerous hitter in the game. A sure-bet first-ballot Hall of Famer.

**2. Kobe Bryant.** Folks in Philadelphia have never liked him, largely because he's a product of Lower Merion. To be honest, we don't much like him either out here in the hinterlands. But there's no denying that Bryant is one of the NBA's greatest talents ever. The owner of three NBA championship rings and one All-Star Game MVP trophy—for which we all booed him at the Wachovia Center (score one for Philly there).

**1. Reggie Jackson.** Where should I start? "Mr. October." Three homers on three pitches in the 1977 World Series. A 14-time all-star, two-time World Series MVP, and American League MVP in 1973. He hit 563 career homers and got into nearly as many scuffles with teammates and managers. You know the funny thing? A friend of mine, Dave Weinstein, who played football with Reggie at Cheltenham High, said Mr. Jackson was five times as good at running back as he was with a baseball bat.

For the record, Glen, Eddie George lived two blocks from my mother in Southwest Philly, so I'm not sure if he should even be on your list. You can have Kobe; ain't no way he'd ever be on any city list.

The dudes who didn't even make my list would top your suburban ten. Check these names out: the late, great Hank Gathers, John B. Kelly, Larry Cannon, Rich Gannon, Gene Banks, Clifford Anderson, Frank Reagan, Rasheed Wallace, Erik Williams, Ernie Beck, Del Ennis, Bo Kimble. Geez, I had to leave Guy Rodgers off the list, who's maybe the greatest player ever to lace them up in the Big 5, because he's not in the Hall of Fame.

Then I had a real dilemma. I had three amazing athletes who will all be in a Hall of Fame one day, yet I could only choose two. So let me just apologize to the legendary Bernard Hopkins—and start running! So eight here are already in a Hall, and numbers nine and ten will be there any minute. One of them is a woman, and I'd take her over stinkin' Kobe any day of the week.

**10. Dawn Staley.** OK, here we go. Three-time Olympic gold medal winner, two-time National Player of the Year at Virginia, where she went to three straight Final Fours. Numerous world championships. North Philly's Dawn was part of that famous 1995–96 national team that went 60-0. This Dobbins Tech grad has a seven-story mural at 8th and Market for chrissakes (go see it and learn, Glen), and was voted by every American athlete (not just her basketball team) to carry the American flag into the Olympic stadium in 2004. We love you, Dawn.

**9. Marvin Harrison.** As much as it pains me as a West Catholic grad to add Marvin, let's face it, this guy is going to smash a ton of records. In fact, he has already teamed up with Peyton Manning for more TDs than any other QB-WR duo in NFL history, and it's not like he's near finished. He's also a three-year letterman in basketball at Roman Catholic. Get ready to book a room in Canton the moment he retires.

**8. Paul Arizin.** Now here's a story for you: Paul didn't even make his high school basketball team at LaSalle. He went to Villanova without a scholarship. A year later, in '49, he set an NCAA record by scoring 85 points in a game. Are you kidding me? He was an All-American and the College Player of the Year his senior year, and went on to a great 10-year NBA career with his hometown Warriors. When he retired he had the third-most points in NBA history. Enshrined in the Hall of Fame in '78, Paul was named one of the 50 Greatest NBA Players ever in 1996, and there's a certain other Philly boy on this list (I'll give you a hint—he once scored 100 points in one game) who cited Paul as one of the top five players he ever saw. So for all you young heads out there, keep your chin up if you ever get cut from a team.

**7. Leroy Kelly.** Quick, name me the player who replaced a legend like Jim Brown, as Leroy had to, and then went on himself to the Hall of Fame. A Simon Gratz grad, this NFL Hall of Famer was one of the great running backs of his time (and an awesome punt returner) who missed just four games in 10 seasons. That's pretty damned incredible, Glen.

You see, city kids are slugging it out for their next meal, not over who gets the keys to the Beemer.

**6. Tom Gola.** Yet another Warrior Hall of Famer, Tom is one of only two players in history to win an NIT (when it truly mattered), NCAA, and NBA championship. Four-time All-American at La Salle College—did I mention that he also won a City Championship at La Salle High? Not only bailed La Salle College out of an ugly mess as a coach, but as a city controller, he also helped the city out of many messes. City kids remain loyal.

**5. Earl Monroe.** Look, I could rattle off a bunch of fantastic stats, but the fact is "The Pearl," a Bartram High grad, just might be the coolest man to walk the planet Earth. He should have played with a sax around his neck. By the way, I once played in a game with Earl Monroe. Got any Hall of Famers on your list, Glen, who you played with? Huh??

**4. Roy Campanella.** Another Simon Gratz alum, Roy was the starting National League All-Star catcher eight straight years. He made five appearances in the World Series with the Dodgers (unfortunately only one win), and was a three-time MVP. He hit 41 homers in '53, a record for catchers that lasted for 43 years. Elected to the Hall of Fame in '69, Roy was paralyzed after a car accident in '58, yet continued to work for Major League Baseball up until his death in 1993, teaching and inspiring all.

**3. Herb Adderley.** Get ready for these numbers by this Northeast High Hall of Famer. Won six—yes, you're reading correctly—six NFL championships, including three Super Bowls. Three of his titles were with the Green Bay Packers before there was a Bowl, then he won two Bowls with the Pack and another with the Cowgirls (and even goes to another Bowl, losing to the Colts in '71 on a last-second field goal). That's sick! Still living in the area, he calls into my show occasionally and once hit a home run off West Philly High's (and former WIP host) Steve Fredericks that Steve told me "still hasn't come down."

**2. Joe Frazier.** I originally wasn't going to have Smokin' Joe on this list because he didn't move to Philly until he was 15. But, Glen, you said if an athlete went to high school in Philly, he's eligible. Although Joe dropped out of school by that age, your qualifier still puts him at high school age, SO HE'S IN! And who's gonna knock him off this list? Not me. He was Heavyweight Champion of the World when that title truly meant something. Joe battled the greatest fighters in the world and, on March 8th, 1971, defeated Muhammad Ali in what might be the single-greatest event in the history of sports. He was elected to the Boxing Hall of Fame in 1990. I have met Joe—a truly gracious man—many times, and even performed with him once at Resorts, when he used to sing with his band, "The Knockouts." Smokin', Joe!

**1. Wilt Chamberlain.** Take every suburban lame-ass on your list, Glen, add them all up, and they still couldn't carry Wilt's jock. The man has his own chapter in this book for chris-sakes. (See page 227.) Do any of your silver spooners merit their own chapter?

## Ten Greatest Athletes from South Jersey (Sorry to Show You Guys Up) :: Reuben Frank

Note: Reuben Frank writes for the *Burlington County Times*.

Nice lists, guys. So where's the varsity?

Hey, Philadelphia and the suburbs have produced some nice little athletes. Clap clap clap.

But consider this: Heisman Trophy winner Mike Rozier of Camden doesn't make the South Jersey list. Olympic track gold medalists Dennis Mitchell of Atco and Lamont Smith of Willingboro couldn't elbow their way on. Merchantville native George Dempsey, who starred on the Philadelphia Warriors' 1956 NBA championship team? No room here. Milt Wagner and Billy Thompson, who both came out of Camden and won an NCAA title at Louisville and an NBA title with the Lakers? They don't make the cut. Check out who does.

**10. Dave Robinson.** Not just a tough, playmaking linebacker, Robinson was a tough, playmaking linebacker on one of the greatest football teams ever assembled. Robinson, a Moorestown native, was one of the key guys on Vince Lombardi's defense when the Packers beat the Browns in the 1965 NFL Championship Game and then beat the Chiefs and Raiders in the first two Super Bowls. Five years into his NFL career, he had won three NFL championships.

**9. Deron Cherry.** One of the most improbable superstars in NFL history. He was a baseball star at Palmyra. A walk-on punter at Rutgers. An undrafted free agent with the Chiefs. The guy nobody wanted became the best free safety in football in the 1980s and is considered one of the greatest undrafted defensive players ever. Cherry finished his remarkable NFL career with 50 interceptions—a record-tying four in one game. He made six consecutive Pro Bowl teams; five straight as a starter. He also received the Byron White Award in 1988 for his tireless humanitarian and charity work. He's now a part-owner of the Jaguars.

**8. Mel Sheppard.** OK, admit it. You've never heard of him. You've probably never even heard of his hometown, Almonesson. But that's what they called Deptford Township in the pre-mall days. And in the 1908 Olympics in London, Sheppard won both the 800- and 1,500-meter runs, setting an Olympic record in the 800. He also won Olympic relay gold in both 1908 and 1912. Since Sheppard, no American has repeated that Olympic 800–1,500 double, and no American has won the Olympic 1,500. He's truly one of the all-time greats, even though nobody knows it.

**7. Leon "Goose" Goslin.** He grew up on a farm in remote Salem, but by his 21st birthday Goslin was on his way to a brilliant Hall of Fame baseball career as a left-hand hitting outfielder. In 18 seasons with the Senators, Tigers, and Browns, Goslin amassed 2,735 hits, 248 home runs, and a .316 batting average. His .379 average led all of baseball in 1928, and he was inducted into Cooperstown in 1968. Goslin played in five World Series, winning one each with the Tigers and Senators. Anybody from Philly ever hit .379?

**6. Irving Fryar**. Personal problems threatened his career early, but once Fryar got his life in order he became one of the most productive wide receivers in NFL history. Fryar, a Mount Holly native and Rancocas Valley graduate, had more catches and yards in his 30s than in his 20s, and finished with 851 catches for 12,785 yards—both eighth-most in NFL history. Now an ordained minister, the Rev still lives in the area and has a church in Burlington County.

**5. "Jersey" Joe Walcott.** Walcott grew up in Merchantville and worked in the Camden shipyards while establishing a reputation as a feared local boxer in the 1940s. He lost his first four heavyweight title bouts and was 37 when he knocked out Ezzard Charles in seven rounds in Pittsburgh in 1951 to become the oldest heavyweight champ in history—a record that stood until George Foreman won the title in 1994 at 45. Walcott retained his belt until 1952, when he lost on a 13th-round KO to Rocky Marciano in what's considered by many the greatest heavyweight championship fight ever. After he retired, Walcott served as New Jersey's boxing commissioner and remained a revered figure in South Jersey until he died in 1994.

**4. Orel Hershiser.** He pitched for 18 years, won 204 games, threw 25 shutouts, received the 1988 Cy Young Award, and pitched in three World Series, winning once. But Hershiser will forever be remembered for his untouchable streak of 59 consecutive scoreless innings to end the 1988 season, a streak that broke Don Drysdale's record by a third of an inning. Hershiser, who grew up in Cherry Hill, extended the streak to 67 innings with 8⅓ scoreless innings to open the 1988 League Championship Series against the Mets. That's the equivalent of 7½ shutouts. In a row.

**3. Ron Dayne.** Forget everything you know about Ron Dayne the NFL running back. An awful lot of people have carried the football in college and none has rushed for more yards than Dayne, a Pine Hill native and Overbrook High graduate. Dayne rushed for 6,397 yards at Wisconsin, breaking the NCAA record of 6,279 set by Ricky Williams. He ranked ninth or better in the nation in rushing all four years in college and won the 1999 Heisman Trophy. And he was a national prep discus champ.

**2. Franco Harris.** Harris was a reliable, durable, productive running back during the regular season. He was picked to nine Pro Bowl teams and still ranks 11th in NFL history with 12,120 rushing yards. But Harris was all about the postseason. His bruising cold-weather playoff performances helped the Steelers win four Super Bowls in a six-year period, and he remains the Super Bowl record holder with 354 rushing yards. He retired with NFL records of 1,556 playoff rushing yards and 17 touchdowns, marks since surpassed by Emmitt Smith. Harris was MVP of Super Bowl IX and was also on the receiving end of the greatest play in NFL history—the Immaculate Reception. Can any Philly guys say that?

**1. Carl Lewis.** Ten Olympic medals, nine of them gold. An unprecedented four consecutive Olympic long jump gold medals. A world record in the 100-meter dash. A ten-year undefeated streak in the long jump. Lewis, who grew up in Willingboro, is the greatest Olympic athlete ever and arguably the greatest American athlete ever. And he's from South Jersey. Not Montgomery County. Not Delaware County. Not the Northeast. South Jersey.

I win.

## Delaware's Top Six Sports Figures :: Peter Mucha

Note: Peter Mucha is the "Early Word" blogger for *The Philadelphia Inquirer*, and once edited a magazine in Delaware—which qualifies him to write this list. Delaware is such a puny state, we only let him name six people.

**6. Valerie Bertinelli.** Oops, I mean Chris Short. (Bertinelli just looked good in shorts.) Anybody who could win 17, 18, 19, and 20 games for the Phillies (1964–68) must have, uh, been in a four-man rotation when relievers stayed in the bullpen playing cards.

**5. Pat Williams.** OK, he's no athlete, but as Sixers GM in '83, he brought Philly its last title in any of the four major sports. Besides, he's an inveterate quipster whose Web site (patwilliamsmotivate.com) has jokes like the Milton Berle groaner, "If at first you don't succeed, stay away from skydiving."

**4. (tie) Dallas Green and Ruly Carpenter**. Hey, if you don't like them on this list, the First State would like back the only World Series title the Phillies ever won, as well as its speedy ratification of the Constitution. (Green managed, and owner Ruly signed Pete Rose.)

**3. Randy White.** Hall of Fame defensive tackle for some stinkin' group of Texans. Nickname: Manster (half man, half monster).

**2. Judy Johnson.** What am I doing picking a guy named Judy who starred for the Hilldale Daisies? Well, this Negro League legend is in baseball's Hall of Fame.

**1. The Phillie Phanatic.** Of course. The alter ego of Dave Raymond, son of Blue Hens coach Tubby, did things in a green suit unrivaled even by the Lucky Charms Leprechaun. At times even funnier than that Milton Berle joke.

# Ten Best Philly Pro Players Not Born in This Country

Well, since we just covered the tri-state area (and with immigration being such a hot topic), why don't we take a look at ten superb athletes to hail from foreign soil. We're excluding Canada not only because it's so close, but because it's . . . uh . . . Canada. They drink so much beer up there we're not even sure if it counts as a country, eh?

**10. Horst Muhlmann.** This German native booted for the god-awful Eagles teams from 1975–77 and, to tell you the truth, Horst wasn't that good himself. But his name is Horst for crying out loud, so how can we leave him off the list?

**9. Kim Johnsson.** Very good stick-handling defenseman from Sweden who was exactly what the Flyers needed in 2006 when they were dumped by Buffalo in the first round of the playoffs (he missed the series, and half the season, with a concussion). This Swede is the last remaining link to Eric Lindros—he was part of the deal that sent 88 to the Rangers.

**8. Vai Sikahema.** Only returned two seasons' worth of punts for the Birds, but Vai sure made every one of them memorable, didn't he? Plus, he's from Tonga! In case you don't know where Tonga is, it's the exit between Academy and Woodhaven on I-95. For the record, you'll never meet a kinder man than Vai.

**7. Peter Forsberg.** As of this writing, he's only played one (somewhat?) disappointing season for the FlyGuys, but when you are referred to as "the greatest player in the world," you must make this list. And how many times have you been reminded that Peter the Great appears on a stamp in his homeland of Sweden? But has anyone ever bothered to check out if this is a big deal? Paul Jolovitz has his picture on a stamp in Sweden, and he's from Alabama.

**6. Pelle Lindbergh.** The first European goaltender (hey, another Swede) to win the Vezina Trophy after posting 40 victories in 1983–84. This after being the goalie on the NHL All-Rookie team the previous season. Unfortunately, they would be the only two seasons for Pelle after he tragically died in a car accident on November 10th, 1985.

**5. Tony Taylor.** "Leading off, Tony Taylor!" Boy, how many times did we hear that in our lives? This Cuban native played 14 seasons for the Phils, including a record 1,003 games at second base. Made the defensive play that saved Jim Bunning's perfect game. A real star at Phils Fantasy Camps because, and this is amazing, he's a nice guy.

**4. Juan Samuel.** Second baseman Sammy still holds a major league record for most at-bats by a right-handed batter in a season with 701 for the Phils in 1984—and that's the most by any National Leaguer in a single season. In six seasons, this Dominican Republic native made the All Star team three times and was the first major leaguer to have double figures in doubles, triples, home runs, and stolen bases in his first four seasons. A fun, vibrant clubhouse presence, Juan ended up being traded by the Phils in 1989 in a deal that brought us Lenny Dykstra.

**3. Bobby Abreu.** Whatever negative thought you might have about our favorite Venezuelan Gold Glover, his offensive numbers are just too overwhelming to ignore. As of this writing, he's into his ninth year with the Phils with a career batting average over .300 and over 800 RBIs. This man can flat-out hit, and there are fans out there who will argue that he's the Phils' greatest rightfielder ever. Just keep him away from any rightfield wall.

**2. Darren Daulton & Darryl Dawkins.** These two aren't just from other countries, they're from other planets. At least we know the name of Lovetron, Darryl's planet, but what whacked-out galaxy is Daulton from? Heard he's thinking of making a comeback—catching for Shirley MacLaine.

**1. Steve Van Buren.** This Eagles great is the only NFL Hall of Famer to be born in Honduras. I would wager he's the only Eagle to be born in Honduras. A real hotbed for churning out legendary NFL running backs. Betcha didn't know that! Huh?

And yes, we've noticed that there are no Sixers on this list. Who were we gonna include? Leo Rautins and Todd MacCulloch are from Canada, and wouldn't have made the list anyway. Samuel Dalembert from Haiti? Don't think so. However, Christian Welp from Germany just missed. Yeah, right.

Note: Billy Cunningham coached the Sixers for eight years, including the 1982–83 championship season. His 454 regular-season wins and 66 post-season wins are both franchise records.

## A Pleasure:

**6. Moses Malone.** A piece of cake. The first time I met Moses, I told him what we expected in terms of rebounding and throwing outlet passes for fast breaks—something he hadn't had to do in Houston. He immediately accepted it and knew how to do it from day one.

**5. Julius Erving.** For him to have to listen to me for eight years, well, that couldn't have been an easy thing for a superstar like him. And if he ever had a bad game, you never had to worry about the next one.

**4. Harvey Catchings.** He pretty much knew his role and accepted it. You really need guys like that: willing to come off the bench.

**3. Caldwell Jones.** He was game for anything. He didn't care if I asked him to cover a guard or a center. He would just nod and go out and do it. Caldwell didn't care if he scored a point, as long as we won.

**2. Mo Cheeks.** He was like a sponge. You only had to tell Mo something once and he had the ability to apply it from that point on. Such a smart and dedicated player.

**1. Bobby Jones.** By far the easiest player ever to coach. Bobby would do anything to help the team win. If it meant him playing five minutes or 35 minutes, he didn't care.

## A Challenge:

**6. Andrew Toney.** He's my sixth man on this team. I loved Andrew, and he sacrificed some individual talent for the success of the team. The challenge with him was that he didn't always make good decisions. I'll never forget playing the Lakers one year, in an over-time game at the Spectrum, with about 14 seconds to go. We called timeout and designed a play that would eventually get the ball to Andrew. But, as we broke the huddle, he said, 'Just give me the ball and everybody get out of my way.' Three Lakers came out at him and he took a crazy shot. Knocked it down. I walked off shaking my head. That was Andrew—he didn't always make good decisions, but they seemed to work out.

**5. Eric Money.** He was difficult to coach because he was a point guard with a scoring guard's mentality of 'shoot first.'

**4. Joe Bryant.** The issue with Joe, and I mean this in a positive way, was that he thought he should be playing more and have a bigger role on the team. Perhaps he should have, but with all the talent we had, I just couldn't find the minutes for him.

**3. George McGinnis.** He was a great player. But I think he just lost his love and passion for the game. He went on to greatness in the business world, which shows what he can do when he is motivated.

**2. Charles Barkley.** I loved coaching him, but he was such a challenge. I think he now understands that I was trying to make him as great as he could be. He showed up the first year at 280 pounds. We had to get him down under 260. He didn't think it was important to run back to half court on defense, but I could see him starting to realize how good he could be and the price he had to pay to get there. I regretted not having the opportunity to push and nurture Charles for more years to help him become his best.

**1. Darryl Dawkins.** I loved him, but I wished he embraced greatness. Darryl didn't want the responsibility night in and night out. He could have been special.

## Best Rookie Seasons

Remember Woody Sauldsberry? We don't either, but he won the NBA Rookie of the Year award for the Philadelphia Warriors in 1957–58, averaging 12.8 points per game.

Also in 1957, the Phillies had the top rookie batter (Ed Bouchee) and pitcher (Jack Sanford). The team still finished at .500. Would you have guessed otherwise?

On the other hand, the Flyers have never had a player win the NHL's Calder Trophy for top rookie.

Here are the top 10 seasons ever enjoyed by first-year players in Philadelphia.

**10. Ted Dean, Eagles, 1960.** His stats were nothing special (just 522 total yards and three touchdowns in the regular season), but the Radnor High grad came through when it counted. With the Eagles trailing, 13-10, late in the 1960 NFL title game, Dean broke a kick-off return deep into Packers' territory. Then he scored the championship-winning touchdown on a five-yard sweep. That was, if we need to remind you, the last championship-winning touchdown ever scored by an Eagle.

**9. Del Ennis, Phillies, 1946.** Fresh back from World War II, the 21-year-old kid from Olney finished fourth in the National League in batting (.313), fourth in home runs (17 in a dead-ball season), and eighth in MVP voting. So why did local fans boo him so much?

**8. Eric Lindros, Flyers, 1992–93.** Can you recall his original mates on the "Crazy Eights" line? We'll name them in a moment. Lindros scored in his first game as a Flyer and set a franchise rookie record with 41 goals in just 61 games. An omen of the Stanley Cups to come . . . oops. He lost out on the Calder Trophy to Winnipeg's Teemu Selanne, who set an NHL rookie record with 76 goals. The Crazy Eights? Lindros (No. 88), centered wingers Mark Recchi (8) and Brent Fedyk (18).

**7. Allen Iverson, Sixers, 1996–97.** AI averaged 23.5 points and 7.5 assists per game. A nice start to a Hall of Fame career. Unfortunately, he was surrounded by drek on Coach Johnny Davis's 22-60 squad. Ask people what they remember about Iverson's break-in season and most mention two things: 1) How the coach called a meaningless timeout in a late-season game to help Iverson continue a streak of 40-point games, and 2) How Iverson wore a white doo-rag to the Rookie of the Year award announcement.

**6. Keith Jackson, Eagles, 1988.** Buddy Ryan's favorite player, and we see why. He caught 81 passes (a franchise rookie record) for six touchdowns as Randall Cunningham's safety valve. Made the Pro Bowl as a starter. We just wish he had held onto that touchdown pass in the Fog Bowl.

**5. Richie Ashburn, Phillies, 1948.** A five-decade love affair got off to a quick start as Whitey hit .333 (second only to Stan Musial) and led the league with 32 stolen bases. He finished 11th in MVP voting on a team that was 22 games below .500. So how did he not win the Rookie of the Year Award? Alvin Dark of the Boston Braves had less impressive stats, but his team won the pennant.

**4. Richie Allen, Phillies, 1964.** Allen entered the National League with a bang and a 42-ounce bat. Give us a little space, please, to roll out the stats: 125 runs, 352 total bases, 13 triples—all of which led the National League. Hit .318 with 29 homers and 91 RBIs. Played in all 162 games. Also led the league in errors and strikeouts, but we're ignoring that. Allen was a transcendent, stunning talent who hit the longest home runs anyone had ever seen in this town. Alas, he was also the Terrell Owens of his era. Who knew back in the balmy summer of '64 how ugly it would all end?

**3. Ron Hextall, Flyers, 1986–87.** Who was this crazy kid from Manitoba? No one had ever played goal like this—wandering into the corners, stick-handling to the faceoff circles, scrapping with the tough guys. His regular-season numbers were terrific: 37 wins and a 3.00 goals-against average, which were good enough to win him the Vezina Trophy as the NHL's top goalie. But his really brilliant work came in the Stanley Cup Finals, where "Hexy" kept the Flyers going to Game Seven against the legendary Edmonton Oilers. He won the Conn Smythe Trophy as the most valuable player of the playoffs and, afterward, Wayne Gretzky called him, "The greatest goaltender I've ever faced." Heady stuff for a 23-year-old.

**2. Grover Cleveland Alexander, Phillies, 1911.** We needed to go old school—real old school—at least once here. Like Ashburn, he came to the Phils as a farm kid out of Nebraska and captured the city. As a 24-year-old rookie, "Old Pete" (no one likely called him that back then) led the league with a 28-13 record. He also finished first in innings (367), complete games (31), and shutouts (7), plus a bunch of stats that no one even knew existed back then, like "fewest hits per nine innings." It started a run in which he won 190 games over seven seasons, before the Phils traded him in 1918 for two marginal players and $55,000. He would go on to win 183 more games, mostly with the Cubs. The Phils would go on to stink.

**1. Wilt Chamberlain, Warriors, 1959–60.** You expected someone else? It's amazing how many lists in this book have Wilt at the top. The Overbrook High grad came home and revolutionized the sport. He wasn't just Rookie of the Year; he also won the league's MVP Award as a 23-year-old, and relegated Bill Russell to the All-NBA second team.

Wilt had passed up his last year at Kansas to tour with the Harlem Globetrotters. When the NBA finally accepted him, much was expected. His $65,000 rookie salary was the highest in the NBA. He was four inches taller than Russell, and broader and more muscular than George Mikan. Columnists worried aloud whether he would destroy the NBA.

He didn't, but he did revolutionize it. Wilt led the league with 37.6 points and 27 rebounds per game. He scored more than 50 points seven times. He played 48 minutes per game. The Warriors improved over the previous season by 17 wins. No one ever made a bigger splash.

**10. Buck–Buck.** Explaining this one is not going to be easy. First, you had to find a cyclone fence. Then you either "bought out" or did "Doggie-Doggie Diamond" to determine the order you would all go. It could be played with any number of kids, but playing with fewer than five was kind of pointless.

The first kid bent over and grabbed hold of the fence with his arms outstretched. Then, the next kid would run about 20 yards, scream "Buck-Buck No. 1!" and jump in the air. He would come down on the first kid's back, attempting to separate the poor guy's hands from the fence. If he was unsuccessful, he had to bend down and hold the first guy around the waist—beginning a small human chain.

The next kid would run down, scream "Buck-Buck No. 2!" and jump on the two guys, attempting to break the chain. On and on it went until someone broke the chain.
And you wonder why I ended up as screwed up as I did.

**9. Wireball, Stickball, Stepball, Boxball, Halfball.** Basically, any game you could play with a pimple ball. After spending a half-hour annoying the old geezer who ran the neighborhood grocery store by bouncing 30 to 40 pimple balls until you picked out just the right one, you would then argue for another half-hour over which game you would play first.

**a). Wireball.** I still occasionally play this game, and the beauty of it is you only need two guys. One throws a ball at a street wire, while the other positions himself under the wire to catch it. If the ball hits the wire on the way up or the way down, and the opposing player drops the ball, it's a home run. If the ball misses the wire and it's dropped, it's a single. Any ball that's caught is an out.

**b). Stickball.** A batter, armed with a broomstick handle for a bat, stood against a wall. Usually there was a strike zone painted on the wall. The pitcher stood about 50 feet from the wall. Before the game began, both players had to agree on a basic set of guidelines—say, a ball hit past the water fountain was a double, past the fence was a triple, into Mrs. McGillicuddy's yard was a home run. Any ground ball in front of the pitcher was an out. Two swing-and-misses, also an out.

There was a kid named Moose Kane in our neighborhood (every neighborhood had a "Moose"), who could bring it so fast, I would have rather faced Sandy Koufax. One other note: Back in 1964, Mr. Pasquale actually painted a strike zone on one of the Patterson schoolyard walls. You know what? It's still there. Forty-two years later.

**c). Stepball.** You found some steps about 25 feet from a facing wall. You could usually find this configuration in a schoolyard. A terrific thing about stepball is that, again, it was a game you could play with just two knuckleheads. One took the ball and threw it as hard as he could at one of the steps. If done properly, the ball rocketed off the step. The other player tried to prevent the ball from going by. If he caught it, it was an out. If the ball went over his head and hit the wall, he could still catch it off the wall for an out. If he dropped it, it was a hit—the type of hit based on how high the ball flew off the wall.

Okay, you don't need a college degree to understand that, do you? Depending on the wall—and I had one in my neighborhood—you could actually play this game by yourself. And boy did I ever. Hour after hour.

**d). Boxball.** Played in a cement yard, exactly like baseball except with no outfielders. The pitcher lobbed the ball to the batter on one bounce, and the hitter punched the ball with his fist. Except he wasn't allowed to hit the ball over an infielder's head. If he did, it was an automatic out. We actually had boxball leagues that were extremely competitive.

**e). Halfball.** The real beauty of this game, the true majesty of it, the social significance of it, was that the game sprung from neighborhoods where kids could barely afford a pimple ball. All pimple balls eventually destruct from the hours of play. Some of them actually split in half. One day, some Einstein, in the middle of despair because no one could afford another ball, said "Hey! Why don't we just use half the ball?"

Not only did we have two balls then, it was almost impossible to do any more damage to half of a pimple ball. Tell me this stroke of genius doesn't rank with the invention of the wheel, air-conditioning, and Viagra.

**8. Flipping Baseball Cards against the Wall.** You stood about 10 feet from a wall and tossed. The guy whose card landed closest to the wall got to keep all the cards everyone flipped. Best played with two or three opponents. All general managers back in the day got their start with this game, because you had to learn which cards to flip early—either players you had multiples of, or a card you couldn't get rid of quick enough, like a Dallas Green. Later in life, the cards got replaced with coins. From that point on it was either a trip to Gambler's Anonymous or a visit from some fat guy wearing a pinkie ring wanting to know why you were late with the vig.

**7. Synchronized Swimming under Fireplugs**. That's "fireplugs," not fire hydrants. Not only was the swimming great exercise, so was throwing early-blooming chicks under the water and running from the cops when they came to turn the plug off.

**6. King of the Hill.** You found a hill and proceeded to throw down anyone who had the nerve to challenge your throne at its peak. Simple as that. King of the Hill was at its best with about 20 guys. A tough "man's" game that Braveheart's William Wallace would have cherished.

**5. Freedom.** In other neighborhoods it was called "Arena" or "Roundup." One team of four or five guys would find spots to hide within a one-square-block radius. Blocks with alleys and shops worked best. The other team then sought to find them, catch them, and imprison them on a "base," which was usually a set of steps.

As one team's guys were caught, they were placed on the steps, which one guy guarded like a hockey goalie. At any time, any member of the sought-after team could spring from his hiding spot and, if he managed to touch the base—even with one little finger—before getting touched himself, everyone in the prison was freed. The game ended when all members of one team were finally caught.

Sometimes you found a hiding spot so good that the game might be over for hours and you wouldn't know it. In fact, I haven't seen my little brother, Gus, in 20 years. If anyone happens to be near 70th and Elmwood Avenue, could you give a look? I'm really getting nervous about him.

**4. Knuckles.** Why would a card game be considered a street game? Well, it was so savage that you couldn't play it in front of your parents, so you had to play it outside. It was sort of like rummy in that you didn't want to get caught holding cards when anyone went out. Except you didn't play it for money, you played for the right to permanently disfigure your friends for the rest of their lives. Nice, eh?

Each red card you were left holding was worth points that counted toward various methods of torture. Ten points were good for a "Choo-Choo Charlie," which gave some lucky opponent the right to take the edge of the deck of cards and run it down your arm. Other players held your arm as you screamed in pain. Twenty points might be worth a "foot sandwich," where your "friends" placed half the deck under your palm and half over it. Then Nicky Scarfo, or Jack Bauer, or Hannibal Lecter, would stomp your hand into dust with his foot. Nice way to kill some time on a summer afternoon.

**3. Hide the Belt.** If you thought "Knuckles" was a fun, sadistic game, then Hide the Belt is right up your alley—where it was usually played. The guy with the biggest, heaviest belt buckle hid it. Then the other players searched for the belt while the guy who hid it barked out hints like, "You're getting hotter," or "ice cold." Whoever found the belt earned the right to whack the other guys with it until they returned to a pre-established base. However, if the guy with the belt accidentally smacked someone already on the base, then everyone got to give him one free whack. And you wonder why Philly's murder rate is so high.

**2. Kill the Man with the Ball.** Pretty self-explanatory. You threw a ball in the air. When someone caught it, you wrestled him to the ground and stomped, kicked, bit, "killed!" Best played with about 20 guys. I often wondered what this game looked like to someone from the 'burbs who might be driving by on the way to the airport.

**1. Running from Cops.** Had this been an Olympic sport, I would have smashed every record Mark Spitz holds.

Not all stars are first-round draft picks. Here are 10 (or maybe a few more) Philadelphia heroes who arrived with low expectations but left in high esteem.

**10. Dave Poulin.** Despite being a finalist for college player of the year awards in 1982, Poulin went unpicked in the NHL draft. He played a season in Sweden, signed with the Flyers, and ended up as the team's captain for six years.

**9. Pete Retzlaff.** The Detroit Lions cut him in 1956, the Eagles picked him up for the waiver price of $100, and he ended up the best tight end in franchise history. Retzlaff played in five Pro Bowls and was a key cog in the 1960 championship team.

**8. Darren Daulton.** A 25th round pick in the 1980 draft, Dutch took a long time to blossom, but was the unofficial captain of the 1993 National League champions. In a decade of poor drafts, the Phils got lucky with this one.

**7. Andy Reid.** Okay, he's not a player. But let's face it: When the Eagles hired the anonymous quarterback coach of the Green Bay Packers to run the show in 1999, who would have thought he would end up the winningest coach in franchise history?

**6. Steve Mix.** Entered the NBA as a 5th-round pick, which is about one step above towel boy. He was waived by the Detroit Pistons, picked up by the ABA, and waived again five days later. Spent the next year out of the game. Mix came to the Sixers in 1973 as the proverbial last-guy-on-the-bench and stayed nine seasons. There's got to be a lesson there somewhere.

**5. Larry Bowa.** Unnoticed and undrafted out of Sacramento Community College in 1965. Bowa wasn't seen as much of a prospect coming up. He wasn't taken seriously when he came to the Phils, hitting just .241 his first four seasons. But he made himself into a Major League hitter and a major league pain in the neck.

**4. Mo Cheeks.** Remember Winford Boynes? Buster Matheney? Terry Sykes? Jeff Judkins? All of those guys—plus 31 others—were chosen ahead of Mo Cheeks in the 1978 NBA draft. But only four of the 35 picked over Mo scored more career points and none had more assists. And just one, some guy named Bird, retired with better Hall of Fame credentials.

**3. Seth Joyner.** Taken in the 8th round of the 1986 NFL draft, Joyner was actually cut before the season, but got called back when another linebacker got hurt. Fortuitous move, eh? Joyner emerged as the most dangerous playmaker on Buddy Ryan's Gang Green defense of the late 1980s. Toss in 9th rounder Clyde Simmons and undrafted free agent Andre Waters, and you've got some real treasures culled off the scrap heap.

**2. Tim Kerr.** The 1979 NHL draft went six rounds and 126 players deep. None of those players was this big center from Tecumseh, Ontario, who got labeled by his junior coaches as too lazy to play in the NHL. Somewhere along the way—taking cross-checks in the back, surpassing the 50-goal mark four straight years, performing heroics even while disabled—he shed that image.

**1A. Wilbert Montgomery and, 1B. Harold Carmichael.** What does it say that the Eagles all-time leading rusher and all-time leading receiver were, respectively, 6th- and 7th-round picks? Perhaps that the draft is less a science than a crap shoot. Anyway, in this town, where 1st-round picks too often end up as Bernard Williams and Antone Davis, we'll take good luck where we can find it.

Note: Angelo Cataldi has been the anchor of WIP's Morning Show since 1990. Before switching to the dark side (radio), Cataldi was an outstanding reporter for *The Philadelphia Inquirer*. In 1986, he was a finalist for the Pulitzer Prize.

**10. Jack McCaffery.** People who don't check out his work in the *Delaware County Daily Times* are missing out on a writer who actually is in touch with the people reading his column. He often anticipates fan attitudes just as they are beginning to form, and he is the one thing that all really good sports columnists should be—provocative.

**9. Glen Macnow.** No one in Philadelphia has done more, in different genres, than Glen. He has written with great distinction about politics, sports business, and sports medicine, the consummate reporter in every venue. Now he writes sports books for kids, sports books for everybody else, and is equally accomplished as a sports-talk host on WIP. The ultimate do-it-all writer, with a tireless work ethic to match.

**8. Stephen A. Smith.** It's no mystery why he has become a national phenomenon. Stephen did such a great job covering the Sixers for the Inky that he was promoted to columnist, which led to radio gigs, which led to an ESPN job, which led to his own national TV show. Stephen combines solid writing with big balls. The guy is intimidated by no one—the prototype of the true Philadelphia sports writer.

**7. Al Morganti.** Yes, he's been a co-host on the radio with me forever, but that's not why Al belongs on this list. In Philadelphia for the past 30 years, Morganti has *been* hockey. There are times when Al knew what the Flyers were going to do before they knew it themselves. He also wrote the absolute best notes column in *The Inquirer.*

**6. Stan Hochman.** A great beat writer for many years covering the pro teams, Stan then became the most reliably honest columnist in the city for decades. His relentless bashing of Norman "Bottom Line" Braman in *The Daily News* was a textbook example of how a columnist should treat a bad sports-franchise owner.

**5. Bill Lyon.** Colleagues at *The Inquirer*, including me, always harbored mixed feelings about Bill. The beauty of his writing was unrivaled in the city. But he usually took the path of least resistance—both in digging for stories and in expressing opinions. Still, his writing stands the test of time, a rare combination of perfectly chosen words and genuine humanity.

**4. Mark Eckel.** The hardest thing for a beat writer to do is offer sharp criticism about the team he covers every day. In an atmosphere of intimidation bred by the Eagles hierarchy, Mark has never blanched. He breaks more Eagles stories than anyone in the city, and he's been doing it for a generation. The fact that he's at *The Trenton Times*—and not *The Inquirer* or *Daily News*—says a lot about the clueless management at those city papers.

**3. Mark Whicker.** When I was a writer, I envied no one more than the quick-witted, memorable *Daily News* columnist in the 1980s and early 1990s. He was so funny and subtle that he would skewer an athlete or coach, and they would often never even know it. The decline of the *Daily News* sports section started when Mark left for the West Coast.

**2. Bill Conlin.** Sometimes his weird and twisted metaphors make his column more a puzzle than a treatise, but no one ever spoke more informatively and fearlessly about the Phillies. I have read most of the best baseball writers in America—it's a personal hobby—and Conlin's work in the *Daily News* is better than any who ever covered the sport.

**1. Ray Didinger.** There can be no debate that he was the best sports writer ever in Philadelphia. His coverage of the Eagles and the NFL was so extraordinary that he was inducted into the Pro Football Hall of Fame. He was also a brilliant columnist at the *Daily News*—the perfect balance of eloquence and fairness. Now at NFL Films, his work is the closest thing to pure art that sports writing will ever reach.

## The 5 Worst Sports Writers in Philly Since 1980. . . .

**5. Howard Eskin.** Most people don't remember that the irascible talk-show host took a stab at writing a column in the *Daily News* for a year or so in the mid-1990s. Designed to be a gossipy version of his radio show, it was an unmitigated disaster, combining unsubstantiated rumors with sophomoric writing. Stick to radio, Howard.

**4. Mark Bowden.** One of the most accomplished journalists of our time—*Black Hawk Down* and *Killing Pablo* are among his bestselling books—Bowden took a hiatus from real reporting to cover the Eagles for two painful years at *The Inquirer*. Bowden's problem was, every sentence on football had a "Gee, whiz" quality that made any sophisticated fan nauseous. If ever a writer proved that you can't be a fan and cover a team, it was Mark Bowden.

**3. Kevin Mulligan.** The Eagles bred a host of duds on their beat over the past twenty years, and Mulligan was one of the biggest. Somehow, he thought the best route to credibility with *Daily News* readers was to tirelessly extol the coaching virtues of Rich Kotite. Mulligan didn't know football. It's no surprise that he ended his career by writing the least-read sports column in the *Daily News,* a people column that should have been marketed as a sedative.

**2. Phil Sheridan.** There are sell-outs in the newspaper business, and then there is Phil Sheridan. As a beat writer covering the Eagles, he deserved a weekly check from the PR department. What Birds president Joe Banner was thinking, Phil Sheridan inevitably wrote. As a columnist, he has maintained his blind allegiance to the Eagles front office, and has combined his utter lack of balls with an uncanny ability to take any topic and make it boring.

**1. Diane Pucin/Claire Smith.** So bad they don't even rate individual entries on this list. Both were part of the feminization of the Inky sports section in the 1990s, and they set back women's sportswriting at least a decade in the city. Both had an extraordinary penchant for stating the obvious, badly. Never have two sportswriters been more ignorant of their readers than these two. Their only saving grace is that they left quickly and quietly.

# Five Things I Love about the NBA :: Al Morganti

**Note: WIP Morning Show co-host Al Morganti is regarded as one of America's foremost hockey journalists.**

5.

4.

3.

2.

1.

Note: Rhea Hughes has been a co-host on the WIP Morning Show since 1997. The Southwest Philadelphia native and Temple University graduate started her career as a WIP producer in 1992.

**10. "We're kind of the gold standard."** Eagles owner Jeff Lurie.
Salary cap winners, yes. Super Bowls, no.

**9. "If you want to get to know me, sorry about your luck."** Phils third baseman Scott Rolen, speaking to fans.
The poster-child in our town for why baseball players can be really unlikable.

**8. "It's kind of like black-on-black crime."** Eagles quarterback Donovan McNabb on Terrell Owens's potshots at him.
    Hey Donnie Mac, I don't think black-on-black crime involves two millionaires having a pissing match from their mansions in Moorestown, N.J. Grow up.

**7. "I'm gonna kill you. I'll kick your ass."** Temple basketball Coach John Chaney to then-University of Massahusetts coach John Calipari.
Deep down in places you don't like to talk about, you wish he had.

**6. "Fans need to learn the game."** Phils Manager Charlie Manuel.
I'd like him to learn the double-switch. Then we'll talk.

**5. "I'd like to thank my hands for being so great."** Eagles receiver Freddie Mitchell after the famous 4th-and-26 play.
If only the talent had matched the ego. What fun that could have been.

**4. "The people who listen to WIP are in South Philly f---ing their sisters."** Phils manager Jim Fregosi, 1994.
Oh, so that's why they double-park like that? Props to Glen Macnow the following day when Fregosi refused to answer questions about the remark with his line, "So how's the team?" Brilliant and witty.

**3. "Next question."** Terrell Owens' agent Drew Rosenhaus. (Repeat 13 times.)
Rosenhaus wrote an autobiography entitled, *A Shark Never Sleeps.* Hmmm, don't you think you are more of a jackass than a shark?

**2. "Practice?! We're talking 'bout practice! Not a game! Practice!"** Sixers guard Allen Iverson.
Reality television at its finest.

**1. "Win today and we walk together forever."** Flyers Coach Fred Shero right before winning their first Stanley Cup.
Um, Jeff, *that* is the gold standard.

**11. "The problem with Philadelphia fans is that they want you to play every game like it's your last one."**
Sixers center Shawn Bradley. When you think about it, the quote really sums up Bradley's relationship with the entire sport.

**10. "I don't have any problem playing outfield, except for the fly balls."**
Phils outfielder Carmelo Martinez.

**9. "This, of course, can in some way hurt his career as a professional ballplayer."**
Ugueth Urbina's defense lawyer, Jose Luis Tamayo, commenting on Urbina being charged with attempted murder in 2005.

**8. "Other than not making the playoffs for eight years, I thought we did a pretty good job."**
Phillies general manager Ed Wade, upon getting fired in 2005.

**7. "Who is she?"**
Eagles backup quarterback Casey Weldon, when told he was going to get a chance to meet ex-Beatle Ringo Starr.

**6. "Morality at this time is not a factor."**
Phils manager Danny Ozark, responding to a question of whether he thought his team had a morale problem.

**5. "Anytime Philadelphia scores over 100 points, and holds their opponent to under 100 points, they almost always win."**
Broadcaster Doug Collins, a former Sixers guard.

**4. "The game was closer than the score indicated."**
Eagles coach Joe Kuharich, after losing a game to the NY Giants, 7-6, in 1968.

**3. "They can do whatever they want. I'll still be eating steak every night."**
Phils outfielder Von Hayes, when asked his reaction to being booed by fans at Veterans Stadium.

**2. "Don't say I don't get along with my teammates. I just don't get along with some of the guys on the team."**
Eagles wide receiver Terrell Owens.

**1. "For who? For what?"**
Ricky Watters, responding to a question of why he didn't stretch out for a pass over the middle. The play, and his comments, came on Sept. 3, 1995—Watters' first game as a Bird. Despite three brilliant seasons, the quote is what most fans remember first about Watters.

# The 10 Best Movies Set in Philadelphia

Remember, this list was written before the release of *Rocky VI*. Hey, you know that sucker's winning Oscars.

**10. *Mannequin*, 1987.** You know how great *Sex and the City's* Kim Cattrall looks now? Just imagine how fine she was when this ridiculous flick was shot in Wanamaker's in 1987. Hello! It also stars *Boston Legal's* James Spader, but who cares? The plot's dumber than dishwater, but we dare you to click past this when you're channel surfing.

**9. *Rocky III*, 1982.** Now Marlon Brando's portrayal of Don Corleone was pretty impressive. Jack Nicholson as R.P. McMurphy? Decent. Jimmy Stewart as George Bailey? We guess he did a passable job. But all these so-called legendary thespians cannot hold a candle to Mr. T as Clubber Lang. He turned down *Hamlet* to do TV shows like *The A Team* and movies like *Eek! The Cat*, but, hey, we all make career mistakes, right? Why the Academy of Motion Picture Arts and Sciences has not honored "T" yet is beyond us. What are they waiting for? Here's one word the critics are in for if they don't award him soon: PAIN.

**8. *In Her Shoes*, 2005.** Yes, we know. It's a dreaded CHICK FLICK. But it features Cameron Diaz at her sexiest (and "loosest"), and it's a funny, good movie. Throw in the fact that it's also written by Philadelphian Jennifer Weiner, and it deserves to be on this list. It might have done better at the box office had they cast Mr. T as Cameron's love interest.

**7. *Blow Out*, 1981.** Directed by Philadelphian Brian DePalma, *Blow Out* is a tight little political corruption thriller starring John Travolta in one of his most underrated performances. It also features slinky Nancy Allen, slimy Dennis Franz, and a completely miscast John Lithgow as the psycho-killer. Despite the fact that it's got trolleys going the wrong way, it shows off Philly cinematically with great scenes along Lincoln Drive and a car crash into the window of downtown Wanamaker's. Look for *The Philly Fan's* Tom McCarthy as a cop.

BDG Alert: I auditioned for this movie and actually had a call back for a speaking role, but it wasn't to be. Years later, Nancy Allen married one of Philly's own, comedian Craig Shoemaker, and I spent a week in their house on Mulholland Drive in L.A. How's that for name-dropping, eh?

**6. *Atlantic City*, 1980.** Atlantic City had been dead for a long time when the casinos hit town, and this terrific film perfectly captures what happens when corporations start pushing out the little guys. Burt Lancaster plays one of those little guys—a wannabe mobster nostalgic of the days when gambling was illegal and more colorful. Tremendous Atlantic City locales, including a scene in the legendary White House, home to some of the greatest sandwiches down the shore. By the way, look for a scene where the gorgeous Susan Sarandon wipes down her "lemons" at a kitchen sink with, uh, lemons.

**5. *Witness*, 1985.** Taut cop drama starring Harrison Ford as a Philadelphia detective hiding out in Amish country from crooked cops. Realistic and gritty local-color scenes include a now-demolished hot dog joint at 15th and Chestnut in center city, plus beautiful shots of Route 30 in Lancaster. It also stars *Top Gun's* Kelly McGillis, bad cop Danny Glover (who used to play great bad guys), and Viggo Mortensen in his debut. Beautiful cinematography is complemented by a suspenseful electronic soundtrack from the legendary Maurice Jarre of *Lawrence of Arabia* and *Fatal Attraction* fame.

**4. *Philadelphia,* 1993.** City Hall looks spectacular in this sorrowful drama about an AIDS-afflicted lawyer taking on the firm that wrongfully fired him. The lead is portrayed by Tom Hanks in an Oscar-winning performance, but Denzel Washington steals the show as a homophobic lawyer who takes the case and learns that prejudice takes on all forms. Great supporting cast of Jason Robards, Mary Steenburgen, Joanne Woodward, and Julius Erving—who hangs with the bad guys and wears a bow tie, no less. Shame on you, Dr. J. The DVD gets extra points for including a Bruce Springsteen video showcasing the Philly skyline from across the river in Camden.

**3. *Trading Places,* 1983.** Other than No. 1 on this list, no film ever shot in Philly shows as many great locations as this comedy satire. The opening credits alone feature over 25 different locales—Boathouse Row, Rittenhouse Square, the Union League, and many, many others. It stars Eddie Murphy as a lowly street con artist and Dan Aykroyd as a snobby yuppie stockbroker. They're forced to unwittingly trade places after a bet is made between the scheming, wealthy Duke Brothers, played with hilarious expertise by Don Ameche and Ralph Bellamy. And all this over a single buck! The movie made huge stars out of Murphy and Jamie Lee Curtis's body. Originally written for Richard Pryor.

**2. *The Sixth Sense,* 1999.** This intelligent, eerie blockbuster—with one of the best you-never-see-it-coming endings in the history of film—holds up even after you know the finale. Haley Joel Osment as the tormented kid got all the press, but it's actually Bruce Willis as a child psychiatrist who makes it work. Willis had shown signs of serious work before, but nothing like this. Known locales like the Striped Bass restaurant are featured, but there are many scenes that, although shot on Philly streets, you're never sure exactly where they are. It all adds to the overall mystery of the film. Did you know that in *Twelve Monkeys,* shot in Philly four years earlier, Willis's character actually says, "All I see are dead people?" If you've seen The Sixth Sense, you'll get the reference.

**1. *Rocky,* 1976.** Yes, we know, it's the obvious choice, but it's the ONLY choice. The Italian Market, the row homes, the el, Convention Hall, dudes on the corner drinking and singing do-wop. And, of course, those Art Museum steps. No film ever felt more Philadelphia than this Oscar-winning classic. Sure, the fighting is ridiculous, but who gives a damn? Like all true Philadelphians, we may not always win the fight, but one thing's for sure: we'll finish it. A soundtrack that is now so embedded in our souls, it truly ticks us off when other towns use OUR theme to pump up a crowd. That theme is ours!

# The Five Best Movies about Coaching and Motivation
## :: Ken Hitchcock

Note: "Hitch" became coach of the Flyers in 2002 and took the team to Game 7 of the Conference Finals in his second year behind the bench. He coached the Dallas Stars to two Stanley Cup Finals appearances, winning the Cup in 1999.

**5. *Cinderella Man.*** The thing that impresses me throughout everything that goes on in that movie, is how James J. Braddock stays so humble. It's the quality you love in an athlete, and it's pretty rare. He fought for all the right reasons—for food and clothing and housing for his family. He didn't fight for notoriety, which never lasts anyway.

**4. *Million Dollar Baby.*** At first Clint Eastwood wants nothing to do with coaching a woman. But he watches her. He sees a work ethic and he sees talent, and that's what excites every coach. We all think we can make someone special when we see that. *Million Dollar Baby* got across the perfect feel for the special relationship that can develop between a coach and an athlete.

**3. *Hoosiers.*** To me, that's the perfect example of a coach accommodating his players and the players learning to perform for him. My favorite scene is in the title game, when Coach Norman Dale calls the final play—a shot for one of his supporting players. His team keeps staring at him, doesn't move, until the coach says, "What?"

The players all look to another teammate, Jimmy Chitwood, their star, who simply says to the coach, "I'll make it."

So Coach Dale, listening to his team, changes the play. And of course, Jimmy hits the winning shot. Sometimes, a coach has to listen to his team.

**2. *Friday Night Lights.*** The class and dignity that the Billy Bob Thornton character shows throughout the movie as the small-town high school football coach gives you a great sense of the combination of stress and pressure that comes with being a coach. Fans come up to him and say, "Hey, we love you Coach, but if you lose, you're finished." Back when I coached in junior hockey, people would talk to me like that every day.

**1. *Gettysburg.*** The whole movie is terrific, but the best part is the 20th Maine sequence. It's an eight-minute scene of Union Colonel Joshua Chamberlain addressing his troops, along with others he had to pull in because their commander was killed. It leads right up to the battle. No movie scene ever gave you a more perfect feel for why people fight and how you can motivate them.

Note: Asked about *Slap Shot,* the notorious and hilarious film about minor league hockey, Hitchcock had this to say:

"I saw Paul Newman interviewed one time saying he thought it was the most realistic movie he ever made. To be honest, a lot of the things that go on in *Slap Shot* aren't far off from minor league hockey. The crudeness and the language are pretty dead on. Hey, that was always the culture of sports at that level—play, drink, carouse, go home. I like *Slap Shot.* But I can't say I'd use it as a coaching guide."

# The 10 Worst Eagles Draft Picks Ever

Boy, we love the NFL draft, don't we? It allows fans to forever say about a player, "Well, he's okay, but for a first-round draft pick, well. . . ." Of course, it works the other way when you find a gem like Wilbert Montgomery in the sixth round. But being the whining folks we are, it's usually more fun complaining about the busts, isn't it?

**10. Mike Mamula.** The Birds moved up to get "Mr. Hurry," picking him seventh overall in 1995, and passing on Warren Sapp in the process. Mamula built up his stock at the pre-draft combine, which has forever changed the way scouts and fans look at that workout camp. He also had problems keeping his pants on—but then again, don't we all?

**9. Leonard Renfro.** A skinny, weak, and useless defensive tackle out of Colorado. When the Eagles lost Reggie White to free agency, they drafted Renfro in the first round to replace him. For that reason alone, he makes this list.

**8. Freddie Mitchell.** Freddie, oh Freddie. A first-rounder in 2001. Freddie was a star at UCLA—on and off the field—having made a couple of appearances on Jay Leno. Actually, that's where the problem started. He was just never as good as he thought he was. A very personable guy, a whacked-out quote machine, there were almost as many FredEx fans as there were detractors. Unfortunately for Freddie, Donovan McNabb was in the second camp, and Mitchell was rarely thrown the ball. The numbers "4th-and-26," however, are permanently tattooed on Eagles fans' souls.

**7. Bernard Williams.** The 14th overall pick out of Georgia in 1994, this six-foot-eight offensive tackle had talent, but preferred playing basketball and rolling doobies. There's not a lot of money in that unless you're Cheech and Chong.

**6. Jon Harris.** Big Daddy was actually with a Virginia alum when the Eagles picked this tall, skinny defensive end with the 25th pick in 1997, and even his friend was stunned. "You got to be kidding me," he cried, tossing his tuna hoagie at the TV. Ray Rhodes swore by Harris and he responded with two sacks in two years.

**5. Antone Davis.** Rich Kotite's first pick for the Birds, which should tell you something right there. A highly regarded offensive tackle out of Tennessee, the Eagles basically traded two first-rounders to get him. To make a long story short, the Packers came out of the whole mess with Brett Favre.

**4. Siran Stacy.** OK, so he's not a first-round pick (second round, 1992), but check out these facts about this running back out of Alabama: Arrested for allegedly beating up his girlfriend two weeks after he was acquitted for beating up the same girlfriend. (She didn't show in court). He was also pulled over for driving his agent's car 100 miles an hour down Broad Street. Now there's a parade.

**3. Leroy Keyes.** If the Eagles lost one more lousy game in 1968, they could have ended up with O.J. Simpson instead of this running back out of Purdue. He got switched over to d-back and lasted all of four years with the Birds. Picked third overall to boot.

**2. Happy Feller**. His name alone earns him a spot here, but there's a lot more. A kicker out of Texas, Happy lasted one season for the Eagles, converting six of 20 field goals in 1971. Not only that, the Birds cut Mark Moseley to keep him. Is everybody Happy?

**1. Kevin Allen.** The Eagles passed on Jerry Rice to take offensive tackle Allen with the 9th overall pick. He passed out from dehydration several times in training camp. He was released a year later after being busted on a Margate beach for "sexual assault." At least we got a great quote out of Buddy Ryan, who said Allen was "a good player if you want someone standing around killing grass."

# The Greatest Duos in Philadelphia Sports History

Because this is famous twosomes, we doubled the size of the list.

**20. David Akers and Koy Detmer.** Koy, for the most part, was an undersized, rag-armed backup quarterback. But he was the Michael Jordan of holders, at least according to Akers. The top kicker in Eagles history always gave credit to the guy who'd catch the ball, spin it, and place it down. Hey, he could have been stuck with Tommy Hutton.

**19. Hank Gathers and Bo Kimble.** Philly kids from Dobbins Tech playing at faraway Loyola Marymount. Gathers led the nation in scoring as a junior, Kimble did it as a senior. We still get choked up remembering how Kimble honored his fallen friend by shooting his first free throw each game left-handed.

**18. Steve Van Buren and Bosh Pritchard.** The original Thunder and Lightning. Van Buren was power and speed, Pritchard was the elusive change of pace in the backfield that led the Eagles to NFL titles in 1948–49. Those two seasons they combined for 3,114 rushing yards and 33 touchdowns.

**17. Andre Waters and Wes Hopkins.** Buddy Ryan's head-hunting tandem of safeties. Remember the infamous "House of Pain" game? Remember which one hit Ernest Givens so hard that his facemask broke and his helmet spun 90 degrees on his head?

**16. Steve Carlton and Tim McCarver.** The first time we ever heard the term "personal catcher." From 1976–79, McCarver squatted for nearly all of Lefty's 140 starts—and rested the other days. This was not an equal partnership; it was more like a remora fish that attaches itself to a shark. Said McCarver: "When Steve and I die, we are going to be buried in the same cemetery, 60 feet, six inches apart."

**15. Jameer Nelson and Delonte West.** The greatest backcourt in St. Joe's history. In 2004, they helped the Hawks become just the second NCAA team in 25 years to finish the regular season undefeated. Both went in the first round of the 2004 draft and look forward to long professional careers.

**14. Larry Bowa and Manny Trillo.** Is it possible they only played three seasons (1979–81) side by side? It seemed so much longer. The best keystone combo (we love those arcane baseball terms) in Phils history—get back to us down the road about Jimmy Rollins and Chase Utley. Together, they averaged just 20 errors a season.

**13. Mark Howe and Brad McCrimmon.** In 1985–86, the Flyers' top defensive pairing combined for 37 goals and 138 points. Not bad. What was astounding was their plus/minus marks—plus-83 for McCrimmon, and an NHL-best plus-85 for Howe. So how did this team lose in the first round of the playoffs to the sub-.500 New York Rangers?

**12. Stan Walters and Jerry Sisemore.** The rock-solid bookends of the Eagles offensive line under Dick Vermeil. They were an odd pair too—Sisemore, the silent Texan, and Walters, the analytical intellectual. The Eagles rushed for 263 yards against Dallas in the 1980 NFC Championship Game. Give Wilbert Montgomery due credit, but know that these were the guys he ran behind.

**11. Jim Bunning and Chris Short.** They combined for 70 starts, 36 wins and even four saves in the fateful 1964 season. Both made the all-star team and got MVP votes. Of course, all that we recall is Gene Mauch losing his grip as the Phils began their September swoon, and pushing Bunning and Short out to the mound on two days' rest. Their arms were spent, the season was lost.

**10. Donovan McNabb and Terrell Owens.** Ah, what might have been. In just 22 games (including the Super Bowl), they hooked up for 133 receptions, 2,085 yards and 20 touchdowns. Prorate that over a few years and you get . . . well, probably two Hall of Fame careers and a title or two. If one of them hadn't been such a jackass and the other so thin-skinned, this could have been the ultimate Philadelphia pair.

**9. Reggie White and Clyde Simmons.** The misconception is that Reggie carried Clyde (you only need first names here). While it doesn't hurt to play with the greatest defensive end of all time, Clyde more than occasionally found himself double-teamed. From 1987–93, the two combined for 162.5 sacks. We're not sure, but that may be a few more than Mike Mamula and Greg Jefferson rang up.

**8. Aaron McKie and Eddie Jones.** The second-greatest backcourt in Temple—and Big 5—history (yeah, we know Jones played some small forward) led the Owls to the Elite Eight in 1993. Both were drafted in the first round of the 1994 draft and went on to fine NBA careers.

**7. Hal Lear and Guy Rodgers.** And now, the greatest college backcourt in city history. Not many folks today can say they saw this superb pair when they starred at Temple in the mid-50s. Lear was a prolific scorer and Rodgers was the prototype for the passing point guard. They set the standard for the thousands of Philly guards that followed.

**6. Ron Jaworski and Harold Carmichael.** What quarterback-receiver tandem holds the Eagles record for touchdown passes? Not Van Brocklin-McDonald. Not Cunningham-Quick. It was the Polish Rifle and his six-foot-eight target, who hooked up 47 times between 1977–83.

**5. Maurice Cheeks and Julius Erving.** Played together for nine glorious seasons on the Sixers. We're not sure exactly how many of Cheeks's 5,023 assists those years ended up in Doc's long fingers. But we've got highlight reels full of evidence.

**4. Mike Schmidt and Greg Luzinski.** The best 3-4 batting combo in the history of the Phils—and exactly what the club was aiming for when it later paired Jim Thome and Pat Burrell. During their eight years together, they totaled 484 homers—Schmidt's parabolic shots and Bull's upperdeck blasts. Schmidt was always the better player; Luzinski the more popular one. Many fans cried when he was sold to the White Sox in 1981.

**3. Eric Lindros and John LeClair.** If you count the seasons they played side by side, LeClair averaged 48 goals and 44 assists per 82 games. The rest of LeClair's career, he averaged a scant 25 goals and 28 assists per 82 games. Lindros' production also went up with LeClair in tow, but not nearly as dramatically. It's fair to say that 88 had more to do with 10's success than the other way around. A scoring pair so good that even right-winger Keith Jones couldn't screw them up.

**2. Allen Iverson and Larry Brown.** The all-time odd couple of Philadelphia sports. They gave this town its biggest NBA thrills over the past 20 years. Like an old married couple, they alternately bickered and embraced. Thing was, they were so much alike—undersized point guards raised without fathers who always needed to prove something. That's probably why they fought with each other.

**1. Harry Kalas and Richie Ashburn.** You expected something other than Harry and Whitey? The finest broadcasting team we ever heard. For 27 years, they went together like coffee and donuts. Like beer and barbecue. Bacon and eggs. We'd better stop—we miss them *and* we're getting hungry.

Note: Bob Saget—an Abington High and Temple University graduate—formerly hosted the popular show *America's Funniest Home Videos,* and also starred as Danny Tanner on *Full House.* But if you have not seen his later work in HBO's *Entourage* or Showtime's *Huff,* or even his hilarious take in the film *The Aristocrats,* well, you're missing a darker, more hilarious side of Bob. Although he's made his home in Los Angeles for years, he never lost his Philadelphia sports roots.

**10. Chuck Bednarik's monster hit on Frank Gifford, November 20, 1960, at Yankee Stadium.**

**9. Villanova plays the perfect game, beats Georgetown in the 1985 NCAA Championship Finals.**

**8. My Phillies beat the Atlanta Braves in the 1993 National League Championship Series.**

**7. The Sixers win Game One in the 2001 NBA Finals in overtime. Remember Allen Iverson hitting that three-pointer over Tyronn Lue?**

**6. The Eagles win the 1960 NFL Championship game over Green Bay.**

**5. The Flyers win back-to-back Stanley Cups in 1974 and 1975.**

**4. Wilbert Montgomery races 42 yards for a touchdown as the Eagles beat the Cowboys in the 1980 NFL Championship game.**

**3. Doc finally gets his ring. The Sixers sweep the Lakers to win the NBA championship in 1983.**

**2. Tug McGraw strikes out Willie Wilson (again!) as the Phillies win the 1980 World Series.**

**1. The Eagles end years of frustration by beating the Atlanta Falcons, 27-10, and go to Super Bowl XXXIX.**

# The Best Pizza in the Area—a Debate

## Big Daddy says:

### 5. Allegro Pizza, City Line Avenue

I wasn't thrilled when WIP moved to City Line Avenue. A longer commute, no more view of Billy Penn and the skyline, too much traffic. It did, however, bring me back to this no-frills pizza joint that's tucked into the Pathmark Shopping Center (next to a no-name "Shoe Outlet" for crying out loud), just south of the Channel 6 and NBC 10 intersection. There's a huge variety (including a terrific tomato pie), all reasonably priced. And they've got clean tables in the back where no one bothers you while you read your Daily News or check out the news on one of their many TVs.

### 4. Mario & Geno's, Upper Darby

Directly across the street from the 69th Street Terminal in Upper Darby, not only is the pizza simply spectacular, the ambiance is straight out of a Tom Waits song; one character after another. To say you never know who you might sit next to is an understatement, and he just might be sleeping. When I lived in Upper Darby I used to ride my bike there every day and eat one plain and one pepperoni slice with a cup of water that they gave you for free. Make sure you eat it over the plate, it's so wonderfully greasy.

### 3. Pizza Villa, 381 S. McDade Boulevard, Glenolden, PA

They were in Southwest Philly, where I grew up, and this is how awesome their pizza is: 215-492-1112. That was their number when they were in Southwest. I ordered so many pies from Pizza Villa that you could, to this day, wake me in the middle of the night and I could rattle off that phone number. Haven't lost a step after 30 years; every bit as delicious and scrumptious as ever.

### 2. King of Pizza, 2300 Route #70 West, Cherry Hill, NJ

Without a doubt the best sausage pizza in the area. It's shredded, instead of chunky, which is the way all sausage pizza should be. Comfortable booths, a friendly staff, plenty of parking (it even has an old-fashioned take-out window), and a good jukebox. Now check this story out: A few years ago, everything but a few brick walls burned down to the ground. In the interim while they rebuilt the joint, someone spraypainted "Eskin Sucks!" on one of the walls. Great taste in pizza and talk show hosts? Nah, it was probably Howard himself.

### 1. Mack & Manco's, 7th & the Boardwalk, Ocean City, N.J.

The undisputed king. I've been eating their paper-thin, unique pie for over 45 years. Forty-five years! No-frills joint with tasty birch beer to boot. They're open year round, and I can't tell you how many times in the dead of winter my wife and I have been in the car, supposedly heading toward a movie, when we glance at each other and say, "What the hell, let's do a Mack's." A tad pricey, but worth every cent. If you want, you can buy a couple slices, grab a bench, and gobble down while looking at the ocean. Can you beat that? It's already in my will that when I die I want to be stuffed and placed in one of their classic green booths.

**Honorable Mentions:** D'Alfonsos on South Street, and frozen Ellio's pizza at any convenience store at 2:30 a.m. Bake it up by the slab. You're usually hammered at the time, and Le Bec Fin couldn't serve up a better meal for the occasion.

## Glen says:

### 5. Lorenzo and Son, 305 South Street
You can have your D'Alfonsos, Big Daddy. I'll walk a block west for the best pizza on South Street. The late-night creatures who form a line snaking to the street know the wait is worth it for the charcoal-touched crust, sweet sauce, and stringy cheese. The piles of strewn paper plates outside attest to its popularity. One other plus: They cut the large pizzas into six slices, not eight, so you always go home with a full belly.

### 4. Boston Style Pizza, 1432 Manoa Road, Wynnewood
This is actually my protest on this list, and here's why: Pizza isn't the kind of thing that you need to travel or make reservations for. Every neighborhood ought to have at least one terrific pizza place and mine actually has two—Boston Style and Cenzo's on Darby Road in Havertown. Boston Style, owned by a Greek family, is living proof that you don't have to be Italian to make a great pie. They make a killer baklava as well.

### 3. Chickie's and Pete's, 15th and Packer
Pete Ciarrocchi opened the city's top sports hangout in the same mall as Celebre (see my No. 2), but they both seem to thrive. Celebre is where I go for a good honest double-cheese-and-pepperoni. Chickie's and Pete's, which started as a crab house, is where I go for something different—a white pizza with chunks of lobster meat. It may not fall under your definition of real pizza, Big Daddy, but—with the sweet lobster and garlicky sauce—it's a heavenly creation.

### 2. Celebre Pizzeria, 1536 Packer Avenue
Anthony Gargano took me here originally, and I try to get back as often as I can before Phils games in the summer. It's been there for more than 40 years, which gives it a great, settled-in feel. I always love a joint where the waitresses call me, "Hon." Nothing trendy about it, just phenomenal New York-style pizza with a thin, crisp crust and tangy sauce.

### 1. Tacconelli's, 2604 E Somerset Street, Port Richmond
The blackened brick oven dates back to World War II, and the millions of pies that have gone through it add to the character of each slice. Some people think "Tac's" is over-hyped. That's fine, stay away. Shorter wait for me. I recommend the garlicky white pie with plum tomatoes, but I always try to go with a large group and order at least a half-dozen different varieties. In fact, it's common to find tables here surrounded by three generations of fans. The ambience is blue jeans and sweatshirts, and the jukebox has some great Italian and lounge-hall favorites that you don't often hear these days.

## Complimentary Nicknames

The best nicknames evolve naturally from fans, from writers, and—especially—from teammates.

We ignored manufactured nicknames for this chapter—did any Eagle fan ever really call Randall Cunningham "The Ultimate Weapon?" And we bypassed commercial hype—because "The Answer" wasn't anything that fans tagged to Allen Iverson; it was the result of some boardroom brainstorming session designed to help sell sneakers.

**15. "The Executioner."** Every boxer worth his title belt requires a decent ring name. Philadelphia boasted "Smokin' Joe," "Willie the Worm," and "Stanley the Kitten." But the name that could best throw fear into opponents, just by hearing PA announcer Michael Buffer shout it, belonged to Bernard Hopkins.

**14. "Wild Thing."** Okay, we're breaking our own rule here, because the handle was stolen from Charlie Sheen's relief-pitching character in Major League. Still, it perfectly fit Mitch Williams (691 major league innings, 544 walks). All the control-challenged Williams needed was Sheen's Buddy Holly glasses from the movie.

**13. "The Hammer."** If you ever met one of Dave Schultz's fists, you didn't have to ask about the nickname. Just check with Dale Rolfe.

**12. "Crash."** Two schools of thought on how Richie Allen earned this one. One has to do with the damage he could do to fastballs with his 42-ounce bat. The other comes from his habit of wearing a batting helmet while fielding first base—the better to ward off showers of fruit, ice, and beer cans. Teammates started calling him "Crash Helmet," which eventually got shortened to "Crash."

**11. "The Polish Rifle."** Ron Jaworski, from Lackawanna, N.Y., earned this for his heritage and his right arm. It's too bad no one uses this for Jaworski anymore. It's much more descriptive than "Jaws."

**10. "Lefty."** You've got to be pretty damned good to have your nickname stem from a body part—Lou "The Toe" Groza, Elroy "Crazy Legs" Hirsch, Muhammad "The Louisville Lip" Ali. According to baseball-reference.com, there were 169 Major Leaguers known as "Lefty" over the sport's history (and none, by the way, as "Righty"). Just three made the Hall of Fame—Lefty Gomez, Lefty Grove, and the guy with 329 wins, Steve "Lefty" Carlton.

**9. "Dr. J."** The name preceded Julius Erving to Philadelphia. In fact, it stems from his high school days when teammates marveled at how surgically brilliantly the kid "operated" on a basketball court. The measure of Erving's greatness is that the nickname got its own nickname, just plain "Doc." How many guys do you know who can be universally identified by one syllable?

**8. "World."** He started out as Lloyd B. Free, and early on, tried out the nickname, "The Prince of Midair." That clearly wasn't going to stick. A friend named him "World"—as in "Around the World"—because of his 360-degree dunks. It sounded like a call to independence—"World B. Free." He liked it so much that, in 1980, Free legally adopted it as his name. We used to hope that former FBI Director Louis Freeh would do the same.

**7. "The Minister of Defense."** The great Reggie White, an ordained minister from the age of 17, would brutalize a quarterback, and then bless the poor sap as he helped him up. Good thing White wasn't Jewish. "The Rabbi of Defense" just doesn't have the same ring.

**6. "Kangaroo Kid."** Like Julius Erving, Billy Cunningham earned his tribute on the New York City playgrounds, in this case Erasmus Hall High in Brooklyn. It is, of course, a nod to Billy C's great leaping ability.

Trivia question: Can you name the other Basketball Hall of Famer who shares this nickname?

Answer: Yeah, we didn't remember James Pollard either, although he coached at La Salle from 1955–58.

**5. "The Big Dipper."** Wilt Chamberlain hated being called "Wilt the Stilt." Felt it made him sound freakish. Didn't like "Goliath" either, for the obvious negative connotation. But he liked "The Big Dipper." Friends shortened it to "Dipper." Real close friends knew him as "Dippy."

**4. "Concrete Charlie."** The thing that no one knows is that the moniker—so perfect for rock-hard Chuck Bednarik—didn't come from anything having to do with football. It came from Bednarik's off-season job of selling concrete up around Bethlehem. At his prime, Bednarik earned just $28,000 a season from the Eagles.

**3. "Chocolate Thunder."** These days, there would likely be protests over the political incorrectness of such an ethnic reference. But Darryl Dawkins was a funny guy who gave himself a funny nickname. Indeed, Dawkins was such a character that he gave titles to his dunks, including the "Go-Rilla," the "Yo' Mama," and—after shattering a backboard over Kings forward Bill Robinzine in 1979—the "The Chocolate Thunder-flying, Robinzine-crying, teeth-shaking, glass-breaking, rump-roasting, bun-toasting, wham-bam, glass-breaker-I-am jam."

**2. "The Voice of God."** We're not sure how many people are still alive who remember John Facenda as a newsman at WIP-AM and, later, as Philadelphia's first prominent TV anchorman at WCAU. But everyone recalls his stentorian baritone voice intoning about "the frozen tundra of Lambeau Field" for NFL Films. Facenda's pipes were so good that he could make a fumble-filled clunker sound like an epic gladiatorial battle. His family trademarked his voice and, after his death, sued the Campbell Soup Co. for using a sound-alike in ads.

**1. "The Boston Strangler."** We'll just leave the words to Larry Bird: "Do I remember Andrew Toney? The Boston Strangler? Yeah, I remember him. I wish we would've had him. He was a killer. We called him the Boston Strangler because every time he got a hold of the ball we knew he was going to score. He was the absolute best I've ever seen at shooting the ball at crucial times. We had nobody who could come close to stopping him. Nobody."

**15. "Bottom Line."** As in "Bottom Line Braman." Credit Daily News columnist Stan Hochman for succinctly labeling the Eagles' cheapskate owner.

**14. "Skates."** Here was a typical game call when Skates was on base: "Lonnie Smith rounds second, he's headed for third. . . . oh no, Lonnie Smith has slipped and fallen down! Again!!"

**13. "Puddin' Head."** The nickname derived from a popular song of the 1930s and, apparently, was common to guys who were, shall we say, challenged by the mental intricacies of the game. We can't be sure whether that applied to Whiz Kids third baseman Willie Jones, but we sure wish the nickname had survived. Wouldn't you love to have seen "Puddin' Head Francona"?

**12. "Arnold."** This one just isn't nice. Flyers teammates insisted that the pug-nosed Bill Barber resembled Fred Ziffel's pet pig in Green Acres, so, well. . . .

**11. "Losing Pitcher."** With a career record of 45 wins and 89 loses, Phils hurler Hugh Mulcahy got this tag because the words "Losing Pitcher" always ran next to his name in the box score. On a separate note, Mulcahy is the answer to the trivia question: Who was the first major leaguer to join the armed services after Pearl Harbor? He probably thought he'd be safer on the front line than on the pitcher's mound.

**10. "Highway 59."** Opponents mocked Eagles defensive end Mike Mamula—playing off his jersey number and his inability to stop the run. "If you want to go a long distance, just go by Highway 59."

**9. "Fat Balloon."** Rhymes with Pat Falloon. Also describes Pat Falloon's physique pretty accurately.

**8. "Big Dog."** Funny thing is, Big Dog was hung on Glenn Robinson back in his college days and was first meant as a compliment, as in, "Leader of the pack." By the time Robinson got to Philly, it was meant as an insult, as in, "What a mutt."

**7. "The Rat."** Kenny Linseman looked like a rat, leaned forward on his skates like a rat, played chippy, nasty hockey like a rat. Today, he says he regrets the nickname. But as a young player he embraced it, once posing for a magazine cover with a rat on his shoulder.

**6. "Head."** Former Phil Dave Hollins carried this one for years because of, a) his extra-large cranium (supposedly he wore a 7-7/8 cap) and, b) he was a major head case. No one, of course, had the guts to call him the name to his face.

**5. "Dirty."** Just like every guy named Rhodes becomes "Dusty," every guy named Waters (or Watters) becomes "Muddy" or "Dirty." In the case of Andre Waters, however, the latter designation fit. We think it was *Monday Night Football* announcer Dan Dierdorf who started it.

**4. "The Fog."** A perfect name for Flyers coach Fred Shero, who seemed in a perpetual daze. Ever hear about the time he went for a walk between periods of a game in Atlanta and locked himself out of the arena?

**3. "Titleist Head."** Teammates hung this on a young Mike Schmidt, comparing his facial pockmarks to a dimpled golf ball. And you thought that Philadelphia fans were rough on Schmitty?

**2. "Five-for-One."** Again, the toughest abuse usually comes from teammates. Von Hayes was a guy cursed by expectations. Scouts looked at his sweet left-handed swing and projected a Cooperstown career. The Phils traded Cleveland a quintet of players just to learn that potential doesn't always translate to performance. Pete Rose used to taunt Hayes by suggesting he change his uniform number to 541.

**1. "Toast."** Marvelous. Just right. What do you call a cornerback who repeatedly gets burned? In Izell Jenkins's case, Toast was the ideal handle. There is debate whether Jenkins or the Giants' Elvis Patterson was the first to be named after singed bread. No matter. We'll take ours with green jelly.

## Fifteen Guys Whose Names Sound Dirty (But Are Not)

**15. Anatoli Semenov,** Flyers center, 1994–96.
**14. Heinie Sand,** Phils shortstop, 1923–28.
**13. Dick Pierce,** Phils outfielder, 1883.
**12. Pete Peeters,** Flyers goalie, 1978–82, 1989–91.
**11. Seth Morehead,** Phils pitcher, 1957–59.
**10. Wagon Tongue Keister,** Phils outfielder, 1903.
**9. Harry Kane,** Phils pitcher, 1905–06.
**8. Dick Harter,** Penn basketball coach, 1966–71.
**7. Charlie Fuchs,** Phils pitcher, 1943.
**6. Karl Dykhuis,** Flyers defenseman, 1994–2000.
**5. Dick Cherry,** Flyers defenseman, 1968–70.
**4. Harry Cheek,** Phils catcher, 1910.
**3. John Booty,** Eagles defensive back, 1991–92.
**2. Jim Beaver,** Eagles guard, 1962.
**1. Jay Baller,** Phils relief pitcher, 1982, 1992.

**10. Bob Froese.** What a perfect name for a hockey player.

**9. Todd Frohwirth.** In fact, the Phils reliever couldn't Frohwirth a damn.

**8. Bill Champion.** Four years with the Phils, eight in the majors—you'd think he would have had at least one shot in the post-season.

**7. Jeff Hackett**. Or, as he was known in pressure situations as Flyers goalie, Jeff "Can't" Hackett.

**6. Darren Rumble.** As the name suggests, a pretty fair hockey fighter.

**5. John Strike.** Eleven Ks in 15 innings pitched for the 1886 Phils. We wish we had more information to go on.

**4. Bob Walk.** Actually, the rookie surprise of the 1980 Phils pitching staff had pretty good control.

**3. Izzy Goodenough.** The answer to the question, unfortunately, was no.

**2. Dave Philley.** This outfielder was destined to play for the Phillies. Too bad that long-time NHL mucker Mike Eagles didn't play football as well.

**1. Mike Quick.** Oh yes, he was. He also could have been named Mike Goodhands.

## Ten Guys with Bad Names for Tough Athletes

**10. Joe Lavender,** Eagles defensive back, 1973–75.

**9. Dean Wink,** Eagles defensive tackle, 1967–68.

**8. Kenny Rose,** Eagles linebacker, 1990–94.

**7. Cliff Politte,** Phillies pitcher, 1999–2002.

**6. Ray Prim,** Phillies pitcher, 1935.

**5. Lance Parrish,** Phillies catcher, 1987–88.

**4. Putsy Caballero,** Phillies infielder, 1944–52.

**3. Jennings Poindexter,** Phillies pitcher, 1939.

**2. Mark Lamb,** Flyers center, 1993–95. Actually played with a bit of an edge.

**1. Todd Pinkston,** Eagles wide receiver, 2000–present. Hey, in this case, the name fits.

## Four Old-Time Phils Who You'd Want to Party With

**4. Johnny Lush,** Phils pitcher, 1904–07.

**3. Lil Stoner,** Phils pitcher, 1931.

**2. Bud Weiser,** Phils outfielder, 1915–16.

**1. Charles Yingling,** Phils outfielder, 1894.

# You Mean the Guy Who Walked on the Moon?

Lots of folks share names with famous people. Hell, for a few seasons in the 1980s, Derek Smith played for the 76ers while Derrick Smith skated for the Flyers. Here's a list of Philadelphia athletes whose monikers matched those of notable folks.

**20. Neill Armstrong,** Eagles end and American astronaut.

**19. Bill Bradley,** Eagles safety and U.S. Senator (yeah, we know he also played for Princeton and the Knicks).

**18. Paul Brown,** Phillies pitcher and football pioneer.

**17. George Burns,** Phils first baseman and age-defying (though finally dead) comic.

**16. Glenn Campbell,** Eagles defensive lineman and "Wichita Lineman."

**15. Rocky Colavito,** Eagles linebacker and Cleveland Indians outfielder.

**14. Phil Collins,** Phils pitcher and Genesis drummer.

**13. Jack Dempsey,** Eagles offensive tackle and heavyweight champion.

**12. Glenn Frey,** Eagles halfback and Eagles guitarist.

**11. Keith Jackson,** Eagles tight end and Hall of Fame college football announcer.

**10. Spike Jones,** Eagles punter and comedic big-band leader (and music video director).

**9. John Kennedy,** first black Phillie and first Catholic president.

**8. Don King,** Eagles tackle and corrupt boxing promoter.

**7. Don MacLean,** Sixers stiff and crooning singer of "American Pie."

**6. Steve Martin,** Eagles linebacker and comic actor.

**5. Russ Meyer,** Phils pitcher and porno director.

**4. Paul Neumann,** Sixers guard and popcorn-manufacturing actor (yeah, we know, that one's spelled Newman).

**3. Ken Reeves,** Eagles guard and "The White Shadow."

**2. Mike Wallace,** left-handed Phils pitcher and left-leaning CBS broadcaster.

**1. Ted Williams,** Eagles halfback and frozen Hall of Fame slugger.

# Spelling Bee

Yeah, we don't understand why ESPN considers this a sport either, but if they're going to cash in on spelling bees, we don't want to be left out.

Here are 20 of the all-time most challenging names in Philadelphia sports history, listed in alphabetical order by last name. If you're reading this, of course, you can't take the quiz. But run these names by a friend. If he can correctly spell 10 of them—first and last names—he'll probably beat you in Scrabble. If he can spell 15, he ought to be working on a newspaper copy desk. And if he can spell all 20, tell him we said thanks for buying the book.

**Porfirio Altamirano,** Phillies pitcher
**Doug Brzezinski,** Eagles guard
**Viacheslav Butsayev,** Flyers forward
**Kurt Gouveia,** Eagles linebacker
**Marc Iavaroni,** Sixers forward
**Andre Iguodala,** Sixers forward
**Pete Incaviglia,** Phillies outfielder
**Joe Lefebvre,** Phillies outfielder
**Billy Melchionni,** Villanova and Sixers guard
**Bill Mlkvy,** Temple forward
**Nazr Mohammed,** Sixers center
**Antero Niittymaki,** Flyers goalie
**Ugonna Onyekwe,** Penn forward
**Branko Radivojevic,** Flyers forward
**Mike Rogodzinski,** Phillies outfielder
**Hank Siemiontkowski,** Villanova forward*
**Junior Tautalatasi,** Eagles running back
**Morris Unutoa,** Eagles center
**John Vanbiesbrouck,** Flyers goalie
**Valeri Zelepukin,** Flyers forward

* Near as we could determine, Hank Siemiontkowski's name is the longest of any athlete who ever played on a major local sports team. The shortest? How about Joe Roa?

Note: South Philadelphia native and comedian Dom Irrera has been entertaining audiences for almost 30 years. He has appeared on *The Late Show with David Letterman, The Tonight Show, Oprah,* and *Late Nite with Conan O'Brien.* He won two cable ACES for his specials on Showtime and with Rodney Dangerfield. He has appeared on *Seinfeld* and other sitcoms, and in numerous films, including *The Big Lebowski.*

If this wasn't enough, Dom also went to Big Daddy's alma mater, West Catholic. Anyone who has seen Dom's live stage show (and if you haven't, shame on you) knows that Dom loves to pepper his routines with colorful Philly street nicknames.

Check out when Dom is performing in the area at www.domirrera.com

**9. "Beaver & Turtle."** Beaver and Turtle were brothers. Beaver had these two big teeth sticking out, and Turtle was a big, slow, hairy bastard. What else would you call them?

**8. "Joey Bag of Donuts."** I'm not even sure where I first heard this one. It was always just floating around. I've known many "Joey Bag of Donuts" in my time. There's no specific reason to even call anyone this, but somehow the name always seems to apply.

**7. "Little Petey."** That's the name I use in my show. But it was actually based on these three relatives I had that we called "Little Lenny," "Medium Lenny," and "Big Lenny." "Medium Lenny," that's the killer name.

**6. "The Nut."** Here's the beautiful thing about this nickname. The Nut's mother hated that we called her son "Nut." So what did we do? We would call his house all the time and say, "Hey Mrs. McGillan, is the Nut home?" We were real nice kids.

**5. "Jimmy the Woman."** There was a "woman" who walked through our neighborhood that we heard was a transvestite. Who knows if it was even true? But we always shouted out, "Here comes Jimmy the Woman."

**4. "Malnu."** This guy came from a big family. They were poor and he was always complaining that they never had anything to eat. He looked terrible. So we called him "Malnu," which was short for malnutrition.

**3. "Mouthpiece."** What else would you call a guy who had no teeth?

**2. "Ritchie the Brick."** An ex-con from a few blocks away who actually served time in jail for killing a man by hitting him in the head with a brick. So what did we do? We reduced this horrible act to a nickname. We were nice kids.

**1. "Barabbas."** He was an older man from around the corner who was fond of saying, "You guys are crucifying me here!"

# The 10 Best Things about the Palestra

**10. It's still great.** I wish everyone would stop waxing nostalgic about it. There are still many, many great sold-out games a year there. Just go.

**9. Those weird windows on the ceiling.** Name another arena where light pours though the roof during a day game. It makes for really odd lighting, which further adds to the building's uniqueness.

**8. You can take a trolley to it.** I have always said that the main reason college football wasn't big in this town was because you couldn't take a trolley to a big-time game. I don't believe the "36" has a stop in Happy Valley. But the greatest teams in the country (Duke, Kansas) have come to the Palestra since it opened in 1927, and you can still get there on Septa.

**7. Everyone shares the same concourse.** Whether you're sitting in the front row or at the tippy-top with your back against a radiator, everyone ends up lumped together in the same tiny hallway at half-time—unlike the Wachovia Center (or whatever they call it these days) which separates its fans by ticket price like the Titanic.

**6. The location.** Plopped right down in the middle of a beautiful college campus. Not a meat warehouse in sight.

**5. It's loud.** Ask any opposing coach to name the loudest venue in the country and to a man he'll tell you it is the Palestra. There's no carpeting anywhere. Not one seat has a cushion. No tiled ceiling. There's nothing to absorb any sound.

**4. The soft pretzels outside.** "Cheaper outside than inside." Not to mention that the guy you buy them off inside isn't wearing crummy looking gloves with the fingers cut out of them.

**3. Divided by two.** When it's a Big 5 battle, you get one team's fans on one side of the building and the other team's fans on the other. This just doesn't happen anywhere else.

**2. Every seat is great.** Granted, very few of them have backs, and you're in big trouble if you're sitting next to anyone even 20 pounds overweight. But every seat is right on top of the players. If Hickory High coach Norman Dale (Gene Hackman) asked a player to tell him what brand of gum an opponent was chewing, well, not only could his player smell the Dentyne, but most of the fans in the stands could as well. And it seats almost 9,000, which makes this even more amazing. This is no small arena.

**1. No luxury boxes.**

**Note: John didn't want to rate this list, so the names are in alphabetical order.**

**Chuck Daly, Penn.** He twice took Penn, an Ivy League school, to the NCAA East Regional Finals, which was a tremendous accomplishment. You just can't overlook what Chuck Daly did before he became such a successful NBA coach.

**Fran Dunphy, Penn** (and now Temple). My pick of the litter because of one reason: He did a lot at Penn with a little. He was perhaps second in the Ivy League to Petey Carril (of Princeton). Fran has won 10 Ivy League titles, Petey won 12. Fran would have surpassed that record if he didn't move to Temple.

**Tom Gola, La Salle.** Tommy is the one who came along at a time when La Salle was going through problems (because of a scandal), and someone like him was really needed. He inherited a team that had many good players and took them to great heights. Tommy was an All-American player. He's in the Hall of Fame. And he happened to be one of our great coaches and someone that I respect highly.

**Ken Loeffler, La Salle.** I did not know him, but I knew of him. He took that La Salle team (in 1954) to the NCAA championship. The next year they went back to the Final Four, against the (Bill) Russell team from the University of San Francisco. He is certainly somebody we should respect as being one of the greats.

**Harry Litwack, Temple.** Harry was one of the creators and another Hall of Famer. Before I got involved in this, coming out of high school, he was always someone I looked at as being special. He produced a number of great players—Guy Rodgers and Hal Lear, among many others. He also was one of the first to produce the 3-2 zone, one of the zones that we still use as well.

**Herb Magee, Philadelphia University.** Herbie should be in the Hall of Fame. He has won a National Championship at the Division II level. He certainly is one of the best-kept secrets in this city. He should have been coaching at the Division I level, but he coached a Division II team and has certainly gone largely unrecognized. He is certainly one of the great minds and one of the great shooting coaches in basketball. I really revere him.

**Rollie Massimino, Villanova.** He won a national championship here against one of the hot-button teams of all time, Georgetown. What else do you need to say?

**Speedy Morris, La Salle.** Speedy is just Philadelphia. He certainly made a great transition from being one of the great high school coaches in the city, to coaching women's basketball, to running a successful men's team at LaSalle. He is one of our overlooked great coaches. I admire him and love him dearly.

**Jack Ramsay, St. Joseph's.** He was always innovative and creative. He is another Hall of Famer from St. Joe's and the one who created, and has written books on, the full-court pressure defenses he employed. One of our most innovative and creative coaches, he won titles here in the Big 5 and also won titles in the NBA.

Note: John Chaney retired from his Hall of Fame career at Temple in 2006. He's been a fixture in Philadelphia sports for decades, not to mention the community.

"These are the places that I attend that are pretty special," John says of his favorite food joints. "It is almost like a sin if you don't find places of this kind to find your niche as far as food is concerned."

**6. Groben's, 2629 W. Girard Avenue.** Groben's has some of the greatest seafood anywhere. They have got the Alaskan king salmon there, which is a little bit different, and the wild Alaskan salmon there, all the great fish—exotic fish—you can get there. And it is the freshest fish ever—fresh fish every day. Open every day except Sundays and Mondays, up until about six o'clock in the evening.

**5. DiNardo's, 312 Race Street.** My seafood place for crabs is DiNardo's. I only get the real big ones, coming out of Texas I think. They serve them with a delicious celery-seed spice on them. I love them dearly.

**4. Tommy Gunn, 4901 Ridge Avenue.** I only go there for one thing, and that is brisket. They have some of the best beef brisket. Try the brisket sandwich, which is so good. And the sauce that he makes is outstanding. You can even take some of the sauce home and use it for your own ribs.

**3. Whooleys, Mount Pleasant Street, Ambler.** It's pronounced "Hooleys," and it's an open-pit barbecue right out there on the street next to the VFW post. It's only open on Friday, Saturday, and Sunday. They've got one of the biggest grills I have ever seen. They start cooking very early in the morning and all day long they are cooking chickens and barbecued ribs and pork. It is one of the best-kept secrets in the area.

**2. The Rib Crib, 6333 Germantown Avenue.** They only open on Thursdays, Fridays, and Saturdays, and they start cooking on Wednesday and stacking the ribs up on racks, where they smoke them. They just keep turning them and smoking them all Wednesday in this big brick house. You see, you are not supposed to soak ribs. You don't put ribs in a boiling pot and then claim they are falling off the bone. You could be eating fat, grease, and everything else. You want to eat meat like a Viking—rip it right off the bone.

I have been around the world with barbecue—even down in Argentina, where they dig holes and barbecue whole pigs. I have been to some of the best places in this country for ribs—South Carolina, Florida, New Orleans, Memphis. The Rib Crib is among the best anywhere.

It is all take-out, it is not eat-in, and it is one of the best-kept secrets in the world.

**1. Colleen's, 2200 Ben Franklin Parkway.** They do just about everything. You can go in there and get short ribs. You can go in there and get chicken or lobster tail and shrimp, or anything you can think of. What I like best is the broiled lamb chops. It's all prepared by Les, who's the best. He opens maybe three or four times a week, but he also performs wedding receptions and other events. We even have our Big 5 banquets there. Les gives you so much. That is one of the best places and it is right on the Parkway.

To be honest, we could push this list past 100, so we limited eligibility to athletes who got in trouble while actually playing in Philadelphia—leaving out the likes of Craig MacTavish (who served a year in jail for vehicular homicide before he got here) and Pete Rose (convicted of tax evasion after he left). The criterion also leaves out Edwin "Alabama" Pitts, who came to the Eagles in 1935 straight from a five-year armed-robbery stretch in Sing Sing Prison. These are not all necessarily the most serious run-ins—just the most unforgettable.

**10. Jason Michaels.** Stupid athlete law No. 1: If you're going to wrestle with bar bouncers, make sure they're not Philadelphia cops. Michaels took umbrage at being tossed from 32 Degrees, a popular Olde City nightspot, in July 2005. The Phils outfielder took a few punches at an officer and was immediately pounced upon by five others. Our favorite part of the story was the reaction of Michaels' drinking partner, Pat Burrell. Upon seeing his buddy in trouble, Burrell instantly split the scene. Isn't there a guy rule about never leaving a friend behind in a fight?

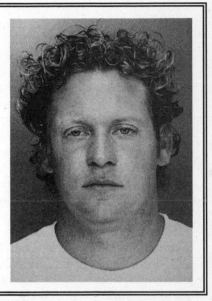

**9. Damon Moore.** Stupid athlete law No. 2: Don't adopt an animal unless you intend to care for it. Moore, an Eagles safety, decided he couldn't handle a three-month-old Rottweiler, so he tied it to a tree at a park in Voorhees and walked away. Cops later found the dog and connected it to Moore, who received a $2,000 fine and 20 hours of community service—sweeping up dog poop at an animal shelter. The case kicked up a box of bad karma for Moore, who soon after injured his knee, got cut by the Eagles and went to the Bears, where he flunked a drug test.

**8. Lenny Dykstra.** Headed home from a teammate's bachelor party in 1991, Dykstra wrapped his brand new Mercedes around a tree in Radnor and broke a few bones. Teammate Darren Daulton, riding shotgun, fractured the orbital socket around his left eye and missed several months. Legendary stories emerged around the late-night romp, but we can only print what we know to be true—or at least what won't get us sued. Anyway, Dykstra was charged with drunken driving, but his record was expunged after he entered a program for first-time offenders.

**7. Mike Mamula.** The under-performing first-round pick was accused of dropping his pants before an Allentown waitress in 1997 after being told he couldn't order a beer after last call. Mamula denied the incident and the Lehigh County district attorney eventually decided not to press charges. That didn't stop Eagles fans from sharing thousands of jokes over the incident, our favorite being that indecent exposure claims against Mamula were dropped for lack of evidence.

**6. Eric Lindros.** As a 19-year-old in 1992, Lindros was arrested after an incident at a Whitby, Ontario bar named Koo Koo Bananas. An innocent young thing accused the Flyers star of spitting beer at her and pouring a pitcher over the back of her head. Lindros was brought to trial, but acquitted when others testified that both Lindros and the girl were in the middle of an Animal House-style food fight, with geysers of suds flying everywhere. Ahh, youth.

**5. Allen Iverson.** In case you slept through July 2002, we'll remind you. A.I. was arrested after police said he barged into a West Philly apartment—toting a gun—and threatened two men (one of whom was wearing hot pants) while looking for his wife, with whom he had fought earlier that night. A judge later dismissed all the charges. All we are left with is the memory of the week-long media stakeout around Iverson's Gladwyne home. Osama bin Laden never drew so much attention.

**4. Eddie Bouchee.** In February 1958, Bouchee, a 25-year-old Phillies first baseman, pled guilty to a series of sex offenses—specifically, indecent exposure involving young girls. He received a sentence of three years' probation and was ordered into a rehab program. Here's the amazing part: In May, the Phils brought him back for the rest of the season. And the season after that. And, by most accounts, there was no uproar from the fans. Somehow, we don't think that putting a pedophile in the starting lineup would go over so well these days.

**3. Sonny Liston.** Sure, we could fill this book with a list of boxers who did time, but we'll limit it to this city's first heavyweight champ. Liston had already served several stretches in the big house before he moved here in 1960. In 1961, Philadelphia cops arrested him twice—once for disorderly conduct and resisting arrest and a month later for impersonating a cop. When he won the belt in 1962, *Daily News* sports editor Larry Merchant wrote: "A celebration is in order. Emily Post would probably recommend a ticker-tape parade. For confetti we can use shredded warrants of arrest."

**2. Ugueth Urbina.** For sheer weirdness, this one takes the prize. The Phils setup man was arrested in his native Venezuela soon after the 2005 season. Several workers on his farm claimed that Urbina accused them of stealing a gun. He then, they claimed, attacked them with a machete and followed that up by dousing them with gasoline and setting them on fire—three times. Urbina was charged with—among other things—attempted murder.

**1. Kevin Allen.** The Eagles reached up to draft this stiff of a tackle in 1985—passing up Jerry Rice, by the way. He played one terrible season and then was convicted of raping a woman on the beach in Margate in October 1986. Allen served 33 months in prison after a jury chose not to buy his story that he "mistakenly believed that the woman consented to have sex" with him at the same time that Allen's partner in crime was 20 yards away, beating up her boyfriend.

# The Worst Quarterbacks in Eagles History
## :: Mike Missanelli

Note: Mike Missanelli is a graduate of Bristol High, Penn State, and Widener Law School. He formerly wrote for the Inquirer and has been a popular host on WIP and WMMR radio.

**10. King Hill (1961–68).** Norm Snead wasn't exactly Joe Montana back then, so we longed for his backup. Ooops, he couldn't play. Besides that, one of the ugliest players of his era, with a crew cut that looked like a bed of nails. I was about seven years old at the time and King Hill scared me more than an episode of *The Outer Limits.*

**9. Mike Boryla (1974–76).** Smart kid. Went to Stanford. Good bloodlines. His dad, Vince, was a former NFL player. His paper arm couldn't cut it in the big leagues.

**8. Rick Arrington (1970–73).** Backup to Snead and then Pete Liske. Did nothing in the NFL, but later produced a pretty hot offspring in sideline reporter daughter Jill Arrington.

**7. Jeff Kemp (1991).** Went to Dartmouth. Should have stayed there and gotten a PhD.

**6. Bobby Hoying (1996–98).** The kid from Ohio State was once a quarterback with promise after filling in adequately for Ty Detmer during the 1997 season. Then, he mysteriously forgot how to play. And unlike A.J. Feeley, he can't blame it on a beautiful female soccer player weakening his legs.

**5. Koy Detmer (1997–forever).** As a quarterback, he was a good holder for David Akers. Research studies conclude that this man cashed more undeserved checks than any player in NFL history.

**4. Pat Ryan (1991).** Randall was hurt. Jim McMahon got hurt. Brad Goebel got hurt. So head genius Rich Kotite was forced to reach out to this former Jet, who had been retired and working on a construction site in Tennessee. Rosie the Riveter may have had a better touch. But in all fairness, he was, at that time, a construction worker—not a quarterback.

**3. Brad Goebel (1991).** A late-round draft pick from that football factory, Baylor. They called him "Gabe." But the only thing he may have had in common with Roman Gabriel is that he wore a single-digit number.

**2. Doug Pederson (1999).** The precursor to the Donovan McNabb era. Interestingly, I have absolutely nothing to say about Doug Pederson. His name leaves me limp.

**1. Mike McMahon (2005).** Maybe I judge him most harshly because he's the most recent. But this guy showed me no discernible skill. He was "horrenable." He was horrendous and therefore left me miserable.

**10. Bill Cowher.** The jut-jawed, froth-spewing head coach of the Pittsburgh Steelers was the last linebacker cut by the Eagles in 1979. He played three seasons in Cleveland, before being traded back here in 1983 for a ninth-round draft pick. He was named the Birds' most valuable special-teams player that season. The following year a knee injury ended his playing career.

**9. Lena Blackburne.** For more than 80 years, umpires have used mud from Blackburne's secret spot in the Delaware River to rub the gloss off new baseballs. Blackburne reportedly made millions selling the "magic mud" to Major League Baseball—a whole lot more than he earned playing infield for the Phils in 1919.

**8. Bud Grant.** You know Grant from those four losing Super Bowls he coached for the Minnesota Vikings. Before all that, he was the Eagles first-round pick in 1950, and finished second in the NFL with 56 receptions in 1952. He then left Philadelphia to play for the Winnipeg Blue Bombers in the Canadian Football League. What was up with that?

**7. Sparky Anderson.** The white-haired curmudgeon who managed both Cincinnati and Detroit to World Series titles played exactly one Major League season. He started 152 of a possible 154 games at second base for the Phils in 1959 as George Anderson, but was not invited back for the following season. Perhaps the .218 batting average had something to do with it. You know the saying, "Those who can't do, teach."

**6. Irv Kupcinet.** You may not know the name, but Kupcinet was a legendary Chicago newspaper columnist for more than 50 years and the host of CBS's first late-night talk show in 1952. He was friends with Humphrey Bogart and Harry Truman. Earlier, he was a bench-warming defensive back for the 1935 Eagles whose most-notable moment was getting into (and losing) a fistfight with Bronko Nagurski.

**5. Greasy Neale.** His bust is there in the Pro Football Hall of Fame, representing the Eagles as the only head coach ever to lead the franchise to consecutive NFL titles, which he did in 1948–49. He was the first NFL coach to seriously scout the college draft, an architect of what has evolved into the standard 4-3 defense, and an originator of the shotgun formation. Before all that, however, Neale played for Jim Thorpe's Canton Bulldogs and also played Major League baseball. He was the leading hitter for the Cincinnati Reds in the fixed World Series of 1919, and spent a less-successful season with the Phillies in 1921, hitting .211. Kind of like a Forrest Gump with brains.

**4. Billy Sunday.** Before there was Rev. Billy Graham, there was Billy Sunday, a booze-hating, Bible-thumping preacher for whom the phrase "fire-and-brimstone" was invented. And before Sunday became the nation's most famous evangelist in the 1920s and 30s, he played eight years in the Major Leagues, including one for the Phillies.

**3. Bill Bradley.** Hey, we consider Princeton a local school, even if they laughed at our admissions application. In the 1960s, Bradley was an All-American hoopster and a Rhodes Scholar for the Tigers, before moving onto a pro career with the New York Knicks and an 18-year stint in the U.S. Senate.

**2. John Madden.** The Eagles drafted him in 1958 out of California Polytechnic College in the 21st round (they actually went 30 rounds deep back then). A knee injury his rookie season ended his career and led to his current fame as a millionaire video game shill. Rumor has it he did some coaching and broadcasting along the way as well.

**1. Bill Cosby.** Who else could top this list? The world-famous comedian attended Temple University on a football scholarship and won a varsity letter as a fullback in 1961. Not sure what that scholarship cost the school, but it sure was a smart move by the Owls—through donations and PR, Cosby has paid back that money thousands of times over.

**10. Pink.** Born Alecia Moore in Doylestown, this singer can drastically change her looks from one day to the next, but thanks to an absolutely killer body, the end result is always the same—sexy.

**9. Lauren Hart.** Keeping a music and television career going is tough enough, but surviving cancer and still looking like a million bucks? That's Lauren Hart. This blonde Cherry Hill East alum—daughter of legendary Flyers broadcaster Gene Hart—sure knows how to rev up a crowd, and that's even before she starts singing. One thing's for sure, Kate Smith would have never looked as great in black leather pants as Lauren. Come to think of it, let's just immediately erase that Kate Smith visual from our minds.

**8. Kim Delaney.** Not many actresses have had more TV success than this dark-haired beauty from Hallahan High. From *NYPD Blue* right on up to *The OC,* Kim even had a brief turn with a show called *Philly.* Rumor even had it she was once romantically involved with WIP's own Rob Charry.

**7. Eve.** When she wears her hair down, this Philly rapper/actress is spectacular. We're not nuts about those strange tattoos on her breasts, but whatever floats your boat, right? Used to strip before she hit it big, but unfortunately for us Philly guys, it was up in the Bronx.

**6. Holly Robinson Peete.** She only spent the first 10 years of her life in Philly, but that's good enough for us. She starred in four different TV series, and her father was the original Gordon on *Sesame Street* as well as being the producer of *The Cosby Show.* Extremely bright and funny (and breathtaking to look at), she's as pretty as ever and she's the mother of four. We forget her husband's name. What is it? He played quarterback for the Eagles. Rodney something. Damn, it'll come to us.

**6A. Judy & Debbie.** You don't think we're stupid enough to leave off our wives, do you? The two most captivating women of all time!

**5. Kelly Ripa.** This blonde is ripped. Grew up in Berlin, N.J. (We knew that town had to be famous for something other than the "Berlin Auction"), attended Eastern High in Voorhees, and was discovered while acting in a play at Camden Community College. This led to soaps and Regis and everything else. Jersey Shore lover too. Someone please call us if you see her walking down a beach.

**4. Maria Bello.** Let's debate. In which scene is Maria the hottest? Her love scenes from *The Cooler?* How about in that cheerleader outfit in *A History of Violence?* (By the way, this Norristown native was a cheerleader at Archbishop Carroll.) Or how about her performance versus Mel Gibson in *Payback?* A terrific actress, as well as being sexy as hell.

**3. Gia Marie Carangi.** First off, how can you not be a supermodel with a name like that? Secondly, what does it say when they choose Angelina Jolie to portray you in a movie based on your life? Are you kidding me? Born in Philly, Gia attended Lincoln High while working behind the counter of Hoagie City, which her father owns. One year later she appeared on the covers of *Vogue* and *Cosmopolitan.* Eight years later she was dead from complications of drug use and AIDS. A sad ending for perhaps the most voluptuous woman who came from our town.

**2. Lola Falana.** This beauty was born in Camden in 1942, and moved to Philly where she graduated from Germantown High. Discovered by Sammy Davis Jr. and Frank Sinatra at the tender age of 21, Lola became the Queen of Las Vegas. What we'll remember most is her regular appearances on Johnny Carson's *Tonight Show.* Not much film work to speak of, but Google around and you'll find out why we've got her at this spot. A real class act. Lola's been ill for a while, but that doesn't mean we forget her.

**1. Grace Kelly.** This selection wasn't difficult at all. Anyone else on this list a princess? After she became Princess of Monaco in 1956, her movies were banned in that country. Thank God you can still see them here. Check out *Rear Window* or *To Catch a Thief.* That way you don't have to take our word for how stunning she was. One of the most gorgeous blondes ever. Her father and brother were Olympic gold medal scullers who practiced constantly on the Schuylkill River by Boat House Row.

## My Favorite Philadelphia Athletes :: Maria Bello

Note: Actress Maria Bello grew up in Norristown and has found great success in Hollywood. Who can forget her performances in movies such as *A History of Violence, The Cooler,* and *Payback*—or her tremendous work on the popular television series *E.R.?* A Villanova grad, Maria is a major sports fan who occasionally calls in to WIP when she's back in town. And by the way, do we have to mention that she's also gorgeous?

In case you're wondering where she did the research for her incredibly sexy turn as a "cheerleader" in *A History of Violence,* Maria was a cheerleader at Archbishop Carroll. But don't even think of making any moves on her. She's a kick boxer. Maria was nice enough to talk sports with us from Vancouver, where she was filming *Butterfly On A Wheel.*

These are her all-time favorite Philadelphia athletes. They are in alphabetical order, because Maria didn't want to place one above the other.

**Julius Erving.** Doc was just so cool, so graceful. I could never take my eyes off him when he was on the court. He had so much style.

**Tommy McDonald.** He was a personal friend of my mom and dad. Tommy is just the nicest guy in the world and really, really funny. What a thrill it was for my family the day he got inducted into the Pro Football Hall of Fame.

**Donovan McNabb.** There was nothing more exciting than when he would take off and run with the ball.

**Mike Schmidt.** Schmidt was simply the greatest baseball player I ever saw. And he made it all look so easy, which is also the secret to great acting.

Every actor thinks he's an athlete, and every athlete thinks he's an actor. Most often, they're wrong. But dozens of Philadelphia athletes have taken roles in movies. While most have been closer to Lawrence Taylor than Laurence Olivier, a handful shined on the big screen. Or at least they didn't embarrass themselves.

Here are lists of the 10 best and 10 worst acting jobs ever by Philadelphia jocks—along with 10 special ones you may have missed. We did not include any in which the athlete played himself (say, Joe Frazier's brilliant cameo in *Rocky*), instead focusing on roles in which our hero extended his wings (say, Smokin' Joe in *Ghost Fever*).

## Ten Best

**10. Joe Klecko.** We include Klecko because of his years at Temple, not his fame as a member of the Jets' "New York Sack Exchange." And we include Klecko because the Chester native was terrific in Burt Reynolds's *Heat*—not to be confused with Michael Mann's slicker movie *Heat*. This one is a punch-'em-up vehicle set in Vegas. Klecko plays a mob bodyguard who, in stunning slow-motion, tosses a guy through a window. And he doesn't even spoil it with a Mark Gastineau sack dance.

**9. Roman Gabriel.** This may be a cheat, since the acting role came four years before Gabriel arrived in Philadelphia in 1973 as the Eagles' so-called savior of a quarterback. Still, we had to include Gabriel in *The Undefeated,* simply because he got to play John Wayne's adopted Cherokee son, Blue Boy. How many actors get to break into the business playing side-by-side with a legend like the Duke?

It didn't do much for Gabriel's thespian career, however. He only ever acted in one other movie.

**8. Tim Rossovich.** You could have predicted an acting career for Rossovich when he first showed up as an Eagle in 1968 with sideburns and a bushy mustache, and drew attention by eating glass and setting himself on fire.

By the late '70s, he was out of football and into Hollywood as an actor and stuntman. He appeared in more than 15 movies, and his finest work came in the Michael Keaton-Henry Winkler comedy *Night Shift,* playing a menacing pal to the coroners-turned-pimps.

**7. Jack O'Halloran.** Back in the 1960s, "Irish Jack" was a six-foot-six heavyweight contender out of Runnemede, N.J., who battled future heavyweight champs George Foreman and Ken Norton. You're more likely to recall him as Kryptonite villain "Non" in *Superman* and *Superman II*. A scarier, more-intimidating mute never lived.

O'Halloran made other notable movies (he was great as lug Moose Malloy in *Farewell My Lovely*), but his *Superman* role brought him a guaranteed lifetime income attending superhero conventions. There's even an action figure doll with his likeness.

**6. Bob Uecker.** Somehow he converted six seasons—including two for the Phillies—as a dreadful backup catcher (career batting average: .200) into a four-decade career in comedy. Uecker had success in standup, television (*Mr. Belvedere*), and dozens of commercials. But his finest work came as cynical flask-sipping announcer Harry Doyle in the feature movie *Major League*.

Think about this: How many times over the years have you heard a wild pitch greeted with the shout, "Juuusssst a bit outside." That's Uecker's tagline from the movie. That's his contribution to the lexicon.

**5. Julius Erving.** Doc plays a hoops superstar surrounded by teammates resembling the Village People in *The Fish That Saved Pittsburgh*. He wears the tightest basketball shorts in history, dribbles in time to disco music, and nearly trips over his platform shoes in one scene. He finds himself upstaged by Flip Wilson and Jonathan Winters and has to deliver lines like, "I've learned to lean and walk on air, and listen to the rhythm inside my body."

Still, it works. And it works because you can tell that Doc is playing it for fun. As seriously and earnestly as he played the game, Erving is in this campy film for the laughs. Watching it, you feel like you're in on the joke.

Erving recently said that Fish was his second-favorite movie of all time, trailing only *The Great Escape*. Us? We'd call it a draw.

**4. Walter "Piggy" Barnes.** What? You don't remember the rugged starting guard for the Eagles' championship teams of 1948 and 1949? No matter. You've probably seen Barnes in any number of classic westerns, including *Rio Bravo* and *High Plains Drifter*, or on TV series like *Gunsmoke* and *Rawhide*. He was one of those "that guy" actors—as in, "Hey, I've seen that guy a million times."

Barnes's most-notable role came in *Any Which Way But Loose*, playing legendary street brawler Tank Murdoch. I don't want to give away the end of the movie, but the final scene, in which Barnes scuffles with Clint Eastwood, is a classic.

**3. Wilt Chamberlain.** Personal prejudice here, but we thought The Dipper stole *Conan the Destroyer* as Bombaata, the seven-foot bodyguard to the queen with the unstoppable finger roll. After all, who—other than Wilt—could upstage a cast that included Arnold Schwarzenegger, Andre the Giant, and Grace Jones?

Watch carefully the scene where Wilt single-handedly crashes down a stone wall. As he picks up the rocks to throw them, you can clearly tell they're made of foam rubber.

**2. Tex Cobb.** The former heavyweight contender has been in great movies (*Diggstown*) and terrible movies (*Ernest Goes to Jail*). But his classic performance comes in the Coen Brothers' comedy *Raising Arizona*, in which he plays Leonard Smalls, the Lone Biker of the Apocalypse. Watch as Tex shoots that tiny little lizard off the rock. Marvel as he figures out the whereabouts of the cons just by sniffing their hair grease.

This, of course, was Cobb's second-greatest contribution to the arts. His greatest was getting pasted by Larry Holmes in a fight so one-sided that it spurred Howard Cosell to swear off boxing forever. For that, we thank you, Tex.

**1. Tim Brown.** You may better remember the great Eagles halfback from the classic football scene in *M*A*S*H* (not exactly an acting reach), but his work in another Robert Altman film, *Nashville*, was far superior. Brown plays Tommy Brown (hmmmm, how'd they come up with that name?), a country singer modeled after Charley Pride. Not only can he act, but he's called upon to warble a tune, "Bluebird," and proves he can sing as well.

## Ten Worst

**10. Todd Zeile.** The former Phils infielder plays "Mullet" in *Dirty Deeds*, a 2004 teen sex romp that bills itself as a poor man's *American Pie*. Very poor man's. Looking at the credits, we couldn't help but notice that the film's co-executive producer is listed as Julianne McNamara-Zeile. Hmmmmm . . . a little nepotism never hurts.

**9. Bo Belinsky.** He pitched two seasons for the Phils in the mid-Sixties. That's the least of Belinsky's accomplishments.

"Bobo" was a New Jersey pool-hall rat who pitched a no-hitter as a rookie with the Angels, hung with Frank Sinatra, and performed truly horribly in the 1967 malt-shop flick *C'mon Let's Live a Little*.

His greatest feat was marrying Hollywood sex bomb Mamie Van Doren. For further research, look her up on Google images. That alone will justify whatever you paid for this book.

**8. John Kruk.** What's Kruk's famous line? "I'm no athlete, lady, I'm a baseball player."

Well, he's no actor either. Ever see Kruk as Lanz in the Wesley Snipes-Robert De Niro flick *The Fan?* Let's put it this way: Compared to that, his work in *The Best Damn Sports Show, Period* was Shakespearian.

**7. Reggie White.** We will always love Reggie for his Hall of Fame play as an Eagle and his commitment to make the world better. His semi-autobiographical flick, *Reggie's Prayer*, is well intentioned, but about as tolerable to most guys as a Dr. Phil marathon.

Reggie plays Reggie Knox, a retired player who coaches and counsels troubled high schoolers. Co-stars include ex-Eagle Keith Jackson as his assistant coach and Brett Favre and Mike Holmgren as janitors. Really.

**6. Tim McCarver.** Steve Carlton's personal catcher plays a preaching, pompous windbag of an announcer in *The Naked Gun*. Wait a second, that's not acting. That's just McCarver being himself.

**5. Bernard Hopkins.** We might as well stick every Philly fighter on the list, eh? Hopkins was nice enough to contribute to this book, so we won't go too hard on his work in *State Property 2*. Let's just say we wouldn't blame him if he sent director Damon Dash on a one-way trip to Palookaville.

**4. Joe Frazier.** His friend, Sherman Hemsley (aka George Jefferson from *The Jeffersons*), roped Frazier into playing Terrible Tucker in *Ghost Fever*, a terrible film that combines boxing, the supernatural, and torture. Trust us, the worst torture is that foisted on the viewers. Remember the beating that Smokin' Joe took from George Foreman? This was worse.

**3. Pete Rose.** Director Mark Tinker had a sense of humor when he cast Rose as Ty Cobb in the 1991 made-for-TV film, *Babe Ruth*. The movie itself is outstanding—better than both the William Bendix and John Goodman versions. But Pete? Well, if you remember Rose's Aqua Velva spots from the '70s, you pretty much know his acting range.

**2. Muhammad Ali.** We'll always consider The Greatest a Philly guy for his years in Cherry Hill and Fairmount Park. And we'll always marvel at his showmanship and skills. But Ali should have never agreed to take a shot at acting in *Freedom Road*. In the 1979 film, Ali stars (if that's the word) as Gideon Jackson, an ex-slave in 1870's Virginia who gets elected to the U.S. Senate. He stares at the camera at inopportune times, mumbles through his monologues, and looks ready to punch out co-star Kris Kristofferson half the time. Actually, that may have helped the movie.

**1. Jeff Lurie.** We're not even considering *V.I. Warshawski, Detective in High Heels*—which Lurie produced and which most experts credit as his best effort at destroying the arts. We're merely focusing on the Eagles owner's brief on-camera gig in the 1998 made-for-TV monstrosity called *The Garbage Picking Field Goal Kicking Philadelphia Phenomenon.*

Lurie plays the taproom pal of Tony Danza's lead character, Barney. Aside from appearing about as comfortable in a corner bar as Snoop Dogg in a nunnery, Lurie utters this immortal line:

"Hey, did you hear about the Eagles new owner? I hear he's a great guy!"

Hey, could you be more self-serving? I hear you're an egomaniac!

# Ten You May Have Missed

**10. Izzy Lang.** Another former Eagles' runner had an ever-so-brief appearance in the 1970 comedy *Where's Poppa?*. He's the character called Muthafucka who mugs star George Segal. Not really a proud moment.

**9. Judy Arnold.** Maybe my favorite. If you've never seen *Kansas City Bomber,* a flick about the dreams of Roller Derby star Raquel Welch, go rent it tonight. That's Welch in the cleavage-heaving close-ups. But in the actual skating scenes, that's Arnold, the pretty blonde bomber of the Philadelphia Warriors Roller Derby team, doing all the dirty work as a stunt double.

**8. Ricky Ledee.** The former Phillie appears as ballplayer Ruiz in Kevin Costner's soapy *For the Love of the Game.* Not much to review, really, except that the Ponce, Puerto Rico native's Latino accent sounded pretty authentic.

**7. Dave Babych.** The one-time Flyer defenseman's wooden performance as Wolfhard wasn't the only reason that *Slap Shot 2* went straight to video. But it sure didn't help.

**6. Dick Allen.** He portrays a scout in *Summer Catch,* a disappointing movie about Cape Cod League baseball. Presumably, he's searching for the next Dick Allen.

**5. Harold Jackson.** Typecast, typecast, typecast. You've got to say that Jackson was convincing as a football player in the biting *North Dallas Forty.* We only wish he'd gotten to wear his trademark No. 29 jersey.

**4. Peter Zezel.** Let's just agree that Rob Lowe wasn't the only babe magnet in *Youngblood.*

**3. Herschel Walker.** Not very convincing as a convict football player in *Necessary Roughness.* Now Ben Davidson, he pulled it off. Too Tall Jones, he pulled it off. Herschel seemed a little too sweet to be doing hard time.

**2. John LeClair.** The Flyers winger plays a good-guy rescuer in the kids' movie *Far From Home: The Adventures of Yellow Dog.* Hell, he saves the dog, so you've got to love him.

**1. Tom Woodeshick and Jack Concannon.** The Eagles' starting running back and former backup quarterback appeared in the hit 1970 war spoof *M*A*S*H* playing—surprise—football players in the movie's best scene. Actually, they're two of the guys passing a joint down the bench.

The scene drew laughs back then. Just to show how times have changed: Imagine if Brian Westbrook and Jeff Garcia appeared in a movie today smoking pot. Imagine the uproar.

Note: Bill Bergey roamed Veterans Stadium as a rough, nasty middle linebacker for the Eagles from 1974 to 1980. He is an authority on toughness.

**10. This space is reserved.** I didn't want to put any current Eagles players here because their careers are still unfolding. But a few of them are vying to earn this spot down the road. My money's on Brian Dawkins.

**9. John Bunting.** A tough outside linebacker. I played seven years with this man. I never saw a guy who had so much football knowledge as a teammate. Not only was he a good solid football player, but he kept the clubhouse loose.

**8. Seth Joyner.** Another rough, tough outside linebacker. He could blitz as well as being an outstanding cover man. He had a tremendous career.

**7. Andre Waters.** If Andre wasn't playing strong safety he absolutely could have been a linebacker. He never left anything in the bag. I would love to have played with him.

**6. Wes Hopkins.** Andre Waters' partner at free safety. Wes was a tremendous free safety who hit harder, pound-for-pound, than any defensive player I've seen. He never took a play off and he played hard every game.

**5. Herman Edwards.** I have never seen a defensive back with such unbelievable instincts as Herm had. He was a fun guy on the practice field and in the locker room. And, boy, was he tough. The Eagles grabbed him as an undrafted free agent in 1977—a great move.

**4. Jerome Brown.** This six-foot-three, 300-pound tackle was so fast off the line of scrimmage that, combined with his power, he could quickly eliminate blockers. That way he could destroy quarterbacks and running backs. He was the jokester and funny guy in the locker room.

**3. Tom Brookshier.** I love the way Tom would attack wide receivers. He challenged them physically before they could get into their routes.

**2. Chuck Bednarik.** I'll never forget the way Chuck cold-cocked Frank Gifford in 1960. No one wants to hurt anyone intentionally, but when you have the perfect hit on one of those pretty running backs, it's very rewarding.

**1. Reggie White.** A defensive end with power, speed, and the smarts to get to the quarterback. I haven't seen that kind of ability from any other player. I put him on the top of the list not only because of his talent on the field, but he was a great guy off the field too.

# The Five Toughest Point Guards I've Ever Faced
## :: Maurice Cheeks

**Note: Mo Cheeks came to the Sixers in 1978 and directed the team's offense for 11 seasons as one of the smoothest, greatest point guards in NBA history.**

**5. Micheal Ray Richardson** (1978–86: New York Knicks, Golden State Warriors, New Jersey Nets). It's a shame that more fans don't remember him—although Sixers fans sure do from when he and the Nets eliminated the Sixers in the first round of the 1984 playoffs. At six-foot-five he was one of the first tall point guards, and that really gave me a lot of problems.

**4. Norm Nixon** (1977–89: Los Angeles Lakers, San Diego/Los Angeles Clippers). Quick and smart—and a real scorer. With all the other great guys he teamed with on the Lakers, he's become a forgotten great player.

**3. John Stockton** (1984–2003: Utah Jazz). He was incredibly competitive. Mean and nasty. He'd bump you, hit you, whatever.

**2. Isiah Thomas** (1981–94: Detroit Pistons). I swear he could play today. The first point guard that didn't always have the "pass first" mentality—yet he was a great passer. He could really break you down off the dribble. Tough and mean. He gave me fits to guard him.

That's my list.

**Note: Wait a minute, here. Isn't Mo forgetting somebody? Wasn't there a No. 32 on the Lakers who broke the Sixers fans' hearts on many occasions? How could he not even bring up you-know-who?**

**1. Magic Johnson** (1979–91, 1995: Los Angeles Lakers). Oh, him? He doesn't count. I mean, he was so great and unique that he's a list unto himself. Plus, he was so tall I only guarded him if my whole team was in foul trouble. The best floor leader ever.

Note: Bob Kelly played 11 seasons for the Flyers, scoring the Stanley Cup-winning goal in 1975. He is better remembered by fans, however, as the aggressive, hard-hitting left winger who amassed 1,285 penalty minutes.

**10. Paul Holmgren, 1975–84.** He went after me when I played for Washington in 1981. Boy was he a hard hitter. "Homer" always went after the toughest guys—Nick Fotiu, the Carlson brothers, anyone with a reputation. He was very in shape, very ripped.

**9. Bob Kelly, 1970–80.** I reserve this spot for myself because it was my jersey number. I don't consider myself a true heavyweight like these other guys, but I could handle myself okay.

**8. Craig Berube, 1986–91, 1998–2000.** He had 1,139 penalty minutes as a Flyer and more than 2,000 during his time in the league. Very inspirational. "Chief" used to drink down in my basement. He'd take out his teeth and put them on the bar, and you'd see his knuckles, all scraped up. He really enjoyed fighting.

**7. Dave Brown, 1982–89, 1991–95.** He was a big, tall, standup guy who would just stand back and throw fists. Sometimes, he would take two or three punches for every one he threw, but his were harder. I remember the 1987 brawl against Montreal in the Conference Finals. Dave came out of the locker room with just pants and skates—nothing else. He went after their toughest guy, Chris Nilan, who wanted no part of Brownie.

**6. Rick Tocchet, 1984–92, 1999–2002.** His 1,817 penalty minutes are a franchise record. He was a fully developed player who could score and play defense, and boy, could he fight as well. Pound for pound, one of the toughest ever. The girls liked him too, eh? When my daughter was 12 years old, his was the jersey she wanted.

**5. Mel Bridgman, 1975–82.** I watched him break in with us. He went after the toughest players we played against, like Curt Fraser of Vancouver, who was a 200-pounder when there weren't a lot of those around. Mel pumped weights when other guys weren't yet into that. A pit bull. Not the best-looking guy around, but as tough as they come.

**4. Glenn Cochrane, 1978–79, 81-84.** He logged 1,110 penalty minutes with the Flyers. Not too shabby. He was a stand-up, throw 'em kind of guy. A good teammate, too. Do you remember what he would do in a fight? He would rip off his shoulder pads, jersey, elbow pads, whatever he could, so his opponent had nothing to grab onto.

**3. Donald Brashear, 2001–.** He's the best legitimate total heavyweight the Flyers have had in a lot of years. He's a fearless player out there, goes into every dangerous corner. With the rules changing to de-emphasize fighting, it's good that he's been able to hone his skills. He doesn't embarrass you as a player.

**2. Dave Schultz, 1971–76.** My teammate, "The Hammer." He was instrumental in changing the way the rest of the league looked at us, the Broad Street Bullies. Dave fought all the heavyweights back then, Noel Picard, Joel Bouchard. A great fighter, threw like a jackhammer.

**1. Behn Wilson, 1978–83.** Not only was he the toughest fighter ever, he was also unpredictable. He would spear you just as easily as look at you. He was even nasty with his own teammates. One day he went after Ken Linseman during a practice. They really went at it before the other guys—led by Paul Holmgren—stepped in.

**Honorable mentions:** Jack McIlhargey, 1974–77, 1979–81; Al Secord, 1988–89; Dave Hoyda, 1977–79.

## A Philadelphia Frankenstein

What if you had the ability to create the perfect athlete from the best attributes of everyone who's ever played in this town? Here's what we came up with:

**Left arm**—Steve Carlton
**Left fist**—Joe Frazier
**Right arm**—Sonny Jurgensen
**Right fist**—Dave Schultz
**Knuckles**—Chuck Bednarik
**Fingers**—Doc Erving
**Hands**—Mike Quick
**Wrists**—Rick MacLeish
**Forearms**—Greg Luzinski
**Elbows**—Gary Dornhoefer
**Biceps**—George McGinnis
**Shoulders**—Wilt Chamberlain

**Hair**—Oscar Gamble (Best Afro ever)
**Sideburns**—Richie Allen
**Eyes**—Mike Schmidt
**Ears**—Donovan McNabb (He can always hear criticism, even when it's whispered)
**Nose**—Rod Brind'Amour
**Jaw**—Mike Keenan
**Mouth**—Buddy Ryan
**Beard**—Cowboy Flett
**Brains**—Billy Cunningham

**Back**—Herschel Walker
**Abs**—Terrell Owens
**Chest**—Reggie White
**Belly**—John Kruk
**Feet**—Randall Cunningham
**Toes**—Brian Westbrook (cuts on a dime)
**Ankles**—Heather Mitts
**Right leg**—Tom Dempsey
**Left leg**—David Akers
**Thighs**—Corey Simon
**Calves**—Charles Barkley (for a guy that size to lead the league in rebounds, something had to give him that leaping ability)
**Rear end**—Rick Mahorn
**Asshole**—Norman Braman

**Heart**—Allen Iverson
**Pituitary Gland**—Manute Bol
**Guts**—Tommy McDonald
**Spleen**—Larry Bowa
**Balls**—Bob Clarke

## Ten Local Athletes Who Don't Need a Mask on Halloween

Mind you, the two of us realize we don't look like Denzel Washington or Brad Pitt. But, as we used to say in the neighborhood, here are some folks who "fell out of the ugly tree and hit every branch on the way down."

**10. Kareem Abdul-Jabbar, George Foster, Tie Domi, and Joe Jacoby.** We realize these good-looking fellas didn't play for any Philly teams, but our teams battled against them so often, it feels like they did. To quote the late, great Rodney Dangerfield, these guys are so ugly that "when they were born, the doctor slapped their mother!"

**9. Lenny Dykstra.** "Pigpen" from Peanuts. The scratching, the spitting. Lenny could have had the starring role in *Caveman*. Even centerfield at the Vet was disgusting by the time Lenny was through with it, thanks to all the tobacco stains.

**8. Rick Tocchet.** Nose broken a dozen times, eight-thousand stitches to his face—just a day at the office for hockey players. Could easily go out for Halloween as Frankenstein—as is.

**7. Ryne Duren.** This Phils pitcher, who could bring it at 100 miles per hour, wore these insane coke-bottle glasses because he was half-blind. If he was an actor, Ryne would portray a very quiet serial-killer type. All of this made him really fun to bat against, eh?

**6. Tex Cobb.** Several claims to fame. As a boxer, Tex's fight against Larry Holmes was so ugly and one-sided that it prompted Howard Cosell to retire as a boxing commentator. As an actor, Tex appeared in more than 30 movies, including some pretty good ones like *Raising Arizona* and *Uncommon Valor*. Somehow he never got cast in a romantic lead. We wonder why. Had a face that resembled a sack of nails. Extremely funny and likeable guy.

**5. Danny Ozark.** This former Phils skipper looked 70 when he was 50. Imagine what he looked like at 70.

**4. Tyrone Hill.** "Skeletor" from *He-Man and the Masters of the Universe*. If you ever want to know how truly bad former NBA star Charles Oakley is, he once punched out this former Sixer—the scariest-looking cat ever to wear shorts. Over a poker bet no less. Tyrone also once got a photo op with Faith Hill when she performed in Philly because of the last-name connection. Wonder if someone has a copy of that adorable portrait.

**3. Chuck Bednarik.** Even these days, in his 80s, Concrete Charlie could cuss out every man in a packed barroom and NO ONE would accept the challenge. His hands are scary looking.

**2. Manute Bol.** We never believed the story that this seven-foot-six former Sixer once killed an African lion with a spear. No way would the lion have gotten that close.

**1. Big Shot.** Are you kidding me? That bad complexion, that awful hair, that veal cutlet of a tongue. Not to mention he was about 150 pounds overweight. No wonder the fans despised this former Sixers mascot.

When you're a kid playing against a team that you had never seen before, sometimes just the mascot of that team could put a little fear in you—the Warriors, Wildcats, Marauders, Pirates, Destroyers, Manson Family. Whatever.

So imagine the obstacle the teams on this list have to overcome before the game even begins. We're not including any high school teams (well, maybe one) because there are simply too many in the area with measly monikers. Sorry kids, but you'll get over it one day.

**10. The Phillies.** We understand the whole "ph" thing. But it's still pretty weak—so much so that over the years all the Phils broadcasters have taken to calling them the "Fighting Phils." Ooooh. We're scared now.

**9. The Haverford College Fords.** This one's really confusing. Should we assume they mean the car? If so, what model? A Ford Mustang would work, but what if the team comes out driving Escorts? What if the car is a rusted out piece of crap Pinto?

**Glen Alert:** This also happens to be the nickname for my local high school, Haverford High. I once suggested to a school board member that the district consider giving the team a new tag. She looked at me as if I had a third eye growing out of my forehead.

**8. The Sixers.** We get the historical significance, but it's a far cry from the Warriors, who used to play in this town. The NBA really is a league full of weak nicknames—the Knickerbockers, the Lakers, the Nets, the Jazz, the Wizards. What the hell are the Wizards supposed to do? Put a spell on you? Hypnotize you? Now Washington's former nickname, the Bullets—that put a scare in you, didn't it?

**7. The La Salle Explorers.** Yes, we know that the nickname honors French explorer René-Robert Cavelier, Sieur de La Salle, who traveled the Mississippi River (now there's a local connection). Still we have no idea what to even make of this one. Explore what? Explore this!

**6. The Philadelphia Kixx.** Yeah, we get it. It's soccer. (As much as we "get" soccer.) You kick the ball, right? Clever. At least the name "Phantoms" has some sort of a scary tone to it. The "Soul" implies that the team is going to play with a lot of heart. Unless this "Kixx" name implies that they're going to be kicking their opponents in the "family jewels" vicinity, it's not putting a big scare in us.

**5. The Lehigh Engineers.** What, do they break out slide rules in the huddle? Hurl protractors at opponents' heads? We'll give you this much—they probably know how to draw up a heck of a play.

**4. The Rowan Profs.** You have to be kidding, right? We're visualizing old guys with gray goatees running out of the locker room smoking pipes and quoting Shakespeare. How do their football teams put up the amazing records that they do?

**3. The Franklin & Marshall Diplomats.** A tad bit out of the area in Lancaster, but the Sixers based their training camps on that campus for years, so they're in. Diplomats? Let's get this straight. If the Dips are getting their ass kicked in a game, they'll negotiate themselves out of a loss?

**2. The Delaware Blue Hens.** Hens? "Mother" hens? You're kidding, right? "Hen" is lame enough as it is, but what the heck is a "blue" hen? Turns out the origin for this nickname goes way back to revolutionary days when there would be cockfights in Delaware. But somehow the school administration didn't think that a mascot name like "Blue Cocks" would sound all that appropriate being chanted by the student section at a ball game. What a shame. That would have been fun.

**1. The Pennsylvania Quakers.** The Quaker Oats man! The cat with the white Beatle haircut and the blue hat. We hope he doesn't see this list because we don't want him to hunt us down like dogs and kick our ass. For crying out loud, the number-one belief in the Quaker religion is pacifism. How does that huddle break? "On three, Peace!"

**Big Daddy Alert:** I have a lot of nerve contributing to this list, since my West Catholic High School mascot name is, get ready for this, the "Burrs." You know, those Velcro-like balls that fall from trees. Watch out, we might give you a rash.

# Big Daddy's Favorite Chrome Domers

In honor of my follicly challenged writing partner (must get cold up there, eh Glen?), I thought I'd salute our skullcap-wearing friends. First up, there must be something about coaching that makes these poor souls pull their hair out. These are in no particular order, except for No. 1. (And don't peek ahead!)

## The Coaches

**10. Terry Francona, Phillies.** See what managing in this town can do? By the time he got to the Red Sox he had no more hair left to lose.

**9. Harry Perretta, Villanova.** Fans think it was coaching women that drove longtime Villanova coach Harry nuts. But Harry's hair started falling out years before that, from all the times I schooled him on the basketball courts of the Observatory on West Chester Pike.

> **Glen says:** "Hey, BDG, I heard it was the other way around!"

**8. Craig Ramsay, Flyers.** Just looking at Craig used to put the Flyers to sleep on the bench.

**7. Mike Keenan, Flyers.** He may have been balding, yet somehow this Flyers coach used that head of his to intimidate.

**6. Rollie Massimino, Villanova.** When he would flip out on the sidelines, his well-placed comb-over would swing from one side to the other.

**5. Jack Ramsay, St. Joe's, Sixers.** Come on, be honest. Give him some gold hoop earrings and tell me Jack couldn't make a good living playing Mr. Clean at conventions.

**4. Alex Hannum, Sixers.** He proved that even coaching championship teams could not stop him from reaching for the Rogaine.

**3. John Lucas, Sixers.** Tell me John didn't look like he popped out of Aladdin's lamp.

**2. Phil Martelli, St. Joe's.** Is there one bald joke left in the world that Phil hasn't used? At least all he has to do before he goes out is straighten his tie. Whoops . . . I think Phil just used that line at a banquet.

**1. Rich Kotite, Eagles.** The first time I saw Richie the K at a press conference, I thought he was there to fix a pipe leaking from the Vet ceiling. Then he stepped up to the podium and started talking!

## The Players

**10. Derrick Coleman, Sixers.** How could a bald head sweat this much? Rumored to have been Marlon Brando's stand-in for *Apocalypse Now*.

**9. Floyd Peters, Eagles.** He was so bald that the players often mistook him for one of the coaches and it actually turned into his nickname, "The Bald Eagle."

**8. Clay Dalrymple, Phillies.** I'll never forget the first time I saw Clay take off his cap to wipe his brow at Connie Mack Stadium. What a shock! Bald. Not strong, virile, Michael Jordan bald, but bald like your Uncle Harry. This couldn't be. Not a Phillie. Not a major league baseball player. Say it ain't so, Clay!

**7. Ed Van Impe, Flyers.** Back in the Flyers' Stanley Cup days when NHL players wore no helmets, there was no hiding it if you had a full head of skin.

**6. World B. Free, Sixers.** Not even a name change from "Lloyd" to his current moniker could stop the erosion on top of his head.

**5. Terrell Owens, Eagles.** Just wanted to see how many different lists T.O. can make in one book. "Are you truly bald or is that just a fashion statement?" "NEXT QUESTION!"

**4. Charles Barkley, Sixers.** I remember when the Round Mound of Rebound had hair, but like everything else about Chuck, he just wanted to "be like Mike" in every way.

**3. Bernie Parent, Flyers.** Television hair ads. Radio. Billboards. Newspaper ads. You have to hand it to Bernie. Not embarrassed in any way by his baldness. Nor should he be.

**2. Eddie George, Abington High.** If you're going to be bald, this is the way to go. The most intimidating, baddest-looking mother on the planet. A dead ringer for actor Woody Strode, for those of you old enough to remember.

**1. Matt Geiger, Sixers.** Just think, we would have been denied years of watching the greatness of Allen Iverson had this handsome fellow not stopped a trade involving A.I. because of a no-trade clause in his own contract.


## Even Announcing Takes Its Toll

The following gentlemen could use a gift certificate from Dr. Pistone Hair Restoration: Sixers announcers Marc Zumoff and Tom McGinnis, and PA announcer Matt Cord. Don't forget Phils' announcers Larry Andersen and Chris Wheeler. Also don't forget the shaved rage that Sixers owner Pat Croce started back in 2001! Anyone still having nightmares over the bald Angelo Cataldi?

Thanks for making fun of my bald pate, Big Daddy. But, as they say, grass doesn't grow on a busy street. I will, however, concede to being envious of some haircuts.

## Guys with Great Hair

**10. Al Harris.** The Eagles' penalty-challenged cornerback appeared to steal his coif from Milli Vanilli. Still, he boasted the boldest locks in any NFL secondary until Troy Polamalu came around.

**9. Tim Rossovich.** Some white guys can sport Afros; some cannot (more about that second category later). The Eagles linebacker grew one that could have made Jimi Hendrix jealous, until coach Eddie Khayat—who was to the NFL what Major Frank Burns was to *M*A*S*H*—forced him to cut it and shave his magnificent bushy mustache. Another time, Rossovich just set the whole thing on fire.

**8. Rick Tocchet.** The Flyers winger boasted a blow-dried pompadour in the 1980s that drove the young girls wild. Recent shots of him show an almost-bald head. Maybe he lost a bet?

**7. Kyle Korver.** We wouldn't be the first to compare his looks to Ashton Kutcher, so let's just note that when the Sixers produced a bobble-head of him in 2006, the figurine came with "real hair." What could possibly be the source?

**6. Chuck Daly.** The Penn coach was impeccable—in dress, in style, in hair. Unlike some of his colleagues (Massimino, Chaney, Speedy Morris), Daly could dress down a referee without his shirt-tail falling out or his hair flapping around. Nova's Jay Wright has a chance to surpass Daly for "best locks in the Big 5" if he and his hairline stick around long enough.

**5. Rick MacLeish.** In the days before all NHL players became faceless, helmeted entities, there was no more exciting sight than to see the Flyers winger speeding up ice, his long mane flying behind him.

**4. Darren Daulton.** A perpetually tanned surfer-dude-with-muscles look. Dutch loved whipping off his catcher's mask and helmet on foul pops, the better to show off his sweet lid. Daulton sold more tickets to females than any player in Phillies history.

**3. Allen Iverson.** Might have topped this list if he didn't keep changing the pattern so often. For a while, Al had someone traveling with him on road trips to do his hair a different style for every game. The results ranged from tragic (that flat tire-tread pattern) to magnificent ("The Crossover," a series of criss-crossed cornrows resembling a basketball net). Probably did more to influence hairstyles among America's youth than anyone since the Beatles.

**2. (Tie) Oscar Gamble, Garry Maddox, Bake McBride.** And every other Phillie who sported an Afro back in the 1970s. My own personal favorite was Gamble, whose baseball cap rested about 20 inches above his eyebrows. I still keep around a 1975 baseball card of Gamble, in which his mass of hair, squeezed under a batting helmet, spills out like earmuffs on steroids.

Of course, the patron saint of Afros is . . .

**1. Julius Erving.** In the ABA days, they actually once presented the "Biggest Afro Award," which Doc lost by a hair (sorry) to Darnell Hillman. The 'do was part of the fashion, the grace, the magnificence of Doc. The greatest hairstyle of all-time, and no one wore it better than Julius.

## Guys with Bad Hair

**10. Don Saleski.** As we said, some white guys can grow a 'fro, some can't. Saleski was definitely in the latter category. They didn't call him "Big Bird" for nothing. Kind of a cross between Art Garfunkel and Horshack.

**9. Curt Simmons.** In the days before every game was on TV, much of our sense of a player's appearance came from baseball cards. Simmons, as we recall, adorned his 2-1/2 x 3-1/2-inch card with a crewcut so square and flat he must have planned it with a T-square. You could have landed a small plane on his head. One other thing we learned from Simmons' card is that he cut off a toe in a lawnmower accident. I think they even had a little cartoon to illustrate it.

**8. Keith Van Horn.** All that gel and the stupid cowlick up front—sort of Prince Valiant meets Eddie Munster. Looked worse when it became soaked with sweat, which is to assume that Van Horn ever broke into a sweat.

**7. Michal Handzus.** Makes you miss the traditional NHL mullet. The Flyers center apparently decided to see if he could go his entire career without cutting it. Began looking like a homeless man sometime late in 2005.

**6. Samuel Dalembert.** You'd think with the $61 million contract Billy King bestowed on him that Dalembert could get himself to a decent stylist.

**5. Donovan McNabb.** Well, sometimes. Forgive us for suggesting that McNabb is an Iverson wannabe—at least follicly—but, between the cornrows, the faux Afro, and the squashed-down doo-rag look . . . well, we just wish he'd make up his mind and come up with his own act. A square guy trying to look cool never fools anyone.

**4. Macho Row.** Call it what you like—the Tennessee tophat, the Kentucky waterfall, the Canadian passport—we'll stick with the traditional name, and tell you that the 1993 Phils clubhouse boasted more mullets than all the Great Lakes combined. The most impressive, of course, belonged to Mitch Williams. We loved when he doffed his hat to reveal it after each save.

**3. Armon Gilliam.** Known to all as "Gumby"—a nickname bestowed by Charles Barkley—during his disastrous three-year stint with the Sixers. Gilliam was six-foot-nine on one side of his head, six-foot-six on the other.

**2. Pete Rose.** Sported the ultimate bowl cut during his Phillies seasons, a tribute to his intellectual hero, Moe. Later shifted to a poorly dyed red crewcut, which resembled a sack of rusty nails.

**1. Freddy Mitchell.** Remember the "Frohawk?" This bust of a first-round pick couldn't draw enough attention to himself as a talented player, so he tried stunts like wearing furs, moping, and transforming his head into something out of Spaceballs. He unveiled this monstrosity for the 2004 NFC Championship, boasting afterward, "Now everybody is trying to get the Frohawk." We're still waiting for the second person, Chief.

## Media Division

**5. Al Morganti.** See Macho Row notes above.

**4. Big Daddy Graham.** Sorry, my friend, but what color do you call that? It's definitely not a tint found in nature.

**3. Michael Barkann.** Ah, so that's what they mean by a "widow's peak." I don't know what's of greater concern to the ecosystem, the deforestation in South America or the deforestation in North Barkannia.

**2. Ed Rendell.** The Guv qualifies as media because of his Eagles post-game work. And he makes the list because, with each passing year, he looks more like Woody Harrelson in "Kingpin." We're just hoping that Rendell and Rudy Giuliani run against each other for President so we can have the first all-combover election. Hey, Ed, here's the news: Everyone knows you're going bald! Accept the facts gracefully.

Of course, the only thing worse than a combover is . . .

**1. Chris Wheeler.** "Wheels" is . . . let's just say that the fright wig Mike Schmidt put on back in 1985 was more convincing than his doll-hair toupee. Chris, there's no shame in going topless. Take it from one who knows.

Note: Phil Martelli grew up a hoops junkie in Southwest Philadelphia. He has been head coach at St. Joseph's since 1995. In 2003–04, he led the Hawks to the first undefeated regular season since 1991, and to the NCAA Elite Eight.

**Guy Rodgers, Temple, 1955–58.** I only know of his greatness by word of mouth and from what the elders have said. But if you believe in Santa Claus, then you believe in Guy Rodgers. And I believe in Santa Claus.

**Cliff Anderson, St. Joseph's, 1964–67.** Undersized, but he pursued every rebound relentlessly. He scored against the giants because he had a giant heart—that's the perfect Philadelphia player.

**Larry Cannon, La Salle, 1966–69.** He always played like the court was running downhill, and he was going in that direction. A power guard before anyone used that term. He played for one reason—so his team could win.

**Ken Durrett, La Salle, 1968–71.** If Guy Rodgers is No. 1, then Ken is 1A. He was his era's Kevin Garnett or Tim Duncan—a big man who could move.

**Howard Porter, Villanova, 1968–71.** A Florida import who was years ahead of his time in terms of being a forward who did everything well.

**Michael Brooks, La Salle, 1976–80.** Smooth, silky, satiny—the "Three-S Man." Of all the Big 5 legends, he was the most understated great player ever in the city.

**John Pinone, Villanova, 1979–83.** John was like a dock worker playing basketball. He had a body like a bouncer but skills that belied his body.

**Lionel Simmons, La Salle, 1986–90.** His nickname befits his game—the "L Train." He loaded that team on his back and carried it to unique places. He may be among the last 3,000-point scorers that we ever see in college.

**Mark Macon, Temple, 1987–91.** The quintessential Temple guard. Everything started with his defense. His demeanor set him apart from a very early age. Remember, he was the national freshman player of the year.

**Jameer Nelson, St. Joseph's, 2000–04.** Every list should have one of my sons on it, and this list does. When Naismith and boys designed the game, they came up with a position called point guard. At St. Joe's, we call it a Jameer.

# The Six Greatest Games Involving Big 5 Teams
## :: Phil Martelli

Note: Phil Martelli was the first coach to take his team—the 2003–04 St. Joe's Hawks—through an undefeated regular season since UNLV's Jerry Tarkanian did it in '91. For that, he was named the NCAA's 2004 Coach of the Year. He's had pretty good seats for some great Big 5 games over the last decade himself. Here is his list of the greatest ever.

**6. La Salle 73, Villanova 69—February 13, 1971, the Palestra.** It was billed as Ken Durrett vs. Howard Porter. But when you look back at the rosters, you see 10 guys and not a single weak link. They had another great match up a year earlier, with Nova winning, 96-85.

**5. Saint Joseph's 71, Villanova 69—January 16, 1966, the Palestra.** The Hawks were ranked fifth in the nation but trailed for most of the game. Steve Donches, a deep reserve, hit a 30-footer at the buzzer to rescue St. Joe's.

**4. Villanova 66, Georgetown 64—April 1, 1985, NCAA Championship Game, Lexington, Kentucky.** Going in, I was delighted to see that Nova had reached that level, but—like most people—I never thought they had a chance. They rolled the perfect seven that night.

**3. Temple 98, Villanova 86—February 10, 1988, McGonigle Hall.** Temple was ranked No. 1 in the country at the time, and both teams would go on to make the Elite Eight that season. It was Mark Macon and Mike Vreeswyk vs. Doug West and Mark Plansky. A rock 'em, sock 'em, up-and-down-the-floor game. More scoring than you would expect in a city series game, especially a Temple game.

**2. LaSalle 91, Western Kentucky 76—January 16, 1971, the Palestra.** Ken Durrett went off for 45 points against seven-foot All-American Jim McDaniels. Durrett had done wonderful things before that night, but when he took McDaniels to school, he became legendary.

**1. Villanova 90, Penn 47—March 20, 1971, NCAA East Regional Finals, Raleigh, N.C.** Penn was undefeated going in, and the Quakers had already beat Nova during the regular season. But this was a different setting. Nova crushed them in a revenge game to get to the Final Four. The teams flew home on the same plane, which must have been uncomfortable.

Note: Merrill Reese has been the Eagles radio play-by-play announcer for 30 years.

### 10. November 22, 1992 at the New York Giants. Vai Sikahema turns into Rocky.

**The call:** *"Here is the punt by Landetta. No block on this time. He drives it. Sikahema backs up. He takes it at the 13. Starts right, across the 20, 25, 30, 35, 40, midfield, 45, 40, 35, 30—Sikahema at the 20, the 10. Touchdown! Vai Sikahema! It happened! He finally broke one! It was bound to happen—and Sikahema is punching the goalposts! The Eagles have taken this game and ripped it apart at the seams!"*

**Merrill remembers:** "I have a few special-teams plays on this list, because they can be so unexpectedly thrilling. This was the best punt return I've ever seen and the longest in Eagles history. Vai put the game away and then he did his Rocky rendition on the goalposts at Giants stadium."

### 9. October 24, 2005. Matt Ware's return of a blocked field goal beats the Chargers.

**The call:** Merrill: *"There's 2:37 remaining here in the fourth quarter. The ball is spotted, the kick is—blocked! The kick is blocked, the Eagles have the football! Running with the football is Matt Ware. At the 30, the 20, the 10, touchdown, Matt Ware! And the Eagles take the lead! Matt Ware picked it up. It was blocked, Matt Ware picked it up and the Eagles take the lead! This is amazing. This is amazing!"*
Mike Quick: *"I think I'm gonna have a heart attack."*

**Merrill remembers:** "The funny thing is, Mike (Quick) and I had talked about Ware earlier that day, wondering when he'd get a chance to do something. Then, the field goal is blocked and I see Matt Ware running toward the end zone. The Eagles trailed, 17-13, and a San Diego field goal would pretty much end any hopes for the day. But Quentin Mikell broke through the line, blocked the kick, it bounced right into Ware's arms, and the Eagles got a 20-17 miracle win."

### 8. December 10, 1995 vs. the Cowboys. Groundhog Day, or Fourth and One— twice.

**The call:**
Merrill: *"The Eagles stopped them once; can they do it again? It will be fourth and one, and Switzer's going for it again."*
Stan Walters: *"I think Switzer should be punting here."*
Merrill: *"I wish he were punting here."*

Stan: *"He's got a lot of confidence in his offensive line."*

Merrill: *"Can they do it again? They could pass, too, to Novacek, who's in motion. Here they go. Fourth down. They go to Smith and the Eagles stop him again! They stop him again! And this time they can't take it away! The same pla—it's Groundhog Day!"*

**Merrill remembers:** "In a 17-17 tie, the Cowboys had fourth-and-inches at their own 29. Their coach, Barry Switzer, decided to go for it, and Emmitt Smith was stopped for a loss by the Eagles defense. But the officials' whistle had blown to signal the two-minute warning, so the play didn't count. Dallas got another chance. Switzer decided to go for it again and called the same exact play. I had just seen the Bill Murray movie, *Groundhog Day,* where he wakes up in the same day again and again, and that's what came out of my mouth."

### 7. October 19, 2003 at the New York Giants. Brian Westbrook's punt return saves the season.

**The call:** *"Westbrook—dangerous every time he has his hands on the football. The snap to Feagles. He gets it away. It's a wobbler, bounces across the 20. Westbrook takes it. Looks for running room, up to the 25, the 30, to the 35, 40, 45, midfield, 45, 30 25, 20— Brian Westbrook! He's going, he's going! Touchdown, Brian Westbrook! Eighty-four yards, no penalty flags! I don't believe it! Brian Westbrook has just exploded, and with 1:16 remaining this place is in a state of shock!"*

**Merrill remembers:** "Brian Westbrook's terrific return beat the Giants at the Meadowlands. This came late in the game when the Eagles needed a big play. It came on the heels of a tough loss in Dallas and launched the Eagles to a nine-game winning streak."

### 6. October 3, 1993 at the New York Jets. Eric Allen's incredible interception return.

**The call:** *"Thornton, the tight end, goes into motion. Esiason, play action, he's back, he's firin—and it's intercepted by Allen! Spinning at the 10, out to the 15, the 20, cutting to his left at the 25, 30, Allen to the 40, Allen to the 45, 50, 45, 40, Eric Allen down the far sidelines, steps over a man, he's going to gooooo! Eric Allen with a miraculous return of an interception, and the Eagles take the lead! Eric Allen with an absolutely miraculous return, getting help from a block by Ben Smith. Ninety-four yards, and the Eagles lead!"*

**Merrill remembers:** "This was as great and exciting a play as I've ever seen. It was a tough game, in which the Eagles lost Randall Cunningham and Fred Barnett to season-ending injuries. They were down, 30-28, with time running out when Allen made this remarkable play. It ended with him seeing Cunningham next to the end zone on crutches and then handing him the ball."

## 5. November 15, 2004 at Dallas. Donovan McNabb becomes the Ultimate Weapon II.

**The call:** *"Back goes McNabb. He steps up, he's being rushed. He gets away from one man, dashes to the outside, still rolling, comes back to the near side ala Randall Cunningham against Buffalo. Pumping. Loading up. He is firing it deep and it is . . . caught by Freddy Mitchell! Down at the 15! Freddy Mitchell! I haven't seen a play like that since Randall Cunningham ran away from Bruce Smith in Buffalo and hit Freddy Barnett."*

**Merrill remembers:** "McNabb ran around for about 14 seconds, leaving would-be tacklers in his wake before firing downfield to Freddy ("I want to thank my hands for being so great") Mitchell. While Donovan scrambled I remarked 'Ala Randall Cunningham in Buffalo'—that's how reminiscent it was."

## 4. December 2, 1990 at Buffalo. Randall Cunningham's amazing scramble-and-pass.

**The call:** *"Cunningham is back. He's being trapped. He ducks under three men. He's looking . . . he's rolling . . . he's heaving it deep down field for Barnett—who leaps and has it! At the 40, at the 35, 30. Barnett's gonna scooooore! Touchdown! Unbelievable! For a 95-yard touchdown to Fred Barnett!"*

**Merrill remembers:** "It ended up as the second-longest offensive touchdown in franchise history. Unfortunately, the Eagles lost the game. Afterward, Randall was asked if he ever amazed himself, and he answered, 'Yeah, sometimes I even amaze myself.' Of course, that got him in trouble, but all he did was answer honestly."

## 3. November 10, 1985 vs. Atlanta. In overtime, Ron Jaworski and Mike Quick hook up for the longest pass in Eagles history.

**The call:** *"Second down and 10 for the Eagles. Jaworski retreats, he's looking . . . he fires the football over the middle. Complete to Quick. He's going to go—25, 30, 35, 40, midfield, 45, 40, 35, 30, 25, 20—Mike Quick, touchdown! The Eagles win! The Eagles win! Forget the extra point! Jaworski to Quick, 99 yards and the game is over!"*

**Merrill remembers:** "I was worried that the Falcons might win the game on a safety. The Eagles had been in five overtime games before this, and lost four of them. So I wasn't that confident before the pass."

**2. November 19, 1978 at the New York Giants. Herm Edwards performs the Miracle at the Meadowlands.**

**The call:** *"Under 30 seconds left in the game. And Pisarcik fumbles the football!! It's picked up by Herman Edwards. He's at the 15, 10, 5, touchdown Eagles! I don't believe it! I do not believe it! I do not believe what has just occurred here ladies and gentlemen. As Pisarcik came forward he fumbled the football, Charlie Johnson hit him and Herman Edwards picked it up and ran it in for a touchdown!"*

**Merrill remembers:** "I didn't realize until the next day what I had seen. And I never thought it would be one of those plays that every fan would see—on ESPN, HBO, highlight shows—thousands of times. It's one of the strangest plays in NFL history."

**1. January 11, 1981, NFC Championship Game vs. Dallas. Wilbert Montgomery scampers 42 yards for the opening touchdown.**

**The call:** *"Second down and 10 for the Eagles. The Cowboys have six defensive backs in the game. Jaworski hands off to Montgomery. Up the right side—25, 20, 15, 10, touchdown! Montgomery exploded up the right side and the Eagles have scored first. Wilbert rambled 42 yards. The block—Sisemore and Peoples. And the Eagles have struck!"*

**Merrill remembers:** "I knew, and I think everyone in the Delaware Valley knew right at that moment that the Eagles were going to the Super Bowl."

**12. Bob Clarke.** I've been doing him on stage since I was 12. He's a pretty lucky diabetic.

**11. Bill Bergey.** Because it pisses him off. He doesn't want to admit his voice is that squeaky, and whenever he hears me do his voice he just wants to snap my neck!

**10. Howard Cosell.** He was the first guy I ever imitated. You never forget your first love. Did I just say that?

**9. Ray Rhodes.** I was once accused of making him sound too black. That hurt me . . . it hurt deep down inside of me. Did I say sodomy?

**8. Rich Kotite.** No material required—just repeat the script he gave. Overbearing, paranoid, obnoxious, uncomfortable, and delicious!

**7. Jim Lynam.** I just like saying "I beat DePaul that year" . . . along with "Charles is Charles."

**6. Charles Barkley.** Because Philadelphia is a racist city. Where else does a brother have to pretend he's Greek, just to have a picnic?

**5. Bill Campbell.** It seems like anything you say in Bill's voice is funny.

**4. Allen Iverson.** A real fun voice to do; he sounds a lot like Tone Loc. And he continually provides plenty of fodder.

**3. Dave Zinkoff.** Al Jolson meets W.C. Fields meets Leon Redbone. The Zink was one of my earliest and strongest inspirations. Who wouldn't want a job yelling stuff out like that?

**2. John Facenda.** Close second to Harry. "Hello there." Doesn't everyone want to play God?

**1. Harry Kalas.** His voice is a Mona Lisa. It's the most instantly recognizable thing I do when I'm on stage and for that, I am eternally grateful to Harry Kalas. Doing Harry in front of a room full of people is like playing Pine Valley.

We've disqualified hilarious people like Dom Irrera, Joe Conklin, Craig Shoemaker, and Cozy Morley because they happen to be friends of Big Daddy.

**10. Chuck Barris.** We don't care if *The Gong Show* set new standards for degrading humor—we thought it was hilarious. Not only was Chuck ineptly funny as the host, he also developed the show. Stars (stars?) such as Gene-Gene the Dancing Machine, the Unknown Comic, Jaye P. Morgan—well, we loved every second. The whole concept of screening out the lousy singers on *American Idol* stems from the thought process behind Chuck and *The Gong Show.*

**9. Larry Fine.** Okay, what exactly did he do? He was a member of *The Three Stooges* and that's enough for us. Questioning his contribution is sort of like asking if Ringo Starr was really a great drummer. Who knows how the Stooges or the Beatles would have turned out with a different roster? Did you know that the left side of Larry's face was so calloused from Moe slapping him that it was permanently numb? He never felt a thing. Out of respect, go check out his mural at 3rd and South.

**8. Seth Green.** Still so young, *Austin Powers'* Scott Evil has plenty of time to move up this list. Also hysterical in *The Italian Job.* And check him out playing a 12-year-old Woody Allen in an underrated film called *Radio Days.* From Overbrook Park.

**7. The Phillie Phanatic.** We know what you're thinking—isn't Big Daddy friends with him? Well, he's a very difficult guy to get to know. He doesn't talk much. Seriously, anyone who thinks his act has grown stale . . . well, let's just say that you've grown old. Watch the kids when he's doing his thing. They're laughing as hard as kids have ever laughed since he burst on the scene back in the '70s. There was a Sixers game back on a Sunday afternoon in '83 when they were making their championship run. During a key timeout in the fourth quarter, the Phanatic came over from the Vet, charged down the Spectrum aisle onto midcourt, and drove the crowd wild. It's one of our favorite memories from that sensational year. Beyond all that, you try working in that heat.

**6. Jack Klugman.** Yes, Walter Matthau's portrayal of Oscar Madison is tough to beat. Jack, however, expertly portrayed Oscar for five years and never missed one joke. A fine dramatic actor also. If you don't believe us, check out *Twelve Angry Men.*

**5. Sherman Hemsley.** Big Daddy's daughter Keely was born the same year *The Jeffersons* ended its 10-year run, but ask her who her all-time favorite TV character is. Without missing a beat, she'll tell you, "George Jefferson." Who doesn't know someone like George? Sherman kept refining him year after year. A really talented guy who's still out there working. Did you know that Sherman has played the same George Jefferson character in five different shows? Can you name them?

**4. Will Smith.** Admit it, you almost forgot how funny he is, didn't you? He's so talented in so many areas that you don't immediately recall all of his funny stuff. Six seasons of *Fresh Prince,* a great comedy in *Men In Black,* countless videos, *Independence Day,* his work hosting award shows, and on and on and on. When his career is done, he might be the biggest star ever to come out of this town. There's not a field he hasn't conquered. And he's still Philly "street" funny.

**3. Peter Boyle.** *Young Frankenstein, The Dream Team, Joe, Steelyard Blues.* Boyle had a stroke in 1990 and couldn't even talk for six months—then goes on to star for nine sensational seasons on *Everybody Loves Raymond.* What a career. Big Daddy once presented this fellow West Catholic grad with an award at a Communion breakfast. A very nice man who came close to entering the priesthood back in his early years. You may know that this La Salle University grad is the son of early Philadelphia TV star "Uncle Pete." But we'll bet you didn't know that the best man at Peter's wedding was . . . John Lennon.

**2. W.C. Fields.** We know the movies seem very dated. But consider this: Today, more than 60 years after his death, people who don't have a clue who he was still affect many of his voice mannerisms. Did you know he turned down the title role in the *Wizard of Oz?* Once the biggest comedy star in the world, Fields was a wiseguy who never refused a drink. Boy, that doesn't sound too Philadelphia, now does it? In the early '70s, you couldn't go into any Wildwood summer rental without seeing that famous poster of him playing cards.

**1. Bill Cosby.** Life has gone so badly for Bill in recent years. We hope it doesn't cloud people's reflections on him. What didn't he do? One of the most influential stand-ups ever, he sold more comedy albums than anyone. A starring role in *I Spy.* Eight years of *The Cosby Show.* Movie success with *Uptown Saturday Night,* among others. *Fat Albert.* All of this, plus he was a great athlete who still carries the torch for amateur sports. Even the words "Jello Pudding" out of the mouths of a million impressionists makes us smile every time.

## Most Entertaining Athletes Ever in Philadelphia
:: Craig Shoemaker

Note: Philadelphia native Craig Shoemaker was named Comedian of the Year at the *American Comedy Awards,* has recorded three successful comedy CDs, and was seen by over two million people in 2005. He has appeared in over 100 television shows—including *Comedy Central Presents,* ABC's *The View,* HBO's *Comic Relief,* and *The Hollywood Squares.* Recently Craig wrote, produced and starred in the film, *National Lampoon's Totally Baked—A Potumentary.* For more information, visit www.CraigShoemaker.com.

**10. Moose Dupont, Flyers.** The "Moose Shuffle" needs to be taught to Donovan McNabb. Those horrible Michael Jackson moves of McNabb's keep him off my list. Moose was an original, and always looked like he was going to pull a hamstring.

**9. Rick Tocchet, Flyers.** He went into the corners and usually came up with the puck. He always reminded me of those psychos in high school who were not very big, but if you fought them the police would be called to break it up.

**8. Andre Iguodala, Sixers.** I was sitting courtside at the Staples Center in L.A. and I swear his vertical leap was so high he could have written his name on the top of the backboard. Plus, that's a hell of a name to have to write, even at sea level.

**7. Manute Bol, Sixers.** He was so skinny, gravity could knock him down. His one-handed three-point attempts looked like he was trying to hit a trick shot to win a game of horse.

**6. Lenny Dykstra, Phillies.** He always had tobacco chew all over him and dirt on his uniform—in the first inning. Always had lots of hustle. Even if he wasn't fast, he looked like he was.

**5. Tony Franklin, Eagles.** Hell, it's 20 below zero and he's kicking barefoot. I tried it in 80-degree weather and it still hurt.

**4. Ben Hawkins, Eagles.** Before wide receivers discovered Sharpies, pompons, and bling, Ben showed flash by simply playing with his chin strap dangling from his helmet. I used to want him to get hit just to see the helmet fly.

**3. Steve Carlton, Phillies.** Watching him twitch his face always made me wonder what kind of stuff was running through his mind. Since I never heard him speak, I was just left to guess.

**2. Willie Montanez, Phillies.** He caught the ball by throwing his wrist forward like a comedian would do a bad imitation of a gay guy. When he went up to bat he flipped the bat from handle to barrel; just wish he could have hit a little better.

**1. Bob Kelly, Flyers.** He had the shortest strides with so much energy. With his long hair flopping and beer belly bouncing, The Hound looked like he was playing for a local bar league.

# Defunct Teams

Sure, the Athletics skipped town for Kansas City and the Warriors left for San Francisco. But what about the Philadelphia Tapers—what happened to them? Many teams and many leagues failed to survive in this great sports city. Here are our 10 favorites.

**10. Tapers.** Before the ABA competed with the NBA, the American Basketball League gave it a shot from 1960–63. The Tapers tried to fill the gap between the time the Warriors left and the Sixers arrived from Syracuse. Unfortunately, the league folded mid-season, on December 31, 1961. The rather lame team name came from their sponsor, Tuck Tape, a rival (apparently unsuccessful) to Scotch Tape. Their most notable star was Sylvester Blye, a six-foot-nine guard whose college career ended after one game when officials at Seattle University discovered he had toured professionally with the Harlem Clowns.

**9. Fury.** Many soccer teams have tried and failed here—the Atoms, the Fever, and the women's Charge. That probably speaks to the discriminating taste of Philadelphia sports fans. Our favorite of these failures was the Fury, who played at the Vet from 1978–80 in the North American Soccer League. No one remembers any of the team's players. But everyone sure knew their owners—rock stars Paul Simon, James Taylor and, particularly, Peter Frampton, who was huge at the time. Before there was Jon Bon Jovi pushing the Soul, there was Frampton Comes Alive.

**8. Bell.** Owned by Jack Kelly and headed by flamboyant quarterback King Corcoran, the Bell were part of the upstart World Football League, which lasted less than two seasons in the mid-70s. The team drew extremely well at the start, prompting team officials to brag they would someday have more fans than the Eagles. Then word got out that nearly all of their tickets were giveaways. The Bell made the 1974 WFL playoffs with a 9-11 record, but only because the team finishing ahead of them didn't have sufficient funds to travel to a road game.

**7. Athletics.** No, not that version. In the late 1970s, some genius came up with the idea of the professional American Slow Pitch Softball League. These A's featured player-manager Johnny Callison, NFL star Billy "White Shoes" Johnson in centerfield, and *Bulletin* football writer Ray Didinger at third base. When Johnson had to report to football camp, he was replaced in center by a softball legend named Johnny Dollar, who wore "$" as his jersey number. They played for one season in Veterans Stadium to a crowd of several dozen friends and family members, and then relocated to a real softball field in Delaware.

**6. Firebirds.** This minor league hockey team—kind of the Phantoms of the 1970s— played at the old Convention Hall and won the North American Hockey League title in 1976. They featured, at various times, future Flyers coach Terry Murray, future Flyers broadcaster Steve Coates, and future Olympic hero Mike Eruzione. When those attractions didn't sell tickets, the Firebirds tried to cash in on the Flyers' success, signing the (less talented) brothers of Dave Schultz, Rick MacLeish, and Bill Barber. Their coach was the colorful Gregg Pilling, who once protested a league mandate that his players wear helmets by coaching the next few games sporting a German Army helmet.

**5. Sphas.** Ever see that Saturday Night Live skit with Michael Jordan about basketball before black players? That was sort of the Sphas—undersized, slow guys in real short pants shooting underhanded foul shots. The Sphas (the name is an acronym of the South Philadelphia Hebrew Association) existed from 1918 to 1946 and featured local legends Eddie Gottlieb and Harry Litwack. Their heyday was the 1930s when, as an amateur team, they beat both the original Celtics and New York Rens, considered the top pro teams at the time. Eventually the franchise evolved, under player-coach Red Klotz, to become the Washington Generals, the Harlem Globetrotters' touring patsy.

**4. Blazers.** The World Hockey Association lasted seven seasons, but just one (1972–73) in Philadelphia. The Blazers arrived with real star power—Bernie Parent, Derek Sanderson, and Johnny "Pie" McKenzie. But their problems began immediately. Opening Night was cancelled when the ice cracked at the Civic Center. More than 8,000 fans rained souvenir pucks down on the poor Zamboni driver. Sanderson played the year so disinterested that the team PR man's list of daily tasks included waking the star up for games. And when the paychecks inevitably started bouncing, Parent sat out the playoffs. One more thing: Yellow and burnt-orange uniforms?

**3. Stars (baseball).** Few folks are still alive who remember when black players were barred by Major League Baseball's color line. But that's how it was until the late 1940s. The Stars originated in Darby, PA, in the early 1930s and won the National Negro League pennant in 1934. They played their home games at a long-forgotten park at the corner of Belmont and Parkside. Their star players included lefty pitcher Slim Jones, whom reporters claimed threw harder than Lefty Grove in his prime, and catcher "Biz" Mackey (not to be confused with rapper Biz Markie).

**2. Stars (football).** The upstart United States Football League (USFL) lasted just three seasons, but certainly helped Philadelphia get through a tough era of Eagles football. While the Birds went 11-20-1 in 1983–84, the Stars went 31-5, and won the league's championship in 1984. They claimed to be the best team in the city, and it was tough to disagree. In 1985, the Stars moved to Baltimore and, the next season, the USFL went under. Serves them right. Plenty of talent on this squad, including running back Kelvin Bryant, quarterback Chuck Fusina, and the "Doghouse" defense led by future NFLer Sam Mills. Carl Peterson was the general manager and Jim Mora, Sr., was the coach. All in all, a solid franchise. Bonus trivia question: What member of the Stars became the last USFL alum to play for the Eagles? Answer: Sean Landeta, who punted for the Birds in 2005.

**1. Frankford Yellow Jackets.** Named for the part of the city where they played, the Jackets were the top team in the early days of the NFL. They went 14-1-1 in 1926, a victory total no NFL team matched until the 1972 Miami Dolphins. Talk about defense—they shut out 11 opponents that season. Because of state blue laws, the Yellow Jackets would play home games on Saturdays. Then they'd take an all-night train to somewhere like Buffalo or Duluth, and beat a fresh team on Sunday. The Great Depression wiped out their finances, a fire destroyed their stadium at Frankford Avenue and Devereaux Street, and they folded after the 1931 season. Two seasons later the Eagles arrived.

Because many of our lists have been top "ten" lists, why not take a look at the greatest players ever to wear the uniform numbers 1 through 10? This was a lot more challenging than we anticipated.

**#10 Lefty Grove.** We expected a battle royal between Maurice Cheeks and Larry Bowa, but the fact is, neither of those players is in the Hall of Fame and Lefty is. Played nine years for the A's and won two World Series, and pitched in other Series in 1929–31. He led the league in strikeouts seven times in a row, wins four times, and ERA nine times (five with the A's.)

**#9 Sonny Jurgensen.** A member of the Eagles last championship team, this quarterback is in the Pro Football Hall of Fame as well as a being a member of the Eagles Honor Roll. His 32 touchdown passes in 1961 is still an Eagles record. Many who saw Sonny play claim that no quarterback in the history of the game had a stronger arm. Still broadcasting games for the Redskins network—where he regularly rips the Birds.

The Phillies' Manny Trillo and the Flyers' Bob Kelly and Pelle Eklund performed admirably also, and don't forget the Sixers' Willie Burton (who was married to Miss Nude Florida) and the Birds' Joe Pisarcik, who was more famous as a Giant for you-know-which play.

**#8 Dave Schultz.** We know what you're thinking—he wasn't a player, he was a goon. But this Flyers bad boy was instrumental in Philadelphia winning two Stanley Cups. No one symbolized the Bullies like The Hammer. Were fellow Flyer Mark Recchi and the Phils' Bob Boone better players? Absolutely. But Schultz transcended mere athletic exploits; he captured the true soul of a city. We also have to say hello to one of the luckiest Sixers ever to cash a paycheck, Marc Iavaroni, as well as hometown hero Aaron McKie.

**#7 Bill Barber.** Although Eagles quarterback Ron Jaworski played a lot of great seasons, Billy won two Stanley Cups and is in the NHL Hall of Fame. No other Flyer in history scored more regular-season and playoff goals than Billy.

**#6 Chris Therien.** Oops, our mistake.

**#6 Julius Erving.** One of our favorite Phils, Johnny Callison, wore this number proudly. But after Doc wore it, no other athlete of any merit ever chose this number again. As our man legendary Sixers announcer Dave Zinkoff used to call him, "Julius Errrrrrrrrrrrrrrrrving!"

**#6 (Honorable Mention) Johnny Callision.** Hats off to our main man, who also wore #6 for the Phils.

**#5 Donovan McNabb.** No Eagles quarterback has as many postseason wins as Donovan. By the time he retires he'll hold every Birds passing record there is. Does anyone remember that the Flyers' Reggie Leach also wore #5 for a spell?

**#4 Lenny Dykstra.** It's hard to select a player who spent much of his time here on the disabled list, but he had three quality seasons in centerfield—one of them (1993) among the greatest seasons any Phil ever put together. A hard-nosed, gritty player, "Nails" is still a fan favorite. Hard to leave off Flyers defenseman Barry Ashbee for emotional reasons; and we must mention the underrated Clint Richardson, who brought consistency off the Sixers bench during the 1982–83 championship year.

**#3 Jimmie Foxx.** Oh boy, this one's gonna stir it up, isn't it? No denying the greatness of Allen Iverson. We love him. And Allen is going to be in the Basketball Hall of Fame one day, no doubt. But Hall of Famer Foxx slugged his way to three World Series with the A's, winning two of them. He won the MVP Award three times. How many Philadelphia athletes can claim that? In '33, Jimmy won the Triple Crown and got rewarded with a PAY CUT from cheapie owner Connie Mack. In his career, Foxx batted .325 with 1,751 runs and 1,922 RBIs. His 534 home runs stood second only to Babe Ruth until Willie Mays passed him in the mid-1960s. He was also the inspiration for Tom Hanks's performance as Jimmy Dugan in A League of Their Own. Phils great Chuck Klein would get more props from us if he had not worn five other numbers besides #3.

**#2 Moses Malone.** "Fo-Five-Fo." He played only four seasons for the Sixers before being traded in one of the darkest days in Philly sports history. (He later returned for a lackluster fifth season in 1993-94.) This relentless rebounder indeed took us to The Promised Land in '83. An NBA Hall of Famer and one of the 50 Greatest ever, no one ever had the work ethic under the boards like Moses. The city loved him for it. Honorable mention to Eagles kicker David Akers and Flyers defensemen Mark Howe, Ed Van Impe, and Bob Dailey.

**#1 Bernie Parent.** Geez, this was hard. Can we actually leave out Hall of Fame Phils centerfielder and beloved sportscaster Richie Ashburn? Well, if it will make you feel any better, it pains us too. But what are you gonna do? In 10 years with the Flyers, (and one with the WHL's Blazers), he led us to two Stanley Cups, was the first Flyer elected into the Hall of Fame, and is still considered one of the top five goaltenders ever to wear the mask. Also the inspiration for the greatest bumper sticker ever: "Only the Lord Saves more than Bernie Parent." Great new hair, too.

**P.S.** The Sixers' Orlando Woolridge and the Phils' Al Oliver both wore #0 for one season. Is that a number? Zero?

Note: For those too young to recall 1964, we'll recap the ecstasy and eventual agony. After finishing 87-75 in 1963—12 games out of first—the Phillies came out strong the following year and had a 6½-game lead with 12 left to play. The city was out of its collective mind and World Series tickets were already printed. But Cincinnati's Chico Ruiz stole home on September 21 to beat the Phils 1-0, starting a 10-game losing streak. In the end, the Phils lost the pennant to the Cards in what, to this day, is considered the biggest collapse in the history of sports.

Who better to talk to about that year then a man who was the first sports idol to many in this town? Johnny Callison played right field and was the driving force behind the Phils' success that year. An Oklahoma native, Johnny has stayed in the area and currently lives in Glenside with his wife, Diane. Here are his top—and bottom—memories of '64.

## 10. Richie Allen.

I took one look at this guy and I knew he was going to be something special. Despite his image, Richie was a great, great guy. They booed him right away, which I could never figure out.

## 9. Jim Bunning's Perfect Game

Everyone says you're supposed to stay away from a pitcher when he's pitching a perfect game, but Jim wouldn't stay away from us. He was stalking up and down the dugout saying stuff like, 'You guys better start diving for balls, I'm pitching a no-hitter!' I went 2-for-4 in that game with a home run, but nobody remembers that—nor should they. It was a great experience to be part of. A special, special day for Jim. Did I want to make the final out? Well, let's just say that would have been alright, but it was just as fine that I didn't.

## 8. Johnny's Walk-Off Three-Run Home Run in the All-Star Game

This was a moment I'll never forget. A major thrill. I hit a fastball off Dick Radatz. My mother-in-law and sister-in-law were in New York for the game with my wife, who was expecting our daughter, Sherrie. When I hit the homer, my wife thought she was gonna deliver right there.

## 7. The City's Mood Through the Summer

I was living in Glenside and everywhere you went—the dry cleaners, the gas station—everyone knew who I was. The town just went crazy. It was a lot of fun. Everyone was rooting for us. They were so starved for a winner.

## 6. Chico Ruiz Steals Home

I wasn't thinking steal at all. I had never seen anyone steal home in a game I was playing. When he started running, I thought, 'What is this guy, crazy? Who steals home with Frank Robinson at the plate?' Ruiz did that on his own. He had to, it was so insane. (Was there any way of knowing that was the beginning of an oncoming disaster?) Oh, no. It was just one loss. Remember, I played for a Phils team that had lost 23 straight in 1961.

### 5. Johnny Hits Three Homers against the Braves in a Late-Season Loss

No one even remembers that. In fact, I hardly remember it at all myself because we lost. I remember it not being any big thrill at all.

### 4. Elimination Day, October 4, 1964

Well, I remember feeling shitty and just plain exhausted if you want to know the truth. We knew that the city had not had a winner for a long time and that we let everyone down. We did our part by winning the final game, but, unfortunately, the Mets didn't do theirs and lost to the Cards.

### 3. Did Manager Gene Mauch Get Tight in Shortening His Rotation?

I don't think so. I think he went with that rotation (Bunning and Short) to try to win it quickly so he could give us all a rest before the World Series. We had been playing every day. In fact, it was the first time all year he was nice to us. Usually he was cussing at us all for something. I still think we would have won the thing had not Frank Thomas gotten hurt. (Thomas was acquired in August and contributed mightily but broke his thumb on September 8th.)

### 2. Losing the MVP Award

Well, everyone says I would have got it had we won, but we didn't. (Ken Boyer of the pennant-winning Cardinals won it.)

### 1. How He Remembers 1964 Now

It was the closest team I ever played for. Everyone was pulling for each other all year. It was a team with no jealousy.

In compiling lists of the best and worst finishes of all time, we decided to leave out championship games which—by their very nature—are all thrilling. How are we supposed to rank Mo Cheeks's exclamation-point dunk against the Lakers in 1983 against the sight of Tug McGraw hopping up and down on the Vet Stadium mound in 1980?

Besides, it allows us to write this book without mentioning Joe Carter even once.

Oops.

Here are 12 of the best and the worst endings in our history.

## Best

### 12. Jaws to Quick for 99 yards, 1985.

The Eagles had the ball at their one-foot line in overtime against Atlanta at the Vet. The Falcons defense overplayed an expected run, and Mike Quick split the secondary with a beautiful slant route. Ron Jaworski hit him at about the 25, and Quick sprinted his way to a victory—and into the NFL record books in a tie for the longest offensive touchdown.

### 11. Afleet Alex stumbles but wins the Preakness Stakes, 2004.

". . . And Scrappy T veers to the right, and he bumps into Afleet Alex! Alex falls to his knees . . . No, Jeremy Rose has him up! And here comes! Afleet Alex down the stretch!"

Just for the record, Alex won by 4¾ lengths and paid $8.60 on a $2-to-win ticket. Long after those numbers are forgotten, the awe-inspiring finish will be remembered.

### 10. Lindros destroys the Rangers, 1997.

The puck slid toward Eric Lindros's stick with 10 seconds left in a tie game. As Lindros skated in front of the net, a Rangers defenseman pushed a glove into his face.

Now there were nine seconds left in regulation. Lindros shook off the defenseman and moved to his backhand. Eight seconds.

He faked a shot that sent New York goalie Mike Richter to his right. Seven seconds. As Richter moved, Lindros rifled a backhand toward the empty side of the net and . . . Goal! With just 6.8 seconds left, Lindros' bullet gave the Flyers a 3-2 win in Game Four of the Eastern Conference Finals. They went on to win the series in five. It was the high point of Lindros' star-crossed career here.

### 9. Shocking the Cowboys, 1996.

This one had all the markings of a crushing defeat. The Eagles clung to a three-point lead at Texas Stadium, but the Cowboys were driving. Dallas had the ball at the Eagles' three-yard line with 15 seconds to go. Damn, it seemed so inevitable.

Then, Troy Aikman threw one into the end zone—right into the hands of Eagles line-backer James Willis. He lugged it a few yards and then lateraled to Troy Vincent, who outran 11 Cowboys the rest of the way. The 104-yard touchdown set the franchise record for longest TD.

As Merrill Reese said, "The Eagles win, the Eagles win, the Eagles win. . . . "

## 8. The pennant-winning comeback against Houston, 1980.

Okay, this one's a little bit of a cheat, because it happened in the top of an inning, rather than directly ending a game. But winning the pennant in extra innings has to fit on this list somewhere.

Game 5 of the 1980 NLCS may have been the most exciting game ever played by the Phillies. They trailed the Astros—and the great Nolan Ryan—4-2, going into the eighth. Then they scored five runs, three on a Manny Trillo triple. But the Astros tied it up and the game went to the tenth.

Mike Schmidt struck out. Del Unser doubled. Trillo flew out to center. Then, Garry Maddox became the hero, doubling to center and driving in the pennant-winning run. Dick Ruthven quickly put the Astros down in the bottom of the tenth and, for the first time in 30 years, the Phils were in the World Series.

## 7. Johnny Callison wins the All-Star Game, 1964.

Played in Queens at the brand-new Shea Stadium, this All-Star Game featured 15 future Hall of Famers. It entered the bottom of the ninth with the National League trailing 4-3. Red Sox ace Dick Radatz gave up a walk to Willie Mays and a looping single to Orlando Cepeda. Two outs later, Phils rightfielder Callison came up and hammered a fast ball into the right-field seats to win the game for the Nationals.

"That homer was the greatest thrill of my life," Callison said later, "but I remember thinking that it was only the beginning. It was going to be the Phillies year. We had everything going our way. Everything."

Until September, at least.

## 6. Keith Primeau ends the marathon, 2000.

The guy who never seemed to connect in the playoffs ended the third-longest game in NHL history by scoring in the fifth overtime to give the exhausted Flyers a memorable 2-1 victory over the Pittsburgh Penguins. Players said that, by the end—2:35 a.m. to be exact—they felt like they were skating in oatmeal.

The seven-hour contest took it all out of the Penguins. The Flyers won the next two games—and the series.

## 5. Brian Westbrook saves the season, 2003.

The Eagles started the season 2-3. Now they trailed the Giants, 10-7, with 1:34 to play at the Meadowlands. Another loss would have destroyed the season. And the Birds' pathetic offense gave no indication it could pull this one out.

As Jeff Feagles went back to punt for the Giants, the Eagles put nine guys on the line, trying for the block. Feagles got off the punt, but didn't get much hang time on a short wobbler.

Westbrook took it on a bounce at the 16. He quickly broke through a wall of defenders. Then he outran Feagles in front of the Giants' bench and tiptoed along the sideline to evade a last-ditch diving attempt by Marcellus Rivers. Westbrook scored, as 78,000 Giants fans sat in stunned silence.

The return started a nine-game winning streak, leading the Eagles to the NFC Championship game.

## 4. Iverson slays Goliath in Game 1 of the NBA Finals, 2001.

The 76ers had already survived two grueling seven-game series to get here. The Lakers, meanwhile, had not lost in 67 days, a string of 19 games. The Las Vegas line was 1-20 that the Lakers would win the Finals, and even money that the Sixers wouldn't take a single contest.

Vegas apparently did not factor in Allen Iverson.

Game 1, in Los Angeles, was tied after four quarters, with Iverson putting up 41. In OT, he shifted into another gear, scoring seven unanswered points in the final two minutes to give the Sixers a 107-101 win. He left the supposedly impermeable Lakers looking frantic and confused.

"People may be shocked," Iverson said afterwards, "but I don't think we shocked ourselves."

The Lakers came back to take the next four games. But there would be no sweep. And there would be one game to always remember.

### 3. Bobby Clarke makes an overtime statement, 1974.

The Big Bad Bruins—two-time winners of the Stanley Cup—seemed invincible in the '74 Finals, especially after winning Game 1. The Flyers trailed in Game 2 at the Boston Garden, but tied it with 52 seconds to go on a wrister from Moose Dupont, of all people.

Twelve minutes into overtime, Clarke took a pass from Bill "Cowboy" Flett and back-handed one at Gilles Gilbert. The Bruins goalie made the save, but was on his back as the puck bounced out. Clarke picked it up and lifted one high into the net for the victory.

It was the Flyers' first win in Boston in nearly seven years, and it made a statement. "I don't see how anybody can have doubts about us now," Clarke said. "We know we can beat them."

Which, of course, they did.

### 2. Fourth and 26, 2004.

The Eagles were down three points with 1:12 left in regulation in this playoff game to the Packers at the Linc. Donovan McNabb had been sacked eight times and the offense was struggling without an injured Brian Westbrook. It came down to a desperation play—the type that teams never seem to convert. Fourth down and 26 yards to go.

McNabb went back, moved to his right a few steps, and hurled one downfield. Freddie Mitchell, the perennial underachiever, split two Packers defenders and snagged it, beautifully, before taking a hit from Darren Sharper and falling forward for the first down.

David Akers followed with a 37-yard field goal to tie the game. The Eagles won it on another Akers field goal, after Packers quarterback Brett Favre catapulted an interception on Green Bay's first play of overtime.

Afterward, Mitchell suggested that the city show its thanks by erecting a sculpture of him next to the Rocky statue. And he thanked his hands for being so great. Thankfully, he was gone a year later.

### 1. Miracle at the Meadowlands, 1978.

The greatest twist-of-fate ending in NFL history. With the Giants leading the Eagles, 17-12, and seconds remaining, all New York quarterback Joe Pisarcik had to do was kneel over the ball. He didn't, of course.

Herman Edwards' 26-yard return of the fumbled handoff with 20 seconds remaining didn't just become one of the most-replayed moments ever in football, or the ultimate lesson to play every game to the very end. It also served as a turning point for the Eagles. They won three of their last five games in 1978 to make the playoffs for the first time in 18 years.

# Top 10 Philadelphia Soul Records of All Time
## :: Harvey Holiday

Note: Harvey Holiday has been a Philadelphia deejay for over 30 years, and currently spins all your favorite numbers on 98.1 WOGL.

**10. "Stay With Me"—Lorraine Ellison.** Yes, Bette Midler did a version—but get the real thing. You'll love it if you can find a copy.

**9. "Some Kind of Wonderful"—Soul Brothers 6.** "Can I get a witness?"

**8. "Cowboys to Girls"—The Intruders.** Little Sunny, Big Sunny Phil, and Bird

**7. "Could It Be I'm Falling in Love"—The Spinners.** Motown's loss is Philly's gain.

**6. "Betcha By Golly Wow"—The Stylistics.** "You're the one that I've been waiting for."

**5. "Only the Strong Survive"—Jerry Butler.** The Iceman comes to Philadelphia and makes a perfect record.

**4. "Disco Inferno"—The Tramps.** A groove to make you move.

**3. "Expressway (To Your Heart)"—The Soul Survivors.** The first top-10 hit written by Kenny Gamble and Leon Huff. Charlie and Richard Ingui sing it like they've been stuck on the Schuylkill for hours.

**2. "La La Means I Love You"—The Delfonics.** The most gorgeous example of Philadelphia's falsetto harmony.

**1. "If You Don't Know Me by Now"—Harold Melvin and the Blue Notes.** "We've all got our own funny moods. I've got mine, woman you've got yours too."

# Ten Best Rock Records to Come Out of Philly

Since our friend Harvey Holiday has covered the soul sound, let's take a look at the best rock records to ever come out of this town. This list will not cover jazz, folk, classical, opera or hip-hop. That'll be for a future book.

A few rules: No ballads. A song must have been on a major label, and if it wasn't, it had to be a hit nationally.

Honorable mention goes to Robert Hazard, Cinderella, Charlie Gracie, Familiar 48, Bill Doggett, the A's, Pink (who can rock it out), Chubby Checker, G. Love (whose two songs I considered for the top ten—"I76" and "Cold Beverage"—were really more rap than rock), the Dead Milkmen, The Roots (some of their stuff has a rock edge to it), Joan Jett, and Hall & Oats, who were too folksy at the start of their career and too R&B later to make this list—though they are undeniably great and "You Make My Dreams" came really close.

**10. "Rock Around the Clock"—Bill Haley & The Comets.** I must admit that if I never hear this song again it'll be too soon, but there's no denying its importance. And that lightning-quick guitar solo still blisters! From Chester, Bill originally scored only a modest hit with "Clock." But after the song was used in the movie Blackboard Jungle, it went on to sell twenty-five million copies. Actually, we like his hit "Shake, Rattle &Roll" even more, and it was the first rock and roll song to sell a million copies.

**9. "One Bourbon, One Scotch, One Beer"—George Thorogood & The Destroyers.** Blues purists like to put George down, but anyone who has ever seen this Delaware native live (and he made his bones at South Street's legendary club J.C. Dobbs) knows that whatever George lacked in originality, he more than made up for with passion and energy. In other words, they blew the roof off. Could have easily went with "Move It on Over" or "Bad to the Bone" or George's kick-ass version of "No Particular Place to Go", but "Bourbon" is over eight minutes long, so you get more bang for your buck with this FM radio classic.

**8. "Rock and Roll Is Here to Stay"—Danny & The Juniors.** These street-corner Philly boys became national sensations after Dick Clark suggested they change the words of a song they sang called "Do the Bop" to "At the Hop." However, "Rock and Roll" holds up better due to its anthem-like (and very true) lyrics.

**7. "I'm Not Your Man"—Tommy Conwell & The Young Rumblers.** Can this Bala Cynwyd native play a guitar or what? Every lick cuts right through your speakers. Well-crafted song, too.

**6. "Sally's Sayin' Somthin'"—Bill Harner.** The "Human Percolator!" A song that fills the dancefloor every time. Granted, there might not be anyone under fifty on that floor, but a great song is a great song. Not a true national hit, but it was released on Kama Sutra—the Lovin' Spoonful's label—and it did chart high in NY and LA, and was a smash here.

**5. "And We Danced"—The Hooters.** If it was up to us, the Hooters song that we would have included would have been "Fighting on the Same Side", but the Columbia version is inferior to the independently released version on Amore. "Danced" is a true classic featuring the great songwriting skills of Eric Brazilian and Rob Hyman (Hyman went on to write the classic Cindy Lauper tune "Time after Time" and Eric wrote Joan Osbourne's hit "One of Us") and the amazing drumming of David Uosikkinen. That whole era of Philly rock was truly exciting.

**4. "Bang the Drum All Day"—Todd Rundgren.** Geez, there's only about a couple dozen great Todd tunes we could have went with here ("Hello, It's Me," "I Saw the Light," "Long Flowing Robe," to name a few), but "Drum" is just too much fun. An anthem for all us lazy sods, it has also become an arena staple after it became the unofficial anthem for the Green Bay Packers in the nineties. Todd, an Upper Darby native, starts out in Woody's Truck Stop, moves on to The Nazz (more on them later), before alternately going solo and playing with his band Utopia. He also has scored tremendous success as a producer (Meatloaf's Bat Out of Hell among others) and as a guest commentator on the Bill Maher show. His son, Rex, is currently a shortstop in the Florida Marlins minor league organization.

**3. "You Can't Sit Down"—The Dovells.** What a groove this baby lays down! A #3 hit in the country back in '63, the Sixers thought enough of this song more than thirty years later to build an entire advertising campaign around it. Their fantastic blue-eyed soul singer Len Barry later goes solo and scores another monster hit with "1-2-3," a tune that the Paul Schaefer Band still occasionally plays on *The Late Show with David Letterman.*

**2. "Wildwood Days"—Bobby Rydell.** Where "Every day's a holiday, and every night is Saturday night." Funny, eh? Of every song that has attempted to truly capture the heart and soul of Philadelphia, it takes a trip to the Jersey shore to truly accomplish it. Tell me you don't feel like hitting the beach every single time you hear this. Born Robert Ridarelli in South Philly, Bobby's songs moved better than many of his fellow Philly contemporaries, and any man who got to kiss Ann Margaret (in the classic flick Bye-Bye Birdie) back when she was ANN-MARGARET! is alright in our book.

**1. "Open My Eyes"—The Nazz.** Almost forty years old and there's nothing dated about this rock classic. Dynamic guitar work from Todd, beautiful lead and background vocals led by Stewkey, and absolutely incredible drumming from Thom Mooney, whose legendary work on "Under the Ice" almost single-handedly bumped this tune off the list. If you don't own The Nazz's first two albums, well, what's wrong with you?

Note: Bernard "The Executioner" Hopkins won the USBA 160-pound championship in 1992 and held it for an incredible 13 years. The brilliant, tough and outspoken North Philadelphia middleweight made a division-record 20 successful title defenses during his reign, dismantling Felix Trinidad and Oscar De La Hoya in career-defining wins.

Certainly he belongs at the top of any list of all-time Philly fighters. But Hopkins chose to omit himself from this list—at least until his career ends. Here is his choice of the 15 greatest fighters ever to come out of the city. Bernard did not want to rank the fighters, so they are listed alphabetically.

**George Benton,** middleweight (62-13-1 / 36 KO). This defensive wizard was one of the smartest and most skilled of the North Philly legends. His scientific approach thrilled purists and befuddled opponents. He never fought for the title during a career that ran from 1949–70, but was elected to the Boxing Hall of Fame as a trainer.

**Bennie Briscoe,** middleweight (66-24-5 / 53 KO). "Bad Benny" from North Philadelphia was a gritty, murderous-punching fan favorite. He had three title shots during a career that ran from 1962–82.

**Jeff Chandler,** bantamweight (33-2-2 / 18 KO). South Philly's "Joltin' Jeff" was a sticker and mover with a big punch who won the world championship in 1980 and successfully defended it nine times. He was elected to the Hall of Fame in 2000.

**Tyrone Everett,** junior lightweight (36-1-0 / 20 KO). Known as "The Mean Machine," Everett was a slick and popular lefty from South Philadelphia who won the USBA 130-pound title in 1974. He was robbed in his 1976 Spectrum title fight against Alfredo Escalera and was tragically shot to death just six months later.

**Joe Frazier,** heavyweight (32-4-1 / 27 KO). "Smokin' Joe" will forever be Philadelphia's heavyweight champ. His Hall of Fame career started when he won Olympic gold in 1964. He took the world title in 1968 and held it for five years. His three battles against Muhammad Ali are among the most memorable in the history of boxing.

**Joey Giardello,** middleweight (101-25-7 / 33 KO). The Hall of Famer from South Philly fought for 12 years before finally taking the middleweight title from Dick Tiger in 1960 in his 123rd fight. Giardello battled everyone during a 20-year career, including Sugar Ray Robinson, Rubin "Hurricane" Carter, and George Benton.

**Gypsy Joe Harris,** welterweight/middleweight (24-1-0 / 8 KO). The flamboyant and entertaining North Philly sensation with a most-unusual boxing style was forced to retire at age 23 in 1968 when it was discovered that he was blind in his right eye.

**Kitten Hayward,** welterweight/middleweight (32-12-4 / 18 KO). A tricky, tough brawler who scored big wins over Emile Griffith and Bennie Briscoe despite a tendency to cut during fights and party before them. "I used to operate under a philosophy of run all night, sleep all day, until the last two days before the fight," he said. "I used to do a lot of praying the night before fights."

**Len Matthews,** lightweight (42-10-3 / 29 KO). A rangy puncher from West Philly who began his career with 15 wins. He never got a title shot. "As a child I was quiet, obedient, and shy," he said. "But I suppose deep inside there always was a lust for battle."

**Willie Monroe,** middleweight (40-10-1 / 26 KO). "The Worm" was a lanky, smooth-boxing pro who gave Marvin Hagler a real beating at the Spectrum in 1976. But losses to Hagler in the two return bouts helped to keep him out of title contention.

**Bob Montgomery,** lightweight (75-19-3 / 37 KO). One of the all-time greats is best remembered for his classic series against Beau Jack (four fights) and Ike Williams (two fights) during two runs as lightweight champion. "Bobcat's" long career ran from 1938 to 1950.

**Wesley Mouzon,** lightweight (23-3-1 / 9 KO). Known as "The Chocolate Blur," this talented teenage phenom from North Philly KO'd champ Bob Montgomery in a 1946 non-title bout. He was knocked out in a championship rematch, and an eye injury suffered in that loss forced his retirement at age 19.

**Matthew Saad Muhammad,** light heavyweight (39-16-3 / 29 KO). "Miracle Matthew" from South Philadelphia was an amazingly thrilling brawler who waged the greatest wars in Philly history. He won the title in 1979 and defended it eight times during a Hall of Fame career.

**Meldrick Taylor,** junior welterweight (38-8-1 / 20 KO). Taylor was a quick all-action fighter who won Olympic gold in 1984 and followed with pro titles at 140 and 147 pounds. Sadly, he is best remembered for a heartbreaking two-seconds-to-go loss to Julio Cesar Chavez in 1990.

**Bobby Watts,** middleweight (38-7-1 / 20 KO). Known as "Boogaloo," this North Philly fighter was probably the most skilled of the 70's Philly middles. He was the first ever to beat Marvin Hagler. A longtime Top-10 contender, he was unable to rise to championship status because of a weak chin.

The records and comments for each fighter are provided by phillyboxinghistory.com.

Note: J Russell Peltz, a member of the International Boxing Hall of Fame, started promoting fights in Philadelphia as a 22-year-old back in 1969. Still active, he has promoted fights at the Blue Horizon Arena and the Spectrum as well as East Coast casinos from Atlantic City to Connecticut. Peltz is respected as one of the sweet science's top historians.

### 10. Joey Giardello decisions Sugar Ray Robinson in 10 rounds, June 24, 1963.

In a battle of aging veterans that should have taken place a decade earlier, Giardello soundly outpointed Robinson at Convention Hall to earn a shot at the world middleweight title, which he won later that year from Dick Tiger in Atlantic City.

### 9. Joe Louis KOs Gus Dorazio, February 17, 1941.

On his Bum-of-the-Month tour, Louis stopped off in Philadelphia to defend his heavyweight title against our own real-life Rocky and won easily in two rounds in front of 15,425 at Convention Hall.

### 8. Sugar Ray Robinson decisions Kid Gavilan in 15 rounds, July 11, 1949.

Robinson had his toughest time as welterweight champion when he barely outpointed future champion Gavilan before more than 27,000 at Municipal Stadium.

### 7. Joe Louis KOs Al Ettore, September 22, 1936.

Louis, the future heavyweight champion, was in his second fight since losing to Max Schmeling. He had a tougher-than-expected time with West Philadelphia tough guy Al Ettore, who lasted until the fifth round. A crowd of 40,407 at Municipal Stadium saw the first of Louis' two fights in Philadelphia.

### 6. Alfredo Escalera decisions Tyrone Everett in 15 rounds, November 30, 1976.

Boxing experts rate this as one of the worst decisions of all-time. Unbeaten junior lightweight challenger Everett, of South Philadelphia, appeared to have handily won the World Boxing Council world championship. The lone Philadelphia judge, siding with a judge from Puerto Rico, voted for Escalera in a scandalous ruling, a split decision with the ref voting for Everett. The Spectrum crowd of 16,019 set a Pennsylvania indoor boxing attendance record.

### 5. Matthew Saad Muhammad KOs Marvin Johnson, July 26, 1977.

Saad Muhammad, of Philadelphia, was then known as Matthew Franklin. He and Johnson, who was from Indianapolis, engaged in one of the most brutal toe-to-toe slugging matches ever seen. The fight, at the Spectrum, was even on the scorecards until Saad knocked Johnson out in the 12th and final round of a light-heavyweight elimination bout.

### 4. Kid Gavilan KOs Gil Turner, July 7, 1952.

Gavilan, a respected welterweight champion from Cuba, successfully defended his title when he broke open a close fight and stopped Philly's Turner (31-0 at the time) in the 11th round before 39,025 at Municipal Stadium. It was the largest crowd ever to watch a world welterweight title fight until June 1980, when Roberto Duran and Sugar Ray Leonard topped it in Montreal for their first fight.

### 3. Ike Williams KOs Bob Montgomery, August 4, 1947.

Williams, from Trenton, and Montgomery, from Philadelphia, each held a piece of the world lightweight title. They settled matters before more than 30,000 at Municipal Stadium. Williams knocked out Montgomery in the sixth round to avenge a knockout he had suffered more than three years earlier to Montgomery at Convention Hall.

### 2. Rocky Marciano KOs Jersey Joe Walcott, September 23, 1952.

Unbeaten challenger Marciano came from behind to knock out Walcott, the heavyweight champion, with a single right-hand punch in the 13th round. More than 40,000 watched at Municipal Stadium in what Hall of Fame promoter Herman Taylor called "the best heavyweight fight I ever looked at."

### 1. Gene Tunney decisions Jack Dempsey in 10 rounds, September 23, 1926.

Tunney upset Dempsey to win the world heavyweight title before 120,757 fans who braved a steady drizzle at Sesquicentennial Stadium, which was later known as Municipal Stadium and then JFK Stadium. That's right—120,757 fans!

**12. Tom Dempsey.** He was born with no right hand, and no toes on his right foot. So what better job than to become an NFL place kicker? Dempsey played four seasons (1971–74) with the Eagles after gaining fame for kicking an NFL-record 63-yard field goal with New Orleans. I can still see him in my mind's eye, using that modified, flattened shoe and smashing the ball with that old straight-on style.

**11. Bobby Clarke.** You may have forgotten that when Clarke was drafted in 1969 as a 168-pound teenager, many so-called experts believed that his diabetes would curtail an NHL career. Clarke proved them wrong and became a Hall of Famer and three-time MVP. His medical condition drove him to play with an ethos—losing is worse than dying—that stuck with the franchise for decades.

**10. Cecil Martin.** His family's financial problems caused them to become homeless when Martin was a teenager. For a while, he lived in the back seat of a car. Martin overcame that to have a four-year career with the Eagles (catching a crucial touchdown pass in the 2001 playoff game against the Bears). No player was more involved with the Eagles Youth Partnership during his time here.

**9. Vince Papale.** Every beer-league ballplayer dreams of trying out for—and making—the big club. Papale actually did it with Dick Vermeil's Eagles in 1976, winning a roster spot at rookie coach Vermeil's open-call workout with a bunch of other regular Joes. He played three remarkable years with the Eagles and did some exceptional things off the field, too. Somebody ought to make a movie about this guy.

**8. Afleet Alex.** Not just for winning the Preakness Stakes in 2005 after nearly falling to his knees. We honor Alex—and his team of owners, lead by Chuck Zacney—for linking their fortunes to "Alex's Lemonade Stand," the fundraising campaign for pediatric cancer research started by Alexandra Scott, who died from the illness at age eight.

**7. Tug McGraw.** As a player, he was all laughs and good times. Facing death in his fifties, he became a model of dignity in the toughest of times. Today, the McGraw Foundation—which he created—honors him by funding brain cancer research and improving the quality of life for brain tumor survivors.

**6. Tim Kerr.** He kept coming back from shoulder and knee surgeries that would have driven a lesser man into retirement. But those setbacks were trivial compared with the death of his wife 10 days after she gave birth to their third daughter in 1990. He came back from that too, to raise his children, play another two seasons, and start a foundation, Tim Kerr Charities.

**5. Troy Vincent.** When *The Sporting News* listed the "100 Good Guys in Sports" in 2003, the guy at the top of the list was Eagles cornerback Troy Vincent. A native of Trenton, Vincent created charities in his hometown to improve literacy and provide medical help for indigent families, among other community endeavors. Vincent doesn't just fund them, and doesn't just direct them. He's out on the streets pitching in.

**4. Bernard Hopkins.** He grew up as a self-described thug on the city's meanest streets. By the age of 17, Hopkins had started serving 56 months in prison for multiple violent offenses. Then he turned himself around, taught himself to read, and earned a high school diploma while incarcerated. He also learned to box at Graterford Prison. He grew as a man to become one of this city's best-ever champions.

"People ask if I think I'm a role model," he said. "Yes, I am. I've done wrong and it shouldn't be forgotten. But good things can happen if you decide to truly turn your life around."

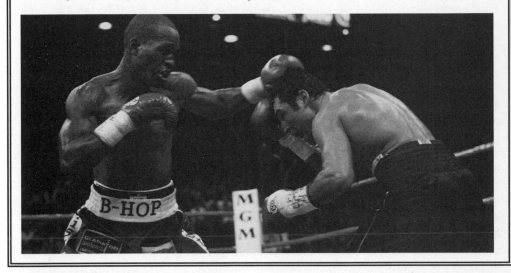

**3. Barry Ashbee.** Leukemia claimed him just 30 days after he was diagnosed in 1977. That was three years after a slap shot hit him in the eye and ended his career at age 34. Those who saw Ashbee go through injuries and illness say he never once complained or succumbed to self pity. "He was the strongest guy mentally I've ever seen," said Bob Clarke.

**2. John Cappelletti.** As a Penn State senior in 1973, he rushed for 1,522 yards on Saturdays and worried the rest of the week about his young brother, Joey, who was dying of leukemia. When they awarded John the Heisman Trophy, he broke from his prepared speech to say, "They say I've shown courage on the football field, but for me it's only on the field. Joey lives with pain all the time. His courage is round the clock. I want him to have this trophy. It's more his than mine, because he's been such an inspiration to me." There wasn't a dry eye at the Downtown Athletic Club.

**1. Jim Eisenreich.** He was so troubled battling Tourette's Syndrome early in his career that he briefly retired. By the time he came to Philadelphia at age 33, medication and his determination to succeed had made Eisenreich into a valuable player. Before nearly every Phillies game in the mid-90s, you'd find Eisenreich giving a pep talk to a visiting youngster, explaining how obstacles could be overcome.

Not a bad list, Glen, but you left out many of my favorites. So here are my choices:

**10. Rollie Massimino.** I know I'll catch hell with this one. Understand, I'm a huge fan of the Big 5. I grew up with it. Lived, breathed and took a bath with it. A lot of people blame Rollie for the breakup of the Big 5. That may be true, and I do not look at him the same way I once did. Hell, I'm a St. Joe's fan for crying out loud. But, damn it, that '85 team took me on one of the most incredible, improbable rides of my entire sports life. Whether or not that "family" mantra he preached ended up being bull or not, I completely bought into it at the time. Imagine, a little Catholic school from Philly (well, close enough) winning the NCAA Championship. Dreams really did come true that magical season.

**9. Joe Conklin.** Let's face it, when I was hired at WIP, I knew what listeners were saying: "Oh, another comic at WIP?" I knew that anything I attempted to do was going to be measured against the brilliance of Joe's work. Lucky for me, I worked solo and had a show to run, while Joe was there to do funny bits only. Thank God for this, because if I had to go toe-to-toe with Joe doing sports humor, I would have been crushed. A true mad genius whose bits never cease to astound and inspire me.

**8. Ron Jaworski.** I don't know if Eagles fans even remember this because he's so revered in this city now, but back in his playing days, this quarterback wasn't liked by everybody. He was the brunt of a lot of cruel, dumb Polish jokes (okay, some of them were funny) when he wasn't having a good game. Tough as nails, Ron hung in there. Hey, if a man can handle 237 concussions, he can surely handle some occasional negative criticism. Now look at him. A successful and beloved businessman who deserves it, because Ron always took the time out for everybody. You'd think he was born and raised in this town, he's so accepted as one of our own.

**7. Dave Zinkoff.** For you youngheads out there, Dave was the Sixers PA announcer for decades. Famous for his colorful way of pronouncing names, his humor, his tremendous charity work, and for just being . . . Zink. Dave did the announcing at my wedding, and I think a lot of people figure I got him there because I was a member of the media. Nothing could be further from the truth. Back then, I was a doorman at the downtown Sheraton, where Dave kept his ticket office. He had befriended me and, when he heard I was getting married, he offered to work at my wedding without charging me a dime. Imagine, the Zink calling out the bridal party: "And noooooow, for the first time EVER . . . ." When he died on Christmas Day 1985, I was in my bathtub in Upper Darby and I cried like a baby.

**6. Joe Frazier.** One time as a boy I was at a PAL sports banquet in a beat-up church basement hall in Southwest Philly. The host introduced an up-and-coming boxer in the audience. "Someday he will make us all proud," the host said. "His name is Joe Frazier, and I would like him to stand up and take a bow." Turned out, Joe was sitting at my table. As a matter of fact, I had just passed him the salt shaker. If you had told me then that that young man would someday be part of the biggest event in sports history, I would have said, "Naah." But, Joe, you sure made us proud.

**5. Allen Iverson.** Someone once asked Joe DiMaggio why he played so hard every game. He replied, "I figure there's some father who has taken his son to see me for the first time and I don't want to let them down." That quote applies to AI. On the court, he has not let me down once in his entire career. Every night, every game, I know I'm going to see the fastest man ever with a basketball thrill me and chill me. How does he do it? He has this intimidating presence that I've always compared to another small, very thin man—Frank Sinatra. When a trumpet player would show up for a session and find out he was recording with Sinatra, you better believe he got his game into gear. Same way with Allen. If you're trying to cover him, you better bring your "A" game. Because you know he is.

**4. Charles Barkley.** The last superstar who never built a wall around himself. He talked to fans during the game, bought folks a drink at a bar after the game. Nowadays it's about that cordoned-off VIP section. Charles's openness got him into trouble every now and then, but I wish more superstars followed his lead. And funny? Forget about it. What I also love about Charles is that he believes every man, regardless of what he does for a living, is entitled to express his opinion. How often do you hear people say that an actor or comic or sports talk-show host has no right to speak out on important issues? Charles speaks out. Boy, does he ever.

**3. Johnny Callison.** He was one of the best players in baseball in the 60s and still had to work in the off-season bartending, selling cars, selling insurance. Soon after his days, the economics changed. You might think he'd be all sour and bitter, right? Wrong. I used to perform at a comedy club where Johnny poured cold ones, and a nicer guy you never met. He was gracious and patient with every fan that approached him. Here's a man who had every right to wish his mother had given birth just 10 years later, which would have made him a multi-millionaire who wouldn't have to work the rest of his life. Yet Johnny kept his chin up and was grateful for everything the game gave to him. There's a lesson to be learned here.

**2. Bobby Jones.** As big as a sports fan as I am, I have to admit that the bling-bling of it all can bring me down. You too, right? So how did Bobby do it? He played in a league with so much selfishness and ego and yet carried himself with dignity. Many self-professed family-oriented, clean-living types are just posers. Not Bobby. He had something kind to say about everybody and always meant it. Come to think about it, have you ever heard an unkind word about Bobby? A religious man, but he never, ever preached. *The Daily News* once did a piece on all of the Sixers' favorite movies. Bobby's all timer—and boy did this one stick out—was Mary Poppins. I asked him about it years later, and he analyzed the movie scene by scene. Explained how the message and spirit of the film was a lesson to all. Now while I'm not going to trade in my copy of Wild Things for Mary Poppins, I admire his stance and actually felt guilty for being my cynical, sarcastic self. Have I mentioned what a truly awesome player he was?

**1. Phil Martelli.** When you grow up in a neighborhood where Big 5 basketball means the world and one of your own ends up not just as the head coach of the St. Joe Hawks, but also one of the better-known coaches in the country, well, it makes you pretty damn proud. Don't let the humor fool you, my man can coach. We grew up five tiny blocks from each other, played in all the same leagues, often on the same team.

**Take a look at this picture of Phil I took with my own
Brownie Instamatic in 1963.**

Note: Pat Croce is the former president of the 76ers and a fitness guru. He is also the best-selling author of *I Feel Great and You Will Too!*, a highly sought motivational speaker, and the creator of Pirate Soul Museum and the Rum Barrel restaurant in Key West, Florida.

**10. Allen Iverson.** He is the David versus Goliath in the game of basketball. I will never forget his ability to carry us to the NBA Finals against Shaq and the Los Angeles Lakers.

**9. Jerry Segal.** Diagnosed as a quadriplegic, Jerry, who through his indomitable spirit is able to play his favorite game of golf, expends just as much energy raising millions for his beloved Magee Rehabilitation Hospital.

**8. Dave Poulin.** A walk-on to the Flyers in 1982, Dave ascended to the prestigious "captain" position and led the team to the Stanley Cup Finals in 1985 and 1987.

**7. Oprah.** She uses her notoriety and power for positive projects on a global scale.

**6. Joe Paterno.** He is living proof that you're never too old to follow your dreams by doing what you believe to be right, despite what the critics may scream.

**5. Senator John McCain.** Anyone who has been tortured and imprisoned for five years—when he could have chosen to been released—and is willing to speak out and tackle sensitive issues like torture and steroids, well, that's my hero.

**4. Bill Bergey.** The Eagles' middle linebacker of the late '70s and early '80s took no prisoners. His teammates followed his leadership to the Super Bowl.

**3. Sister Mary Scullion.** This marathon-running nun has single-handedly tackled the city of Philadelphia's homeless problem and cut the score in half.

**2. Michael Jordan.** His leadership was demonstrated on the court, but it was his "breakfast club," where he motivated his teammates to weight train with him, that set the Bulls' championship pace.

**1. Bono.** The fabulous lead singer for the rock band U2 is the leader of a movement to eradicate debt and AIDS in Africa. A worthy role model and motivator for anyone.

You think you work for a cheapskate or a numbskull? Consider these front-office losers.

**10. Brad Greenberg.** Pat Croce's first choice as general manager of the Sixers quickly proved to be in way over his head. What we'll remember most is Greenberg's complete disdain when forced by Croce to listen to season-ticket holders' laments one night at the arena. These days, Greenberg is an associate basketball coach at Virginia Tech (now there's upward mobility), where his resume brags of him picking Allen Iverson first in the 1996 NBA draft, but ignores his hiring Johnny Davis as coach.

**9. Jack Ramsay and Don DeJardin.** It's tough to tell where the bad work of Ramsay ends and DeJardin's begins but, together, these two general managers turned the Sixers from a 68-13 NBA Champion to a 9-73 disaster in just six seasons. The hideous Wilt trade. Giving away Chet Walker and Wali Jones. Making first-round draft choices from 1967 through 1972 of—are you ready?—Craig Raymond, Shaler Halimon, Bud Ogden, Al Henry, Dana Lewis, and Fred Boyd.

**8. Russ Farwell.** Since 1973, the Flyers have missed the playoffs just five times. Four of those seasons—1990–91 through 1993–94—make up Farwell's tenure as general manager. You can also give him and Jay Snider credit—or blame—for the trade to get Eric Lindros.

**7. Jerry Wolman.** Owned the Eagles from the 1964 through 1968 seasons, during which they went 28-41-1. Awarded a 15-year-contract to Joe Kuharich, whose name you will see again very soon. Went bankrupt during his tenure as owner and was forced to sell. That's a triumvirate of terrible. A nice guy, by all accounts. But you know the saying. . . .

**6. Ed Wade.** Spent eight years as Phillies general manager overvaluing his talent and making deadline trades for washed-up middle relievers. Kept Terry Francona for four losing seasons and later hired Charlie Manuel. Wade also had a perpetual sour-milk expression and alienated fans every time he opened his mouth. It says something about our town's legacy of bad management that there are five guys who could be considered worse.

**5. John Quinn.** Like this guy. Quinn was the Phillies vice president and general manager from 1959–72. That's an astounding 14 seasons with no post-season appearances. Quinn ran an organization that was infamous for being paternalistic toward black players and cheap toward everyone. Once, he was caught paying a young Bahamian outfielder, Tony Curry, several thousand dollars under the minimum because Curry didn't know any better.

**4. Jack Pastore.** Here is a list of all first-round pitchers picked during Pastore's two stints as Phils scouting director in the 1980s: Tony Ghelfi, Kevin Romine, Brad Brink, Derek Lee (no, not that one), Blas Minor, and Pat Combs. Over five drafts, he picked dozens of pitchers. Not a single one enjoyed a Major League career in which he retired with at least 40 victories and a winning record. Seriously, you could throw a dart and come up with better results.

**3. Joe Kuharich.** Take Rich Kotite as a coach and Harry Gamble as a general manager, combine the weakest elements of the two, and you've got Kuharich, who ran the Eagles under Wolman from 1964–68. We'll deal with his coaching in another chapter, but as general manager he traded stars like Sonny Jurgensen, Tommy McDonald, Irv Cross, and Maxie Baughan for virtually nothing. A franchise that entered the 1960s as the NFL champs, left it as one of the weakest. Plus, he had the kind of paranoid demeanor often compared with Captain Queeg.

**2. Gerald Nugent.** He owned the Phils from 1933 to 1942, a decade when they finished last six times and next-to-last the other four. After Chuck Klein won the Triple Crown in 1933, Nugent traded him rather than give Klein a raise. Nugent was finally forced out by baseball's other owners, leaving the franchise to be run by the Commissioner's office for a season. Eventually it was sold to a lumber tycoon named William D. Cox. Nine months later, Cox was banned for life by Commissioner Kenesaw Mountain Landis for gambling on Phillies games. We can't imagine he was betting on the Phils to win. (Isn't it something how Phillies executives dominate this list? We guess that's why the franchise has won exactly one world title in more than 120 years.)

**1. Norman Braman.** You were expecting anyone else? No owner ever alienated the fan base like "Bottom Line Braman." He seemed like an evil character from a Dickens novel (or Disney: think Scrooge McDuck), constantly squeezing the joy from our football team and the nickels from our pockets. He was a native Philadelphian who ran the club as an absentee landlord, monitoring player holdouts from his villa in France. He ran the most profitable franchise in the NFL, yet kept players' and coaches' salaries among the bottom five. Hell, he even charged his players for sanitary socks. And when free agency arrived in 1992, and Braman could no longer keep players under his penny-pinching prices, well, that was the end of any success the Eagles had under his tenure.

# Top Sports Bars :: Pete Ciarrocchi

Note: When we decided to list the area's best sports bars and restaurants, we asked an expert's opinion. Pete Ciarrocchi, of Chickie's & Pete's, has been serving up his legendary crab fries since 1977. There are currently four Chickie's and Pete's; the South Philadelphia location (1526 Packer Ave.) was recently named by ESPN as the nation's third-best sports bar.

Here are Pete's favorite places—other than his own great restaurants—to watch a ballgame. His criterion include versatility, action, food, alternative fun, and the pick-up factor.

**10. Top Dog America's Bar & Grill, 2310 W. Marlton Pike (Rt 70), Cherry Hill.** Sometimes a sports bar, sometimes a night club. Sometimes the fans aren't quite sure who's playing. Well, we're talking Jersey here, but everybody seems to be having a great time.

**9. Champps Americana, 25 Route 73 South, Voorhees.** A South Jersey haunt for the occasional sports fan. Nice cars, hot crowd, and a lot of attitude.

**8. Cheerleaders, 2740 S. Front St., Philadelphia.** Don't let the name fool you. What you'll find here is sports fans, TVs, beer, and boobs. Sounds like fun to me. (Of course, you can walk around the corner and check out Big Daddy's Monday Night Football parties at Club Risque. Boy, that's a tough job, isn't it?)

**7. Mc Fadden's at Citizens Bank Park.** During a Phillies game, it's always a home run.

**6. Brownie's, 23 East Lancaster Ave., Ardmore.** Delaware County's institution for the sports enthusiast. Great sports and great rock.

**5. Dave & Busters, 325 North Columbus Blvd., Philadelphia.** Huge. Huge! Not only can you lose your date here, but if the games on TV stink you can play one of theirs.

**4. Finnigan's Wake, 537 North 3rd Street, Philadelphia.** A great Irish bar with great blue-collar sports fans. They watch American football and European football (soccer). LOUD, wet and wild.

**3. PJ Whelihan's, 400 North Haddon Ave., Haddonfield.** A suburban-style sports bar with good food, good TVs, friendly service, and a casual sports atmosphere.

**2. McNally's Tavern, 8634 Germantown Ave., Chestnut Hill.** Lots of local flavor at this non-smoking establishment. Lots of folks wearing button-down oxfords. The "Schmitter" sandwich is one of the greatest things you could eat while watching a game.

**1. O'Neal's, 611 South 3rd St., Philadelphia.**
A Queen Village hotbed for sports. Located right off of South Street, a unique location for the unusual sports watcher. Some of the customers are even worth watching. Piercings are requested, not required.

# The Best Cheeseburger in the Delaware Valley—a Debate

"Hamburgers—the cornerstone of any nutritious breakfast."

—Jules Winnfield, Pulp Fiction

**Glen Says:** In 2005, I went in search of the greatest burger in town. Over the course of six weeks, I ate 28 cheeseburgers at 19 different places in three states. Anything for radio.

I gained five pounds during my quest, raised my cholesterol level about 200 points, and received one angry phone call from my doctor.

There were just two ground rules. First, I set a price cap of $10. A $100 Kobe-beef-and-truffles special in fancy Center City establishments might be the best, but how many Regular Joes can stop there on the way home for a slider and a beer?

Second, I tried to order the same thing at each place—bacon cheeseburger with grilled onions and/or mushrooms. No boursin, broccoli rabe, or goat cheese to confuse things. Just a basic, All-American burger. Bring me a draft beer or black-and-white milkshake on the side.

Here were the best:

## 5. Standard Tap, 901 N. Second Street, Philadelphia

This Northern Liberties hangout offers a big, fat burger with gooey cheese. They dress it up with a wedge of sweet onion and grilled mushrooms, put it on a homemade crispy bun and charge you $8.50. It's well worth the price.

Standard Tap is a loud, busy place with a crowd that probably knows more about Indie Rock than the Iggles. To be honest, I didn't recognize 90 percent of the artists on the juke box. What I did recognize was a magnificent creation of red meat. And that's why I was there.

Well that, plus the beer. "The Tap's" choices are all on draught and all local—Stoudts, Yards, Victory, Flying Fish—basically all of the microbrews that do Philadelphia proud.

## 4. Five Guys Famous Burger and Fries, several local locations

Five Guys is a small Virginia chain climbing its way up the East Coast. Bottom line: The food is delicious, and—for $5—I got more burger than I could finish.

Start with the freshly ground 100-percent USDA-grade quality beef. The patties are handmade every day—no machines here. I ordered the regular bacon cheeseburger, which is actually two stacked patties with cheddar and three strips of extra crisp bacon. It looks and tastes more like something you'd get at the neighborhood barbecue than from an inexpensive franchise that hands you your meal in a paper bag.

That bag, by the way, was stained with the beautiful grease coming from Five Guys' hand-cut fries. Even if you're a vegetarian, you should go there just for the fries.

## 3. Phil's Tavern, 931 West Butler Pike, Ambler

First, deal with the parking lot, which overflows so much that there was an attendant directing traffic at noon. Then, ignore the menu, which is as large as Andy Reid's play chart. Just ask for the 10-ounce burger. They are not stingy at Phil's. It came with melted cheese on both sides of the bun and 13(!) slices of bacon. Not even a glutton like Big Daddy could put down that much bacon in one sitting.

The burger was fresh-from-the-butcher sirloin, and hand-formed into a thing of beauty. If you're on the Atkins Diet, just lose the bun and enjoy the rest.

## 2. Black Bull Steakhouse, 1470 Buck Road, Holland

Okay, this is not my usual greasy spoon kind of joint, and it's rare that I'll chomp down a burger at any restaurant boasting a wine list the size of a phone book. But if you can get past the upscale surroundings, you'll savor one of the great burgers of your life.

The Angus Steak Burger comes loaded with cheddar cheese, shoestring onions, a smoky homemade steak sauce, lettuce and tomato on an oven-fresh onion-poppy-seed roll. I ordered mine medium-rare (anyone who demands well-done deserves the shoe leather he gets) and was thrilled to find it cooked to the perfect tint of pink. This is a magnificent piece of meat, almost too beautiful to eat. It comes with steak fries and sells for a lusty $9.50.

Wash it down with one of the Black Bull's dozens of beer offerings. I recommend the River Horse Belgian Frostbite.

## 1. Rossi's Bar & Grill, 501 Morris Avenue, Trenton

Who would have thunk that Philly's best burger would come from Trenton? But this is it. This is the place for nirvana on a bun. It's worth the drive, and I'm a guy who hates crossing the bridges to Jersey. Rossi's is the quintessential corner hangout—nothing fancy, just a raucous bar near the dining area and the best burgers in the Middle-Atlantic.

These babies are huge. They've got the right amount of grease. They're tender, they're tasty and they're fresh—Rossi's must keep the Grade-A cows right out in the back. I ordered mine medium-rare and a cross-section revealed the perfect coloration, like a beautiful red sunset.

You can get them at Rossi's with provolone, American, or Swiss (what, no cheddar?), and be sure to ask for lettuce and tomato on the side, or you won't get any. The prices are cheap enough to order two, but I wouldn't recommend that unless you're planning on entering Wing Bowl. The beer selection is sturdy.

The only downside is that Rossi's—halfway between New York and Philly—considers itself a Yankees bar. If you can stomach the shrine to Joe DiMaggio and the bar chatter about A-Rod, you'll be rewarded with a spectacular slab of red meat.

**Big Daddy Says:** Burger and Fries. Does it get any more American? If I donated any of my organs to science (and who the hell would want them?), doctors would cut me open and thousands of burgers and fries would come falling out of my body. I am always—always—in the mood for a burger. When all else fails on a menu, you can never fail with a burger. NEVER! There's no mood that doesn't fit a burger, is there?

I am going to get no fancier on my list than a bacon cheeseburger. That's as complicated as I like my burgers to get. And although I have eaten 467,348 Roy Rogers' Double-R-Bar Burgers in my life, my list has no national chains. I also have to give a special shout out to the defunct downtown H.A. Winston's that was the greatest burger this town ever produced.

Here are five of my favorites:

## 5. Hollywood Café, 940 Mantua Pike (Rt. 45), Woodbury Heights, N.J.

Every blue moon, I order a burger instead of breakfast when I'm at a diner, and I'm always surprised at how terrific a diner burger can be. Not that the Hollywood is just a diner. It's a great sports bar and between October and May you can always find me on Friday sipping a Johnnie Walker Black at their great "Happy Hour." All their burgers are 10 ounces of succulent Black Angus beef served on dynamite toasted sesame seed buns. Must be eaten with two hands.

## 4. P.J. Whelihans, 799 DeKalb Pike, Blue Bell

Start off with eight ounces of Angus Beef. Throw in two slices of yellow cheddar cheese and two strips of smoked-apple bacon with a healthy dose of lettuce, tomato, and onions. It's all served up on a Kaiser bun that's kind of "snowflaky." You got a real winner. The 30-plus TV screens make it a great place to watch a game, and the servers ain't bad on the eyes either.

## 3. Steve's Cheesesteaks, 7th & South, Philadelphia

These babies just melt in your mouth and it's all in the bun. (When are chefs going to realize that burgers are meant to be served up on "buns" and not Kaiser rolls? A Kaiser absorbs all the grease, rendering the burger dry.) We all know burgers are meant to be greasy and you better wear a bib at Steve's. They use oversized soft Vilotti buns, which make all the difference. The joint itself is old-fashioned (and not in some fake "Happy Days" way) with counter seats and big red booths. And be sure to only order one side of fries if you're with a friend because the serving is big enough for two, and they are greasy too.

## 2. Charlie's Hamburgers, 336 Kedron Ave., Folsom

Remember the "Cheeseburger-Cheeseburger" skit with John Belushi and the gang on Saturday Night Live? (By the way, I was in the real joint in Chicago.) That's the feel of Charlie's. It's one of those places where, when you call them on the phone, the guy answers by saying "Yeah?" The burgers are so tiny that you gotta eat about five of them, but believe me, these greasy suckers are worth it. They butter the bun, which is a unique touch. They've been around since 1935, and when I lived in Upper Darby I must have gone to their old location off Baltimore Pike a zillion times. Fantastic shakes too.

## 1. New Wave Café, 784 S. 3rd Street, Philadelphia

First off, it's one of our favorite Queen Village watering holes. Nothing fancy, just a good old-fashioned tavern with a strong jukebox and cold beer. There's even a dartboard in the back. When we questioned the owner, Aly, if we could ask the chef what goes into these tasty babies, he replied, "Are you kidding? It's a secret!" But he did reveal that they're cooked with eight ounces of Angus beef that's hand formed, never pressed, never frozen, and cooked on a grated surface and not a flat grill. Not sure what that all means, but they sure taste great. Many unusual cheeses to choose from, and they're all served up on Vilotti Pisanelli bread (which, you might notice, I'm partial to.). You must check these out.

Sometimes the most unexpected of mortals can reach up and turn in a magical moment.

**10. Steve Jeltz.** The weakest of all weak-hitting shortstops hit all of five homers in eight Major League seasons. Somehow, on June 8, 1989, he hit two in one game—one lefty, and one righty.

**9. Bobby Hoying.** In his first three starts for the Eagles in 1997, he threw for 835 yards, with six touchdowns and just one interception. Some of us were seeing the next Van Brocklin. Unfortunately, in his next 11 starts, he tossed four touchdowns and 15 interceptions. Turns out he threw more like the next Van Morrison.

**8. J.J. Daigneault.** His only mention in the NHL record book is this: Most Teams Played For, career (10). But his two-season stop in Philadelphia produced one of the most memorable goals in franchise history—Daigneault's slap shot past Edmonton's Grant Fuhr with 5:32 left was the winner in Game Six of the 1987 Stanley Cup Finals. It was his only postseason goal for the Flyers.

**7. Kim Batiste.** The seldom-used infielder had just one post-season at-bat for the 1993 Phils, but made the most of it. In the bottom of the 10th in Game One of the NLCS, he beat the Braves, driving in John Kruk with a walk-off double. Career regular-season average of Kimothy Emil Batiste: .234. Career post-season average: 1.000.

**6. Koy Detmer.** When Donovan McNabb got hurt in Week 11 of the 2002 season, Eagles fans figured a promising season was ruined. Detmer stepped in against the 49ers on Monday Night Football and went 18-for-26 for 227 yards and two touchdowns. Then, God appeared to wake up, see how ridiculously well Detmer was playing, and immediately dislocate his elbow before things really got out of hand. That, of course, led to. . . .

**5. A.J. Feeley.** When Detmer went down we knew all hope was gone. So here comes Feeley, who proceeds to win four of the next five games. He did so well that the Eagles were able to parlay the feat by trading him to Miami for a second-round pick, which later became wide receiver Reggie Brown.

**4. Al Hill.** Made his debut with the Broad Street Bullies on February 14, 1977. And what a debut it was. Hill set an NHL record by recording five points—two goals, three assists—in his first big-league game. We don't know if Gordie Howe lost sleep that night, but it turned out that Mr. Hockey's scoring records were never really in jeopardy (at least not until Wayne Gretzy came along).

**3. Marty Bystrom.** Probably the Phils' best-ever September call-up. Bystrom started five late-season games in 1980 and won all of them. Then he won a playoff game and another in the World Series against Kansas City. After that, well. . . . Imagine what it's like to have your career peak at age 22.

**2. Willie Burton.** Just three Sixers have ever scored 53 or more points in a game. Wilt did it eight times (that's just as a Sixer; he did it an astounding 108 times overall). Iverson did it six times through 2005–06. The third man? This career 10-point-per-game scorer who went off for 53 against the Heat one night in 1994. No Sixer ever scored more points in one game at the Spectrum. "He played tonight with the sparrow on his shoulder," said Coach John Lucas. We still don't know what that means.

**1. Andy Delmore.** Came up late in the 1999–2000 season to help the Flyers' exhausted defense. Played so-so in the regular season. Then, in the playoffs, he has a two-goal night against the Penguins. Two games later, he pops in three more. No rookie defenseman had ever scored a hat trick in the playoffs or five goals in one series. A year later, Delmore was gone.

**6. The ride home from the Jersey shore.** We watched the Cup winner down in Sea Isle at "Quack's" parents' house. (Hey, this is Philly, right? Everybody gets a nickname, including our "Broad Street Bullies.") Immediately following the conclusion of the game, we headed back toward Southwest Philly. We always took the back roads because no one had money for tolls. As we started cutting through Jersey, everyone was honking car horns. With each passing intersection, more and more people were gathered, holding signs and makeshift Stanley Cups. You could literally feel the noise as we headed to the Walt Whitman Bridge. By the time we started slicing through South Philly, you couldn't even drive through an intersection. They were all closed; clogged with jubilant, drunken maniacs. I'll never forget the spontaneity of it all. Like God ordered everyone to immediately party. Hey, maybe he did.

**5. The size of the parade.** We all took the '36' trolley downtown for the parade. I lived at 70th Street, which was pretty much the beginning of the line, and still there was barely room for us. By 67th Street it wasn't even stopping for passengers anymore. We were all singing. Chanting. Nothing, however, prepared us for when we came out of the subway tunnels. A sea, an ocean of people. Flyers orange was everywhere and it was blinding. I had been to the Mummers Parade almost every year of my life, but nothing had prepared me for this. Whatever the official estimate of the crowd was, I know this much, they underestimated.

**4. Kool and the Gang.** I got separated from my boys and ended up sharing a quart of Ripple with Maurice, a black West Catholic buddy of mine who I bumped into in front of Jerry's Records on Market Street. He laughed and said he never had seen so many white people in his life. To help me celebrate, he went into Jerry's and bought me a copy of "Wild and Peaceful" by Kool and the Gang, claiming he needed to bring some black pride into this lily-white celebration. This was before Kool had crossed over to mainstream. The album was full of savage funk like "Jungle Boogie," "Hollywood Swinging," and "Funky Stuff." Albums were just $2.99 then. I carried the record around with me for the rest of the day. It became the official party record back at our pad. To this day I can't hear any of these songs without thinking of this grand and glorious day. I still own this album. Thanks, Maurice, wherever you are.

**3. Dirty Franks.** What was the one place on Earth that day where I knew I would find somebody from my crowd? Dirty Franks at 13th and Pine. You had to wait for people to come out before you could enter. Not that Dirty's had a doorman. There simply wasn't any room to get in. Somehow, however, I pushed though the crowd and found my buddy Jimmy "Elliot" Ness, who had somehow conned some Jefferson nurses into buying him pitchers of beer. With seats at a booth we stayed till last call. When we walked back onto the downtown streets at 2 a.m., the crowd had barely dissipated.

**2. Elmer Chestnut.** Almost 72 hours after Bernie Parent hoisted the Cup, we were still partying back at our rented dump in Southwest Philly. We had this goofy extended garage with a roof on it, so we would sit on the roof and drink. Suddenly a car pulled up and out of the passenger seat climbed one Elmer Chestnut, clad in nothing but black high-top Chuck Taylor's. Nothing else. I had the feeling he hadn't worn any clothes since the end of the regular season. He climbed onto the roof, we held our beers high and Elmer toasted, "To the Flyers!" To the Flyers, indeed.

**1. The parade.** To this day it remains the greatest parade. Ever. Period.

**The '74 parade was so much fun,
we did it again in '75 (shown here).**

Note: Edward Malcolm Snider brought the National Hockey League to Philadelphia when he founded the Flyers in 1966. He has been the driving force behind the franchise since then. In 1988 he was elected to the Hockey Hall of Fame.

## The Greatest

### 5. 1974 Semifinals, Game 7, Flyers vs. NY Rangers, May 5, 1974.

We beat them, 4-3, at the Spectrum in a vicious, exciting contest. I really believe this game proved to us that we had what it took to win the Cup. The entire series was hard fought, and each team won every game at home. Thank God we had the home ice advantage.

### 4. 2000 Eastern Conference Semifinals, Game 4, Flyers at Pittsburgh, May 4, 2000.

If Keith Primeau hadn't scored the winning goal in the fifth overtime, we would have had players crawling up and down the ice on their knees. I personally don't know how any of the players could withstand that long of a playoff game—6 hours and 56 minutes—under that kind of pressure. The game ended around 2 a.m. with us winning, 2-1. My friends and I flew home and had breakfast at the Melrose Diner at dawn.

### 3. 1975 Stanley Cup Finals, Game 6, Flyers at Buffalo, May 27, 1975.

We won it in Buffalo, 2-0, on goals by Bill Clement and Bob Kelly, and, of course, more great goaltending by Bernie Parent. Then we came back for another humungous parade—again two million people.

### 2. Flyers vs. Soviet Army Team, January 11, 1976.

The Soviet Army Team was, in reality, the Soviet All-Star Team. They had won all of their games against NHL teams to that point, and it was up to us to show that we were the cold warriors. We beat them emphatically—so much so that they walked off the ice during the game and refused to come back until (NHL Commissioner) Clarence Campbell and I told them they weren't going to get paid. They came back on the ice but were little competition for what I think was our best team ever. We beat them 4-1, and the game wasn't really that close. If Parent hadn't gotten hurt, there is no doubt that we would have won our third consecutive Cup in '76.

### 1. 1974 Stanley Cup Finals, Game 6, Flyers vs. Boston, May 19, 1974.

The most incredible game ever, not only because we were the first expansion team to win the Cup but also because Bernie Parent played the greatest game I have ever seen a goalie play against one of the most high-powered offenses ever—Bobby Orr, Phil Esposito, et al. No one wanted to go back to Boston for Game 7, and the 1-0 lead against that team kept everyone on edge for every second of action. I've never seen anything like the celebration when the final buzzer sounded. For that matter, I've never seen anything as amazing as the parade that brought two million people out onto Broad Street. The parade was the largest crowd I've ever seen in professional sports history, and remained so until the next year.

## The Worst

### 5. I will always have more good memories than bad memories, so there is no Number 5.

### 4. Flyers at Buffalo, April 3, 1972.

It was the last game of the season, and all we needed was a tie against a bad Sabres team to make the playoffs. We had the tie with seconds to play, but Buffalo's Gerry Meehan wristed a 45-footer past our goalie, Doug Favell, who had misplayed the angle. We got knocked out of the playoffs with :04 left on the clock. It was heartbreaking.

### 3. 1980 Stanley Cup Finals, Game 6, Flyers at New York Islanders, May 24, 1980.

This was the season we went 35 games without a loss, setting the all-time professional record. If we won Game 6 on Long Island, there is no doubt in my mind we would have won the Cup back home in Game 7. But during the game, Islanders defenseman Denis Potvin clearly and illegally batted the puck into the net from over his head. The refs counted the goal. Then, to add insult to injury, Leon Stickle made his infamous non-call on a pass that was two feet off-sides which led to the Islanders' tying goal. That game is etched in my memory. I'll always believe it cost us the Cup in 1980.

### 2. Flyers vs. Chicago, January 30, 1969.

The worst loss ever, as the Blackhawks beat us 12-0. Our fans couldn't believe it. I wanted to crawl under the stands when the game was over. I wondered that night if we would ever win another game.

### 1. Flyers vs. St. Louis, November 7, 1968.

We lost to St. Louis, 8-0, on our own ice. If that wasn't bad enough, Red Berenson, their great left winger, had six goals, just one short of the all-time record. St. Louis, believe it or not, was our biggest rival and archenemy at the time. What a humiliation.

Sure, players get catchy nicknames, but sometimes a team is worthy as well. Or even a part of a team. Here are the 10 best in Philadelphia history.

**10. LCB Line.** It wasn't as catchy as Buffalo's "French Connection" of the same period, but it was more potent. Among them, Reggie Leach, Bobby Clarke, and Bill Barber collected 141 goals and 181 assists in 1975–76. Still, for us, the name always calls to mind the Pennsylvania Liquor Control Board.

**9. Fire High Gang.** The Eagles of the mid-70s featured quarterback Roman Gabriel (6-foot-4) throwing them high and deep to Harold Carmichael (6-8), Charles Young (6-4), and Don Zimmerman (6-4). Considering that the average defensive back of the era was about 5-10, it seems like they should have hooked up for more than 43 touchdowns over four seasons.

**8. Mighty Mites.** We're going way back on this one, so if you remember Coach Bill Ferguson's undersized St. Joe's basketball teams, you're well into collecting Social Security. The "Mites" consisted of 6-foot-3 passing guru Matt Guokas, Sr., plus four guys who didn't reach the "you must be this tall" line for most carnival rides. Still, they compiled a 54-17 record over four seasons in the mid-1930s.

**7. Steagles.** When 600 NFL players went to fight in World War II, teams found themselves with depleted rosters. For one season, 1943, the Eagles and Pittsburgh Steelers merged resources and personnel. Officially they were the Phil-Pitt Eagles-Steelers. Rather than toss out that mouthful, most people referred to them as the "Steagles." Together they went 5-4-1—the first winning season in Eagles history. Sort of.

**6. Gang Green Defense.** Buddy Ryan's defense demanded a worthy nickname. With their all-black shoes and nasty swagger, the players behaved like a street gang. So "Gang Green" fit nicely. Funny thing is, the unit had its best season in 1991, after Buddy left and Bud Carson took over the defense. That season they finished first in the NFL against the rush and the pass, first in sacks, and first in takeaways.

**5. Legion of Doom.** No one recalls Jim Montgomery of the Flyers, but everyone remembers his contribution to history. Watching Eric Lindros, John LeClair, and Mikael Renberg bully their teammates in practice one day, Montgomery was reminded of the group of supervillains who regularly battled Superman.

"They look like the Legion of Doom out there," Montgomery remarked. The trio—with an average size of 6-foot-3 and 228 pounds—combined for 305 goals from 1994–97. Then, of course, personality issues turned the Flyers into a real-life Bizarro World.

**4. Macho Row.** Let's give credit to our colleague, Mike Missanelli, for assigning the perfect handle to that manlier-than-thou squad of Darren Daulton, Lenny Dykstra, Dave Hollins, John Kruk, and the rest of the '93 Phils. Lots of testosterone in that clubhouse—some of it reportedly from hypodermic needles.

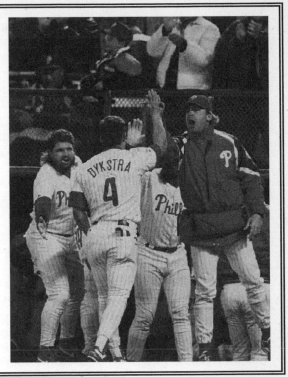

**3. Whiz Kids.** By some accounts, the 1950 NL Champion Phillies were the youngest pennant winners ever assembled. We can't verify that, but consider this nucleus—Richie Ashburn, 23; Robin Roberts, 23; Curt Simmons, 21; Del Ennis, 25. Perhaps the most amazing thing is that the group never won the pennant again.

**2. Wheeze Kids.** In this case, the sequel nickname beats the original. Bill Conlin's moniker for the 1983 Phils summed up the last-gasp effort by a thrown-together collection of aging mercenaries. Pete Rose was 42, Joe Morgan 39, and Tony Perez 41 when they tried to reassemble the Big Red Machine in Philadelphia. On a side note, isn't this the most forgotten league champion our city has ever seen?

**1. Broad Street Bullies.** Give credit to another newspaperman, Jack Chevalier of the defunct Bulletin, for being the first to come up with the phrase, "the Bullies of Broad Street." The name reflected a team that regularly prompted opponents to come down with the Philly flu—a mysterious illness that struck just as the team bus turned onto Broad Street.

The Bullies won back-to-back Stanley Cups and produced three Hall of Famers, but the highlight was probably the 4-1 thrashing of the Soviet Red Army team on January 11, 1976.

**10. The fact that fans put up with ties as long as they did.** Now, I'll admit, before the lockout ties would have been No. 1 on my list. But I'll give the NHL credit for finally fixing it. Now, at least you know there will be a winner. Glen, I know that it's possible for a football game to end in a tie, but I can't even remember the last time that happened in the NFL. And of course there's never been any such thing in basketball. And a tie isn't like kissing your sister, it's like having sex with Roseanne Barr.

**9. How if you bumped into Bobby Clarke walking down Chestnut Street and you asked him for directions to Atlantic City, he would still, to this day, find a way to bitch about the Lindros family.**

**8. Don Koharski. Seriously, does he ref every single game?**

**7. Guys skating around with no sticks.** They resemble Herman Munster on skates out there. Who cares if your stick is broken or if you dropped it? Pick it up!

**6. The face-off dance.** "You put your right skate in, you put your left skate out. . . ." Drop the stinkin' puck already. I know jump balls in basketball are also ridiculous, but there's only a couple of those a game.

**5. Players with no vowels in their names.** I know I'm sounding like some ugly North American here, but please, bring back players like Marty Murray and Keith Jones. Names I could pronounce.

**4. Records like 16-12-8 OTL?** What the hell is an OTL, Glen? Oh, I'm sorry, it's not a new home shopping network, it's the network that carries the NHL. Or is that the OLN? Who the hell knows?

**3. Third-period officiating.** How ridiculous is it that hockey refs swallow their whistles during the third period? Basketball refs don't ignore a shooter getting hacked or goaltending or whatever during the fourth quarter. If they did, there would be no scoring in the fourth quarter. Why can't hockey refs call the entire game the same way?

**2. Switching lines during play.** OK, let's get this straight, Glen. If basketball played with this insane rule, a great defender could block a shot, run out of bounds and be replaced by a great shooter on the other end, without ever calling a timeout. It's proof that Canadians love their beer, because they must have been hammered when they came up with this ridiculous rule.

**1. The Columbus Blue Jackets.** Why? Just why?

First off, let me address a few of your lamer points here, Big Daddy. You miss the days when hockey players had easy-to-pronounce Anglo-Saxon names? Okay, try these NBA tongue twisters on for size—Sarunas Jasikevicius, Primoz Brezec, and Didier Ilunga-Mbenga. Not exactly Joe Smith, eh?

Then you rip the officiating in the NHL which, I'll admit, is not good. But, seriously, are you going to defend a league that employs both Bennett Salvatore and Violet Palmer? Sometimes I think the NBA refs should pull an "Opposite George," and try doing things exactly the opposite of their instincts. It couldn't be worse than it is now.

And feel free to tease the Columbus Blue Jackets. Then, explain the Utah Jazz. There's a franchise that, A) Plays in a city that fits the lifestyle of exactly zero NBA players and, B) Is named for what? That swinging sound coming from the Mormon Tabernacle Choir?

Now that I've cleared that up, here are a few things that I don't get that didn't quite crack my list: The slam dunk contest, the draft lottery (fix!), Larry Brown's wanderlust, why fans can't keep balls that go into the stands, and how come they call them "shorts" when they go below the knees. More like culottes.

Here are my top 10:

**10. The rules make no sense.** Like being able to call time out while flying out of bounds. Like the "advance-to-half-court-on-a-timeout" rule. That's my favorite. I want to put that in football, so the Eagles can gain an extra 10 yards before attempting a game-winning field goal.

**9. Why does the first round of the playoffs take forever?** Seriously, when the Sixers beat the Hornets a few years back, they opened the series on an April Sunday, rested three days to put Game Two on TNT, gave the players time off for good behavior, traveled to New Orleans for game Three, broke a week for Easter and wrapped things up under Independence Day fireworks.

**8. Whatever happened to the talented big man?** Once upon a time, the NBA was dominated by Hall of Fame Goliaths like Wilt, Kareem Abdul-Jabbar, Walt Bellamy, Dave Cowens, Elvin Hayes, Bob Lanier, Bob McAdoo, Willis Reed, Nate Thurmond, and Wes Unseld. All at the same time! Today, we've got Shaq and Tim Duncan (if you call him a center), and, uh . . . Samuel Dalembert?

**7. The league has more dead wood than Gilligan's Island.** If you under-perform your contract in baseball or hockey, they can send you to the minors. In the NFL, they just cut you. In the NBA, you just keep hanging around (Hello, Derrick Coleman). Or they make the NBA-Special trade: My junk for your garbage. So Dikembe Mutombo becomes Keith Van Horn becomes Glenn Robinson. It's basketball's version of the poker game Pass-the-Trash.

**6. Why can't a $12-million-a-year player make half his free throws?** The basket isn't moving, no one's defending you—explain all the bricks and air balls. My 15-year-old niece sinks 70 percent from the so-called "charity stripe," so how come Ben Wallace hits just 42 percent? Maybe this is why NBA players feel the silly need to congratulate teammates after every free throw attempt, make or miss.

**5. Why does the last minute take an hour to play?** Hey Coach, your team is down 14, there are milli-seconds left. Stop fouling! You're not coming back! Please, just let us go home already.

**4. The NBA assaults its fans with more bright lights and screaming barkers than the Las Vegas strip.** I don't get PA announcers who think they're part of the show (like that braying jackass in Detroit). I don't get blaring hip hop while the ball is in play. I don't get why it takes 20 minutes and a laser light show to introduce the home team.

**3. The cap.** Nobody can explain it. Because, really, no one understands it. There are exceptions, exemptions, and enough pie charts to impress a Penn math professor. The NFL and NHL salary caps have ceilings and floors and, basically, that's it. In the NBA, there are special cap rules for injured players, retired players, and slovenly indolent wastes of space—also known as Geigers. There literally have been guys counted against the NBA salary cap who were dead.

**2. I honestly believe that many, many NBA players care more about style points than winning.** Getting your dunk on SportsCenter becomes more important than getting to the playoffs. Spending hours getting a new hair style for each game takes precedence over attending practice. Promoting your latest rap album overtakes reporting to training camp. Gaining "street cred" becomes more essential than working with teammates. Hockey is all about the sport; the NBA is all about selling sneakers.

**1. Latrell Sprewell on turning down a $30 million contract extension: "I've got my family to feed."**
Enough said.

Note: Simon Gagne had his best year as a Flyer in 2005–06, reaching star status in the NHL and setting personal bests in goals and points. Here are his top five restaurants in Philly, listed in alphabetical order. We're sure these establishments will see a marked spike in female customers hoping to catch a glimpse of Gags.

**Anjou Sushi,** 1957 Locust Street. Very sophisticated and yet laid back. Anjou is a Korean-Japanese fusion restaurant with a great lounge and great music. In addition to sushi, it's known for sake-scented dumplings, teriyaki dishes, tempura, and bi bim bap, a Korean specialty of vegetables and eggs served over rice.

**Buddakan,** 325 Chestnut Street. Another great Asian fusion restaurant with a creative, delicious menu. A good place to share. Try the pad thai, broiled Japanese black cod, Singapore noodles, and Angry Lobster, a wok-seared three-pounder served with lobster mashed potatoes.

**Capital Grille,** 1338 Chestnut Street. Great service and a great place to meet people. Great food and wine as well. The steaks are phenomenal, and if you get them with onion strings and cottage fries, it's one great meal.

**Morton's, The Steakhouse,** 1411 Walnut Street. You always feel like a VIP when you go there, and the steaks are delicious. You even get to choose your own steak knife. Famous for the Gachot ribeye, which is 20 ounces. The truffle-oil mashed potatoes and creamed leeks make it a perfect meal.

**Smith & Wollensky,** 210 W. Rittenhouse Square. Another great Philadelphia steakhouse, where it doesn't get any better if you're looking for a fabulous piece of red meat. The servings are huge and the desserts are worth saving room for.

**One more thing:** I love cheesesteaks. My two favorite places for those are Geno's and Pat's.

We know we'll get slaughtered for leaving Buddy Ryan off the list, but his three winning seasons and zero playoff victories make it easier than you think when you see what the rest of these coaches accomplished. It was tough leaving Flyers coach Pat Quinn off the list, too. He coached the 1980 team through its 35-game unbeaten streak and trip to the Stanley Cup Finals. Eddie Sawyer also received some consideration for managing the Phillies' 1950 Whiz Kids, but he only had one other winning season in a short career.

**10. Mike Keenan.** He made Stanley Cup Finals appearances in '85 and '87, losing both times to an Edmonton Oilers team that may be the greatest of all time. Mike was a true mad genius who coached the Flyers in a franchise-record 57 playoff games. Before Ken Hitchcock came along, there was always a rumor that Keenan would come back. That would have been fine by us. We docked him a slot or two for winning the Cup years later with the hated New York Rangers.

**9. Dick Vermeil.** It kills us to rank him so low, but as you'll see, we reserve the top slots for coaches who won championships. Still, the Dick Vermeil Era of Eagles football remains so popular that, to this day, his face smiles down from dozens of ad billboards scattered throughout the Delaware Valley. Dick came along after 10 straight Eagles seasons under .500. Within two years he had the Birds in the playoffs. They stayed there for four straight seasons, including an appearance in the 1980 Super Bowl. With a driving work ethic and a tremendous loyalty trait, he was the right guy at the right time. We're getting all choked up just writing about him.

**8. Andy Reid.** Say what you want about those boring post-game news conferences, but you cannot argue with the success of Reid's Eagles. The numbers are staggering. After enduring his excruciating rookie year with the totally inept Doug Pederson, Reid coached the Eagles to five straight playoff appearances, including four NFC Championship games and an appearance in Super Bowl XXXIX. Fans love to bring up the weak competition in the division, his arrogance, and his reliance on the brilliance of Jim Johnson. True, but Reid has been the head coach of very good teams and his franchise-record number of wins speaks volumes. "Time's yours."

**7. Larry Brown.** He drove us nuts, too. The creator of all that is basketball. He knows the game, you don't. The ultimate carpetbagger. But remember, before Brown arrived, the Sixers didn't make the playoffs for seven straight years. Seven! Do you know how hard that is to do in the NBA? Brown pushed his team to five straight playoff appearances, including that great run to the Finals in 2001 with Allen Iverson and four guys named Moe. We put him over Reid because of Brown's continued success with other teams—a lot of other teams—including Detroit, where he won a World Championship.

**6. Dallas Green.** We hate to rank Dallas so high because he only managed two full seasons with the Phils and was lucky enough to have one of the more loaded teams in this town's history. When you factor in his poor record as a manger after he left, it makes you wonder. But for 1980, Dallas, you'll always have a special place in our heart. It's still the only World Championship this pathetic franchise ever produced.

**5. Alex Hannum.** Coached the '67 Sixers to a title. For years, that Chamberlain-led team was considered the greatest ever in the NBA. An amazing 68-13 regular season record that stood for decades. Hannum coached 12 Hall of Famers, including Wilt, Billy Cunningham and Hal Greer. He also coached the St. Louis Hawks to an NBA Championship. Later coached the Oakland Oaks to an ABA Championship, becoming the second coach to win titles in both leagues. Don't shrug off the ABA; it was a fantastic league.

**4. Billy Cunningham.** The Kangaroo Kid. Our last championship in 1983. Who will ever forget a "slightly" inebriated Billy C. gingerly walking down those airplane steps, with the NBA Championship trophy in one hand, a cigar in the other? Tough as nails. Took a giant collection of egos and went to the playoffs eight straight years. Three trips to the NBA Finals. Also, without a doubt, the greatest player on this list. How's this for a regular season record? 454-196. Are you kidding me? He remains funny and a class act.

**3. Fred Shero.** "The Fog." Sure, he coached the Flyers to two Stanley Cups. Yes, he remains the winningest Flyers coach in history—308 regular-season wins plus 48 more in the playoffs. Yes, he's a brilliant tactician and a cunning motivator. But we'll always remember Fred as the architect of the two greatest parades this city has ever had. When he died on November 24, 1990, we all thought back to that glorious time and quietly (the way Shero would have) shed a tear or two.

**2. Connie Mack.** Yes, we know he managed the A's for 217 years before stepping down at the age of 240. Who was gonna fire Connie? He was the owner. Seriously, Mr. Mack didn't stop managing until age 87. However—and this is a big however—he won nine pennants and five World Series with those teams filled with guys like Home Run Baker and Stuffy McInnis (God, those names are great), and later Jimmie Foxx and Mickey Cochrane. You've got to respect those numbers. Plus he wore a suit in the dugout. How cool is that?

**1. Greasy Neale.** After coaching the Eagles to losing seasons in his first two years, Greasy and the Eagles ripped off seven straight winning seasons, including NFL Championships in 1948 and 1949. His overall record in 10 seasons, including playoffs, is 66-44-5. He gains extra points for having the coolest name on this list. My man, Greasy!

Note: Dallas Green managed the Phillies to their only World Series championship in 1980. In his four-decade career as a player, manager, and general manager, the legendary tough guy often used the word belly to describe a player who had the guts and balls to face hard times—whether mental or physical—and still go out there and perform.

**10. Tony Taylor.** My teammate back in the early 1960s. Tony came from Cuba. He could barely speak English, but he was determined to be a Major League player. He overcame a lot to make it. That takes a different kind of belly, and he sure had it.

**9. Darren Daulton.** He's probably as tough as anyone ever to put on a uniform. Dutch was a leader because he could intimidate, but he also had a tremendous feel for his team and for winning. He refused to let peer pressure interfere with playing the game right. He would call out anyone if he thought the guy wasn't hustling. That takes belly, and you don't have that enough in baseball today.

**8. Gary Matthews.** I loved Sarge. He played the game the way it's supposed to be played—with heart, soul and enthusiasm. He had so much determination. He was a special guy, with the great inner strength you need to succeed.

**7. Jim Bunning.** A great teammate, and one of the toughest competitors I've ever been around. You did not dare look at Jim eye-to-eye on days when he pitched—even in our own clubhouse. He was a lot like Curt Schilling is today, with the focus, the intensity, the desire. And he'd knock you down in a second if you looked at him wrong.

**6. Tug McGraw.** It took belly to do what Tug did back in those days. The closer's job wasn't as fanciful or protected then as it is now. He had an unbelievable run for me and the team in 1980. He didn't always have great stuff, but he had grit and determination, and he did it with a great sense of humor.

**5. Dickie Noles.** I think he's one of the toughest kids I've ever known. On the mound, he was a nasty SOB, not afraid to knock down anyone. And he had the guts to face his (alcohol) demons off the mound and finally come to control them. I've seen a lot of so-called tough guys fail at that.

**4. Paul Owens.** Not a player, but if you talk about belly and balls, the Pope has as much as anybody who was ever in the game. He had the guts to change an organization that wasn't respected and become the architect of a championship club. And of course, everyone remembers 1980, when he got tired of hearing our players bitching about my managing. He called a team meeting in San Francisco and, at age 56, challenged each and every player to fight him. Nobody took him up on the offer.

**3. Bob Boone.** He excelled because he was hard as nails. He refused to get hurt—at least, to admit he was hurt. He would tell the trainers, "Never come out to me unless I call you." So even if Booney was lying on the ground unconscious, the trainer would sit still, waiting for a signal. He took a big, bad shot on a slide at home during the 1980 playoffs, which killed his ankle. Still, he played through the rest of that series and into the World Series.

**2. Steve Carlton.** Who else would you ever want on the mound facing a big game or a big situation? People say I had a slow hook with Lefty. Really, I didn't have a hook at all. Check his record during his first 10 years here—157 complete games. He just had complete focus.

**1. Pete Rose.** Of course the famous story is when he was playing for us during spring training one year. His first wife was at the game, and his girlfriend hired a plane to fly over, trailing a sign that said, "I love you Pete." I think he had three hits that day. No one was ever better at putting aside adversity—whether on or off the field—and playing at such an extremely high level.

**10. Flyers get forward John LeClair, defenseman Eric Desjardins, and forward Gilbert Dionne from the Canadiens for forward Mark Recchi and a third-round draft pick, 1995.**

Recchi was no slouch, but he scored 40 goals three times before this trade, and never again afterward. LeClair and Desjardins (forget Dionne, who was a throw-in) were keys to the resurgence that pushed the Flyers 178 games above .500 over the next decade. Desjardins was named the Flyers top defenseman seven separate seasons, and LeClair surpassed 50 goals three times. Now, if only Big John had been able to score in the playoffs. . . .

**9. Phillies get pitcher Curt Schilling from Astros for pitcher Jason Grimsley, 1992.**

Glen's story: Working for the Inquirer back then, I was the only reporter around spring training the day Schilling first arrived from Houston with a reputation as an underachiever. I watched as pitching coach Johnny Podres taught him a big roundhouse curve, which Schilling mastered in about five minutes.

"He's gonna be a good one," Podres said to me, as he walked away.

What an understatement. Schilling won 101 games as a Phillie—the most of any righthander since Robin Roberts. He was a three-time all star here and MVP of the 1993 League Championship Series against Atlanta. Rumor has it that he did a few things after leaving town, but that's coming up in the next list.

**8. Eagles get quarterback Ron Jaworski from Rams for tight end Charle Young, 1977.**

Young, a tight end, made three Pro Bowls as an Eagle—and none after he left here. Jaworski, meanwhile, became the quarterback that the Birds had been searching for since tossing aside Sonny Jurgensen (more about that later, as well). "Jaws" set a ton of team passing records, was the NFL Player of the Year in 1980, and, of course, led the Eagles to the Super Bowl that same season.

**7. Sixers trade guard Lloyd Free to Clippers for a future first-round pick, 1978.**

Free—in his pre-"World B." days—went on to become a very good scorer for some very bad clubs. He averaged more than 20 points per game for eight straight seasons—although seven of those seasons his team failed to make the playoffs.

So how is this trade a good one for the 76ers? Well, the pick didn't pay off for six full years. But when it did in 1984, the Clippers—as usual—had a lottery spot, and the Sixers used it to draft . . . Auburn forward Charles Barkley.

Free was a nice player and fun to watch. But Sir Charles—along with Wilt, Al, and Doc—is in the pantheon of all-time great Sixers.

Every trade from this point on directly contributed to a Philadelphia team winning a championship.

## 6. Flyers get winger Reggie Leach from the California Golden Seals for Larry Wright, Al MacAdam, and a first-round pick (Ron Chipperfield), 1974.

MacAdam became a nice scorer after the trade; the other two guys never panned out in the NHL. But Leach—possessor of a 100-mile-an-hour shot—flourished as Bobby Clarke's right winger on the famed LCB line (with Bill Barber) of the mid-to-late-70s. He scored 61 regular-season and 19 playoff goals in the Cup year of 1975–76, both still franchise records.

## 5. Eagles get quarterback Norm Van Brocklin from Rams for tackle Buck Lansford, defensive back Jimmy Harris, and a first-round pick, 1958.

Lansford and Harris are best remembered as "Who?" and "What?" Van Brocklin spent just three seasons here, but he turned a last-place club into the 1960 league champion. Looking at the prehistoric NFL passing stats in today's context doesn't do justice to Van Brocklin's greatness, but in 1960 he threw for a career-high 24 touchdowns and averaged 8.7 yards per attempt. More than that, he had a toughness that rubbed off on all his teammates.

## 4. Sixers get center Wilt Chamberlain from Warriors for guard Paul Neumann, center Connie Dierking, forward Lee Shaffer and $150,000, 1965.

Wilt had left town when the Warriors moved west in 1962. Philadelphia sulked for two-plus years and then, on the day of the 1965 NBA All-Star Game, he came home again. He was not quite as extraterrestrial the second time around, which sounds ridiculous when you consider that he won the MVP in 1966, '67, and '68. We'll still argue the 1966–67 championship team is the best in NBA history.

And, the last we checked, Dierking, Shaffer, and Neumann weren't getting mentioned as the best athlete of the Twentieth Century. Although Neumann, we're told, makes a pretty good salad dressing.

Oh, that's another guy?

## 3. Sixers get center Moses Malone from Rockets for center Caldwell Jones and a first-round pick (Rodney McCray), 1982.

You all know this story: Doc couldn't do it alone for years . . . Magic jumps center in the '80 Finals and embarrasses Darryl Dawkins . . . "We Owe You One" . . . "Fo', Fo', Fo.'"

The trade was hastily hammered out after the Sixers signed Malone to a free-agent offer sheet. Jones was nothing more than a nice defensive player; McCray was a decent pro—certainly not the player he was expected to be coming out of Louisville.

Moses, inarguably, is the guy who delivered Philadelphia its last major sports championship in 1983. He was the league MVP, and destroyed Kareem Abdul-Jabbar and the Lakers in the Finals. He is, perhaps, the best offensive rebounder in the last 30 years. We just wish he'd stuck around longer.

## 2. Flyers get goalie Bernie Parent and forward Larry Goodenough from Maple Leafs for goalie Doug Favell and a first-round pick (Bob Neely), 1973.

Bernie had been with the Flyers once before. They traded him in 1971 in a three-way deal that brought scoring punch in the form of Rick McLeish. He was a decent goalie the first time around here, a little better in Toronto, and seemingly disinterested after defecting to the Philadelphia Blazers of the WHA.

When he returned to the Flyers after two-plus years elsewhere, he was a changed goalie. He credited Leafs great Jacques Plante with teaching him the position. Regardless, he was the backbone of two Stanley Cup teams, twice winning the playoff MVP award. He retired as one of the 10-best goalies ever and, for our money, the best player ever to wear the Flyers uniform.

## 1. Phillies get pitcher Steve Carlton from Cardinals for Rick Wise, 1972.

One of the greatest heists in sports history. The amazing thing is that it was proposed to the Phillies by St. Louis owner Auggie Busch. John Quinn, the Phils GM, probably had to restrain himself from kissing Mr. Busch.

Carlton won 20 games his final season in St. Louis. That was a mere precursor. His first season as a Phillie—27-10, 310 strikeouts, 1.97 ERA, all for a last-place club—remains one of the greatest accomplishments in baseball history. Four Cy Youngs and 16 post-season wins for the Phils. Only Warren Spahn has more career wins by a lefty than Carlton's 329.

**10. Eagles trade offensive tackle Bob Brown (with defensive back Jim Nettles) to the Rams for cornerback Irv Cross, tackle Joe Carollo, and guard Don Chuy, 1969.**
Cross was merely playing out the string (in preparation for a TV career) in his second term with the Eagles. And you never heard of Carollo and Chuy—for good reason—although Chuy later sued the Birds in a medical dispute that reached federal court.

Brown—nicknamed "Boomer" for the sound it made when he hit someone—was a perennial Pro Bowler here, but demanded a trade when the club fired Coach Joe Kuharich. We can't attest to his judgment, but we can speak to his continued talent. He made three more Pro Bowls after leaving and was twice named the NFC Lineman of the Year. He had a Hall of Fame career—unfortunately, just the first half was in Philadelphia.

**9. Eagles trade a first-round and fourth-round pick to the Colts for guard Ron Solt, 1988.**
Buddy Ryan hated drafting offensive lineman, so he figured, eventually, he had better trade for one. And Solt was coming off a Pro Bowl season. Perhaps it's just a coincidence that when the NFL began testing in earnest for steroids, Solt's body withered down to the size of Kate Moss. Regardless, the guy who lined up to protect Randall Cunningham was nothing like advertised. He lasted three-plus seasons and earned the nickname, "The Incredible Shrinking Man."

The Colts, meanwhile, used their first-round pick obtained from the Eagles to draft five-time Pro Bowl wide receiver Andre Rison.

**8. Phillies trade third baseman Scott Rolen, pitcher Doug Nickle, and cash to the Cardinals for infielder Placido Polanco, pitcher Bud Smith, and reliever Mike Timlin, 2000.**
That this trade only rates as the eighth worst tells you something about this town's history of general managers. It was one of those Ed Wade specials. Made at the trade deadline, with no leverage, Wade would swap a superstar for a bunch of spare parts—praying that some of it might pan out. Of course, it never did.

**7. Eagles trade quarterback Sonny Jurgensen and defensive back Jimmy Carr to the Redskins for quarterback Norm Snead and defensive back Claude Crabb, 1964.**
The rumors surrounding the reasons for Jurgensen's curious departure continue to this day. Let's just say that Kuharich—a prude and proud of it—didn't approve of Sonny's lifestyle.

We don't know whether Snead was as clean-living as a pastor's wife. What we know is that he wasn't much of a quarterback. Here's the easy way to break down this deal: No quarterback threw more touchdowns in the 1960s than Sonny Jurgensen; no quarterback threw more interceptions than Norm Snead.

## 6. Sixers trade forward Charles Barkley to the Suns for guard Jeff Hornacek, forward Tim Perry, and center Andrew Lang, 1992.

Charles kind of forced his way out of town, but is this the best Harold Katz could do? Perry, a Temple alum, was a tall guy who couldn't shoot, couldn't pass, couldn't rebound. Lang was downright worthless. Hornacek was more infuriating—he was a good player before he got here and after he left, but had no interest in performing for the Sixers.

Barkley took the Suns to the 1993 NBA Finals. He had a few more great seasons until his knees betrayed him. He is one of the 25 best players ever in the NBA and someone who should have spent his entire career as a 76er.

## 5. Phillies trade pitcher Curt Schilling to the Diamondbacks for pitchers Omar Daal, Nelson Figueroa, and Vicente Padilla, and first baseman Travis Lee, 2000.

Ed Wade special No. 2. We'll always recall how the Phils GM said of Schill, "One out of every five days he's a horse, and the other four he's a horse's ass."

Maybe so, but the horse went on to win World Series with both the D'Backs and Red Sox—making Ed Wade look like the ass. Schilling also led both leagues in wins and has made a strong case for future induction into the Hall of Fame.

Padilla was hit with the cliché "million-dollar arm and 25-cent head" so often that it seemed to become his legal ID. Lee was a truly despicable player who could sleepwalk through an entire season. Daal and Figueroa never panned out to anything.

## 4. Sixers trade center Wilt Chamberlain to the Lakers for forward Jerry Chambers, guard Archie Clark, and center Darrell Imhoff, 1968.

Glen note: I had Jack Ramsay on my show in 2006 and he said the toughest thing he ever had to do was trade Wilt. But he felt he had no choice after Chamberlain, a) refused to take a single shot in the second half of Game 7 vs. the Celtics in the '68 conference finals, and b) insisted that ownership had backed out of a promise to make him player-coach.

We don't know, Dr. Jack, but trading him for Manny, Moe, and Jack made it tough for the rest of us. Darrell Imhoff? Wasn't that the guy against whom Wilt went off for 100 that night in Hershey?

**Weird footnote:** In the 1965 trade to get Wilt, the Sixers sent out Connie Dierking. Fast forward to 1970, and they unload Imhoff for . . . Connie Dierking?! Like a bad penny, he kept coming back.

## 3. Phillies trade shortstop Larry Bowa and second baseman Ryne Sandberg to the Cubs for shortstop Ivan DeJesus, 1982.

The Phils considered this merely as a swap of veteran shortstops. Sandberg was regarded as a minor league third baseman whose path was blocked by Mike Schmidt.

But Dallas Green—who left Philadelphia for the Cubs in 1981—knew a little bit about the Phils farm system. While Sandberg produced a Hall of Fame career as Chicago's second baseman for 16 years, the Phils ran out seven guys to man the position, including Tom Herr and Mark Lewis.

**2. Phillies trade pitcher Ferguson Jenkins, outfielder John Herrnstein, and outfielder Adolfo Phillips to the Cubs for pitchers Larry Jackson and Bob Buhl, 1966.**
John Quinn swapped a future Hall of Famer for two starters (combined age 73) who, together, won just 47 games the rest of their careers. Jenkins, converted to a starter by Cubs manager Leo Durocher, won 20 games in each of six straight seasons starting in 1967—and 284 for his career.

**1. Sixers trade center Moses Malone, forward Terry Catledge, and two first-round draft picks (Anthony Jones and Harvey Grant) to the Bullets for Jeff Ruland and Cliff Robinson. At the same time, the Sixers also trade first-overall draft pick (Brad Daugherty) to the Cavaliers for Roy Hinson, 1986.**
June 16, 1986—the Mother of All Bad Days in Philadelphia Sports History. We combined these two deals because they were made within minutes of each other—on a day when someone should have stuffed Harold Katz in a duffel bag. One wonders what the Sixers might have been had Barkley's front-line teammates entering the '90s been Daugherty and Malone, rather than Armon Gilliam and Rick Mahorn.

**A couple of extra thoughts:**
• As much as everyone always ranks the Von Hayes "Five-for-One" deal among the all-time losers, that's an unfair rap. Yes, it was a bad trade and, as Julio Franco plays into his eighties, it looks even worse. But the other four guys in the deal—including Manny Trillo—never panned out to much of anything. Or maybe it's just that this town has seen far stupider trades.

• Perhaps the weirdest deal ever made by a Philadelphia team came in 1978, when the Flyers swapped Coach Fred Shero to the Rangers for a first-round pick that later became Ken Linseman.

• Where to rank the Terrell Owens deal? That is, TO for Brandon Whiting and a fifth-round pick. It certainly worked out for one glorious season. After that. . . .

## My Favorite Places to Go in Philadelphia (Before I Got Married) :: Hugh Douglas

Note: Defensive end Hugh Douglas played seven great seasons with the Eagles and ranks third on the franchise's all-time sack list. Off the field, he is one of the most entertaining players to come through Philadelphia in recent years.

**7. Delilah's,** 100 Spring Garden Street, Philadelphia. The classiest of all the strip clubs. Everyone went there—local guys and the out-of-town players visiting here. The best-looking women at Delilah's are the waitresses.

**6. Cuba Libre,** 10 S. 2nd Street, Philadelphia. A real nice club in Olde City. The music is great, the food is too, and there's a real nice ambience. It attracts a different crowd, a very nice mixed crowd—beautiful women of all shapes and shades.

**5. The Inn of the Dove,** 725 Cuthbert Boulevard, Cherry Hill. It's a very romantic hotel where you can take a woman. Plus, they have in-room TV channels dedicated to porno.

**4. Glam Restaurant and Lounge,** 52 South Second Street, Philadelphia. That's the place where Bobby Taylor used to have his parties all the time. Every night you went there, there were different celebrities wandering around. I met the singer Eve just hanging around there.

**3. Manayunk Brewery and Restaurant,** 4120 Main Street, Manayunk. I haven't been there in a while, but I always liked it because I could go there and no one cared that I was a football player. I could just blend into the crowd. It attracted some interesting people. The lot was always full of exotic cars.

**2. Wizard's Lounge,** 3801 Chestnut Street, Philadelphia. It's a real hole-in-the-wall strip club near Drexel University. You could sneak in through the back door, see what you wanted, and get out without anyone noticing.

**1. Anywhere in Atlantic City.** There's so much going on, you really can't go wrong at any of the hotels or casinos. Of course, football players are always comped, which helps. But I really like the restaurants, the casinos, and the clubs. Sometimes you want to go out and be around people and just not be recognized as an athlete. That's tough in Philadelphia, but A.C. was always a place you could do that.

# Top 10 Most Hated Personalities—Football

**10. Jeremy Shockey.** A loudmouth showoff. Not that we wouldn't have wanted the big tight end for our own squad.

**9. Warren Sapp.** Always starting fights and jabbering to the refs. The thing about Sapp is, even when the Bucs would beat the Eagles, we don't recall Sapp ever having a productive game here.

**8. Lee Roy Jordan.** From this one on, every guy on the list is a hated Dallas Cowboy. Jordan started the whole thing in 1967 by taking a cheap shot at Timmy Brown that knocked out most of the Eagles' halfback's teeth.

**7. Bob Lilly**. And Chuck Howley and Roger Staubach and Jethro Pugh and any others from those smug squads in the 1970s who had the nerve to call themselves "America's Team." Hey, America started in Philadelphia, Bub. And the eagle—not the star—is the national symbol.

**6. Tony Dorsett.** Constantly ran out of bounds rather than take a hit. We despised him for that.

**5. Erik Williams.** A Philadelphia lad who went over to the dark side. Also one of the dirtiest players ever in the NFL. He always seemed to be jamming his thumb into the eye of one of our defensive linemen.

**4. Hollywood Henderson.** As much of a showboat as the nickname suggests. Henderson was never a great player, but CBS (the Cowboys Broadcasting System) loved to show him on the sidelines, waving to his mom or, perhaps, making a quick coke deal. Last we heard about Henderson, he won $28 million in the Texas lottery. Nothing in history ever served as greater proof that life isn't fair.

**3. Deion Sanders.** In the first Eagles game that Glen ever took his son to, in 1998, Sanders returned a punt back for a touchdown and proceeded to dance like he had just discovered oil under the Vet Stadium end zone.
"Someone should deck that guy," said Ted Macnow.
That's my boy!

**2a. Tom Landry, and 2b. Jimmy Johnson.** Landry was a Bible-thumping hypocrite who loved to rub it in against bad teams. We always wanted to knock that Stetson off his head. Although we never got that chance, we did get to muss up Johnson's perfect hair with a few snowballs back in 1989.

**1. Michael Irvin.** Okay, we cheered as he lay sprawled on the Vet turf, his career over. We didn't know he was hurt that bad. We're sorry.
Sort of.

**10. John Rocker.** We couldn't stand him before the Sports Illustrated article. Why? Being a Brave. Running in from the bullpen. What really bothered us most about that article was that afterwards he had the nerve to say that he was simply saying what all of us really think, but didn't have the nerve to utter. So let us say this, you dumb redneck: We're glad you're out of the game. And you're not out of it because of the comments, but because you stunk.

**9. Marge Schott.** We all know about Marge's dumb dog, Schottzie, and her Nazi memorabilia collection. How about this? The Reds' MVP Eric Davis got hurt in the '90 World Series. After the Reds won it, Davis was in the hospital getting an MRI, so he missed the team charter. Ol' Marge made him pay for his own flight home. Classy broad.

**8. Ken Boyer.** This St. Louis Cardinal third baseman won the National League MVP for the '64 season—beating out our beloved Johnny Callison. For no other reason than that.

**7. Ken Griffey, Jr.** Here's the question. Was he a whining prima donna in Seattle and we just didn't know, because it's on the other side of the planet? What the hell happened to this once-revered centerfielder? What does he have to be so miserable about?

**6. Bobby Valentine.** You know why this hack stays in Japan? It's not the money. It's because the fans over there actually believe him when he tells them it was he who invented baseball, and not Abner Doubleday. Plus, he managed the Mets for seven years. 'Nuf said.

**5. Gary Carter.** And he played for the Mets. Enough said. Plus a bunch of Expo teams that, believe it or not, always gave the Phils a hard time. There was something annoying about this catcher's constantly cheery disposition.

**4. Steve Garvey.** Oh, brother, speaking of cheery dispositions. This first baseman from the Land of La-La always got under our skin. Bad enough that he played for those Dodger teams that always got in the Phillies' way, he had to do it with the phony baloney smile of a Disneyland ticket taker. We all found out later why he was smiling all the time. He was knocking up half of Southern California while married. Or engaged. Or was it both?

**3. Barry Bonds.** Ballplayers have been wearing earrings since Dave Parker. Barry is certainly far from the only one to wear one now. And truth be told, we don't give a rat's ass. Barry's earring, however, dangles and glimmers and says, "Look at me, I'm wonderful." Even his earring is on 'roids. Going way back to the Pirates, you have to hand it to Barry: We've hated him for 20 years now. Twenty years! You just don't wake up and be that despicable. It takes discipline and hard work.

**2. Leo Mazzone.** We had to have someone from the dreaded Braves besides the goon above, and while we wouldn't mind drop-kicking Bobby Cox, this guy particularly made us grind our teeth. That incessant rocking back and forth. The sunflower seeds. Those awesome rotations which he coached year after year, pennant after pennant—always at our expense. We're thrilled he's gone to the American League. We'd rather look at Dick Cheney on the Braves bench. Well, maybe not.

**1. Pete Rose.** That's right. Number 1. We're being brutally honest. No one in the history of the game got on our nerves more as an opposing player. The hurling of his bat and the bush-league running down to first base when he drew a walk. The glancing back at the ump—challenging, daring him to have the nerve to call a strike against The Great Pete Rose. The slamming down of the ball after the final out of an inning. All those unnecessary head-first slides.

Funny how it all worked out, isn't it? Those same irritating traits were exactly why we loved him as a Phil. Guess that kind of makes us a little shallow, doesn't it?

**He even managed to get his biggest supporter to hate him.**

**10. Chris Chelios.** He put a terrible cheap-shot on Brian Propp in the 1989 playoffs and—even after Ron Hextall's slashing act of vigilantism—we've held a grudge ever since.

**9. Jaromir Jagr.** Consider this a group entry and add Ron Duguay, Garry Unger, and any other pretty-boy visitor who sashayed onto Philadelphia ice over the years. How great was it when the sound system would play Aerosmith's "Dude Looks Like a Lady" whenever one of them skated out for warm-ups?

**8. Tie Domi.** Remember the time that fat slob from Havertown fell through the glass behind the penalty box trying to get at Domi? It's still worth a chuckle.

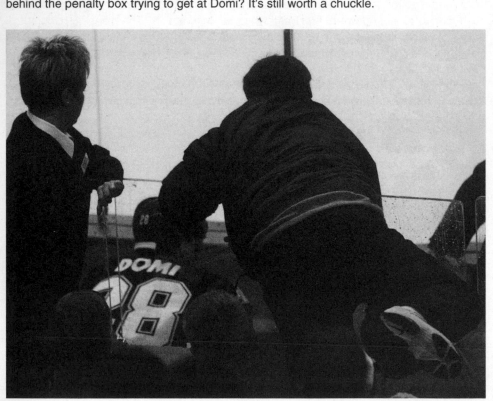

**7. Billy Smith.** Because you need a goalie on this list. Smith earned the nickname "Battle Ax" for the way he swung his stick at opponents' knees. Dishonorable mention goalie: Dominik Hasek.

**6. Every Soviet in 1976.** All those Vladimirs and Aleksandrs from the Red Army team got their clocks cleaned at the Spectrum in a game that had ramifications in both sports and politics.

**5. Matthew Barnaby.** The ultimate pest. This undersized, grinning ninny had the persona of a pro wrestling heel who would smack someone with a roll of nickels and then sidle away with an angelic look on his face. "Who, me??" You always wanted to see Barnaby get thrashed, but he seemed to weasel his way out of fighting the tough guys. In fact, the only time we ever saw Chris Therien drop the gloves was against Barnaby—which pretty much affirms the previous sentence.

**4. Scott Stevens.** The anti-Barnaby. When Stevens hit people, there was nothing furtive about it. And his victims often didn't get up. Just ask Eric Lindros.

**3. Claude Lemieux.** He transformed from Mickey Mouse in the regular season to Superman in the post-season. Three of the Flyers' most-notorious playoff moments involved this jackass—the pre-game skirmish in the 2000 Conference Finals, the fluttering goal he scored over Hextall's shoulder to clinch the 1995 Conference Finals, and, of course, the 1987 pre-game brawl he initiated that had Flyers running on the ice in shower slippers to take a shot at his ugly puss.

**2. Barclay, Bob, and Billy Plager.** The brothers all played defense for the Blues and, in the early 1970s, regularly tuned up undersized Philadelphia forwards. But thank them for this—their bullying (as well as that from teammate Noel Picard) persuaded Ed Snider to invest in tough players which, of course, helped lead to those two Stanley Cups.

**1. Dale Hunter.** He was a great and tough player, but we'll always remember him for 19 years of cheap shots. We were once at a game where Hunter fought two Flyers—Valeri Zelepukin and Roman Vopat—and beat them both up. Now, neither of those players was a noted tough guy, but that was the thing about Hunter. He'd pick a fight with Lady Byng if she laced them up. Amassed 4,292 penalty minutes over his career, and probably deserved twice that amount.

**Other hated goons:** Keith Magnuson, Tiger Williams, Terry O'Reilly, Steve Durbano.

**10. George Karl.** He claimed that the league was fixing things against his team when the Bucks played the Sixers in the 2001 Playoffs. Called a time out and spent the entire two minutes staring at the refs. Shut up and coach.

**9. Jim Boeheim.** Longevity alone puts him here. Not one Syracuse player in history has ever committed a single foul according to this guy, while every shot ever taken by an Orangeman (how would you like to be called an "Orangeman") was put up while being hacked to pieces. You would think old Ichabod Crane would have dropped dead years ago from all his nonstop whining. Because he's been around so long, he's now considered respectable. Not by us.

**8. Shawn Bradley.** We know this is a list for opponents. But we despised him so much as a Sixer that the fact that he stayed in the league for a decade after leaving here drove us crazy. We cringed every time we saw this heartless praying mantis.

**7. Patrick Ewing.** Four years as a Hoya, then another 15 as a Knick. What did we do to deserve this, Lord? Always thought he was overrated from the moment he disappeared the entire second half in the NCAA title game against Nova. Always came up short in big games. For him to be ranked in the NBA's Top 50 is a joke.

**6. Scottie Pippen.** Tell us, how great was he without MJ? A $15 mil a year so-so player, that's what he was. When Jordan wasn't around, Pippen played when he felt like it. Once, when Bulls coach Phil Jackson tried to put him back in a game, he refused to get up because he was pouting that the next play hadn't been called for him. As Sixers fans, we constantly hear that Iverson has no Pippen. Our take: Jordan would have turned Mike Gminski into his "Pippen."

**5. Kobe Bryant.** We could list a long litany of reasons why we felt no sympathy over his All-Star Game tears, but we'll just tell you this: Big Daddy interviewed Kobe while he was still at Lower Merion High and long before he decided to go to the NBA. The brat acted like he was doing Big Daddy a giant favor. And he was wearing shades. Indoors. For a radio interview.

**4. Red Auerbach.** The older Red gets, the funnier we find him. But has there ever been a more arrogant gesture in sports history than Red's practice of lighting up a victory cigar on the bench? While the game was still being contested? At Big Daddy's first-ever Warriors-Celtics game, a fan had to be restrained from going after Red when he lit up that bad boy. The usher should have let the guy go.

**3. John Calipari.** Someone should have let John Chaney lay his dukes on this preening holier-than-thou coach as well. It would have saved us the misery of having to see him coach team after team, year after year.

**2. M.L. Carr.** Another Celtic. A completely talentless, sucker-punching, trash-talking, towel-waving arrogant prick. Now let us tell you how we really feel.

**1. Bill Walton.** Another Celtic. That's right. A Celtic. Bad enough he ripped our hearts out with the Portland Trailblazers in the 1977 Finals. He then reincarnated himself as an annoying sixth man for the Green-and-White and won another championship in '86. Now, we're forced to listen to the Grateful Dead relic ramble on and on as an analyst. Someone should have strangled him with that dumb bandana decades ago.

**10. Joe West.** A surly, vindictive man who should have forever lost his job when the umps went on strike. Once body-slammed Phils reliever David West (no relation) during an on-field rumble between players—no easy feat considering the pitcher's pear-like physique. Also once tossed Lenny Dykstra for, essentially, complaining that West—umping second base that day—was interfering with Dykstra's view of the pitcher's delivery.

**9. Jerry Jones.** Flirted up Glen's wife at the 1990 NFL owners' meeting. We hate him for a lot of things besides that. On a side note: Worst face-lift of all time.

**8. Jim Gray.** This is probably like putting Howard Cosell on the list. People in every city hate this broadcaster, so why should we be any different?

**7. Kevin Collins.** The NHL linesman who skated with a peace-sign medallion around his neck. Let 'em fight, dammit. Although, we always enjoyed hearing Steve Coates rant as Collins would break up a scuffle before it could get started.

**6. Birdstone.** It was bad enough he beat Smarty Jones at the Belmont, costing Big Daddy's wife $100, but did you see the contract he signed the next year? Smokinggun.com has it. No hay for this jackass. M&M's—and no brown ones. No horse trailer, but instead an Escalade limo. No whip; a feathered boa. All horses this prima donna races against must wear blinkers at all times around him. No eye contact. And where do you think Terrell Owens got the idea that if the media wanted to interview him they had to pay him? You got it.

**5. Johnny Most.** His shrill, ear-piercing voice could be heard throughout the Spectrum when he was serving as a Celtics' radio broadcaster and chief cheerleader. This entry gives us an excuse to tell our favorite Johnny Most story: In 1989, he went to the team doctor, complaining of hearing loss and headaches. The doctor took a look, and extracted a TV earplug that had been lodged in Most's ear for nearly two years.

**4. Leon Stickle.** Edges out Collins and Don Koharski as our least-favorite hockey official. Infamous, of course, for the case of brain-lock that caused him to miss an obvious offsides call in the 1980 Stanley Cup Finals, costing the Flyers a goal, the game, and the Cup.

**3. Scott Boras.** The second-sleaziest agent in sports represented J.D. Drew in his 1997 contract stalemate with the Phillies. If you look at Boras very carefully, you can actually see the horns growing out of the back of his head.

**2. Dan Dierdorf.** As a player with the St. Louis Cardinals, we regarded him as a cheap-shot artist. As an analyst for Monday Night Football, we regarded him as worse. Imagine the nerve of that guy, trying to convince people that Eagles safety Andre Waters was a dirty player.

**1. Drew Rosenhaus.** Never in the history of mankind has one man so mishandled a delicate situation. While we do not exonerate Terrell Owens for any of his inane behavior, we still think the episode could have been avoided had Rosenhaus exhibited just a shred of common sense. Our lasting memory will be Rosenhaus, with his lavender shirt and slicked-back hair, wearing that smug grin and repeating his mantra—"Next question"—while Owens' reputation slipped even further away that November afternoon in New Jersey.

**Next Question.**

Note: The late Eric Gregg—a Philadelphia Native—worked 25 years as a Major League umpire, gaining acclaim for his roly-poly physique and his fun approach to the game.

After leaving baseball in 2000, Gregg worked as a columnist for the *Metro,* a greeter and bartender for Chickie's and Pete's, and commissioner of WIP's Wing Bowl.

Shortly before he passed away in 2006, Gregg wrote this list of his favorite—and least favorite—players to work with over the years.

## Five Who Were a Pleasure

**5. Fred McGriff.** He was the guy I called out on strikes in that famous 1997 NLCS clincher. I had a big strike zone all day, but for both teams, so no one complained. Livan Hernandez had 14 strikeouts with two outs in the ninth, and here comes the big curve ball. To be honest, I jumped the gun. I signaled strike three. Even as my hand's going up, I'm thinking, "Holy shit, the ball's outside."

With any other hitter, there would have been hell to pay right there. But McGriff just looked at me, shook his head and smiled. He knew I blew it, but he didn't embarrass me or make me an enemy.

**4. Greg Luzinski.** "Bull" didn't say much to umps. He was a quiet, respectful man. But when he did talk to you, he was very serious. I remember one time during the playoff series against Pittsburgh in 1979. The pitch comes in, it's borderline, and I shout, "That's one!"

Bull looks back at me. He's not happy.

Then the next pitch. It's borderline also, and I shout, "That's two!"

Now Bull turns around and screams, "Two what?"

"Too high," I said. "One ball, one strike!"

I don't often change calls, but I was afraid he'd rip my head off. Manny Sanguillen, the Pirates catcher, just laughed. What could he say?

**3. Jay Bell.** When he was with the Pirates in the 1980s and 90s, it was almost like having another umpire out there. He'd break up fights, he'd intercede with the players, but he'd never show you up. Every batter is your friend when he's four-for-four, but Bell wouldn't gripe about a close call even when he was in an 0-for-19 slump.

**2. Larry Bowa.** The crew I started with, headed by Bruce Froemming, didn't talk to Larry. They were still angry that he showed them up over that play in the infamous "Black Friday" game in 1977 where the ball bounced off of Schmidt to Bowa and he didn't get the call trying to throw out Davey Lopes. But I talked to Larry, and I liked him.

You know, Larry pulled the riot act many times, but never with me. When he had a problem with one of my calls, he was always reasonable and respectful about it. A lot of people don't believe that.

**1. Gary Carter.** He was a great guy with a sense of humor. He'd always talk to the ump—bust your balls, but in a good way. Gary caught my first playoff game in Montreal in 1981. Before the game, he comes up to me and asks, "Tight?"

"Oh yeah," I said. "A little bit."

He said, "Not you, fat guy, your pants. They're about to explode."

It was just his way of trying to keep everyone loose.

He'd double-cross you, though. I'd call a close pitch a ball, and he'd say, "Good call, E." Meanwhile, he'd be signaling to his pitcher that it was a strike.

## Five Who Were Not a Pleasure

**5. Chris Sabo.** What a pain in the butt. Remember that Budweiser dog, Spuds MacKenzie? The dog looked just like Sabo. He and (teammate) Paul O'Neill were two sour-pusses. Always griping, always yelling. He'd say to the umps, "You're lucky to be here. You should have to buy a ticket."

**4. Tug McGraw.** I liked him off the field, but in games, he'd just go nuts all the time. He'd come into a game, load up the bases, and scream at the umps for squeezing him.

One time we ran him, and it was only a spring training game. There's a six-year-old kid in the stands, and he's heckling the umps. We learned that it was Tug's son, so we tossed him, too. It's the only time I ran a father and a son.

**3. Mike Schmidt.** One game I called Mike out four times, all on inside strikes. He didn't like that and started reminding me who he was. I said, "I don't care who you are, a strike's a strike." He's yelling at me, saying, "You're showing me up."

It turns out that my son and his daughter went to school together. The next day, his daughter tells my son, "Your dad called my dad out on a bad pitch and he's not happy."

My son said, "Your dad makes all that money. He shouldn't complain."

I was real proud of Eric, Jr. that day.

**2. Eddie Murray.** He thought every call went against him during his entire 21-year career. So no umpires liked him. One time I was with (umpire) Joe West after a World Series game in which Joe made some tough calls against him. Eddie sees Joe after the game and walks right by him without saying a word.

Joe says, "Where are you going, Eddie?"

Murray says, "I'm getting on the bus. I don't even want to breathe the air you're breathing."

**1. Tim Foli.** Every umpire hated him for his entire career. He was a Gene Mauch disciple, which means he knew the rules inside and out and felt he needed to tell you them all the time. He knew how to get under your skin, and then he knew how to stop just before you were ready to toss him out. Just a real pain.

## 8. Penn State gets jobbed by the clock, October 15, 2005.

Joe Paterno's Nittany Lions had come from behind in the final minute to take a 25-21 lead at the University of Michigan in a classic Big Ten matchup. But a long kick return, followed by two quick passes, brought the Wolverines into Penn State territory with 28 seconds left. At least we thought it was 28 seconds. Somehow, Michigan coach Lloyd Carr convinced the refs to add another two seconds to the clock. No explanation, no review, just give the man more time for no good reason.

Two plays later, Michigan landed at the Penn State one-yard line with one second left. The Wolverines scored as the clock ran out—although, by any impartial account, it should have run out before the last play started. Final score: Michigan 27, Penn State 25, Idiot Timekeeper, 1.

"They took the two seconds back and it was the difference," Paterno said afterward. "What can I do?"

Nothing, really. The loss was the Lions' only defeat on the season. But it was enough to take away any chance they had to play in the 2005 BCS title game.

## 7. Phantom roughing call, December 10, 1961.

The year after the Eagles' last championship, they were 9-3 with two games left, despite losing quarterback Norm Van Brocklin and cornerback Tom Brookshier. They met the New York Giants at Franklin Field with a chance to win the division, and were leading 24-21, late in the game.

With about five minutes to go, Eagles special teamer Leo Sugar dived to block a Giants punt—a play that would have clinched the contest. Giants punter Don Chandler—although not touched by Sugar—executed a writhing, twitching dive that would have done Greg Louganis proud. A blind referee called a roughing-the-kicker penalty, giving the Giants a first down. A few plays later they scored the winning touchdown.

The Giants won the division, the Eagles' season was over, and the local 11 didn't make the playoffs for another 17 years.

## 6. Two seconds from victory, March 17, 1990.

Look, we would never rip a ref for trying to protect an athlete. But Richard Steele's zeal to shield Meldrick Taylor in his legendary fight against Julio Cesar Chavez cost the Philadelphia native the junior welterweight crown.

Taylor, from North Philly, was 24-0-1 going into the fight. He led on two of the three judges' cards after 11 rounds. All he had to do in the 12th was stay away and the win was his. But he couldn't, of course, and with about 13 seconds left, Chavez caught him with a right and dropped him.

Taylor rose with five seconds left in the fight. Steele asked him a few questions, but Taylor was distracted by his corner men. Steele, getting no response from Taylor, stopped the fight. Two seconds remained on the clock—not enough time for Chavez even to cross the ring. And that was that. The ref had done what he thought was right. But in doing so, he cost Meldrick Taylor the title.

## 5. The set-up to disaster, September 15, 1997.

You know the chaos theory, in which one tiny act leads to cataclysmic results? A butterfly flaps his wings in Africa and we've got a hurricane 10 days later?

Go with us here.

The Eagles led the Cowboys, 20-15, on a Monday Night game in Dallas, as Troy Aikman tried to rally his team on a last-minute drive. On a fourth down at the Eagles 45, Aikman threw a pass that was clearly tipped by Mike Mamula before ricocheting toward Cowboys receiver Anthony Miller. Eagles cornerback Charles Dimry flattened Miller before the ball got there. The pass fell incomplete.

End of drive. Eagles win.

Except a ref called interference on Dimry. Dallas's drive continued, and the Cowboys scored two plays later.

Now, everyone knows—and replays showed—that when Mamula tipped the ball, any interference call should have been negated. But none of the seven officials saw Mamula's rare good play. So the Cowboys scored a touchdown that shouldn't have happened.

You know the rest. A miracle pass to Freddie Solomon . . . a last-second gimme field goal attempt by the Eagles . . . Tommy Hutton botches the hold . . . Eagles lose. Ray Rhodes's team—which had won 21 of its previous 33 games, goes on to win just eight of the next 29. The officials' failure to see Mamula's play was the tipping point that set it all into motion. As we said, a butterfly flaps its wings. . . .

## 4. Allan Ray's phantom travel in the 2005 NCAA Sweet Sixteen, March 25, 2005.

Let's set the scene. Underdog Villanova was down 10 to North Carolina with 3:45 left. But freshman guard Kyle Lowry started hitting threes and, with 20 seconds to go, the Wildcats cut the deficit to 66-63—and had the ball.

Junior guard Allan Ray penetrated, jumped and—despite being bumped—hit a layup with 9.4 seconds left. The whistle blew and Nova fans went wild, knowing that Ray—an 83-percent foul shooter—was about to tie the game and send it to overtime.

But wait. The ref wasn't signaling a foul against UNC defender Rashad McCants. Instead, he was calling Ray for traveling. Traveling? What the . . . ? Even most of the CBS announcers (save Carolina shill Billy Packer) deemed the call outrageous. And McCants conceded afterward, "I thought I fouled him. When the ref called it a travel, that was a big break for us."

Big break indeed. Nova lost its chance to advance and Carolina went on to win the national championship. To this day, no one has actually seen Ray take steps.

## 3. Playing through pea soup in Chicago, December 31, 1988.

The Eagles never won a Super Bowl—let alone a playoff game—under Buddy Ryan. Funny thing, most players from that era agree the best shot was their first, the 1988 team. Those Eagles swaggered into Soldier Field to play the Bears with both Randall Cunningham and the Gang Green defense on top of their games.

You know what happened next. A thick fog rolled across the stadium in the second quarter with the Bears up, 7-6, but the Eagles driving. Despite protests to halt the game, referee Jim Tunney ordered the teams to play on. In the end, the Bears won, 20-12. At least we've been told that. We never saw the rest.

Randall threw for 407 yards that day. But tight end Keith Jackson dropped a touchdown in the gloaming, and fullback Anthony Toney nullified another touchdown by going into motion because he thought he saw the ball had been snapped.

Who knows if the Eagles would have won had the game been delayed until the fog lifted. This much we do know: It was a damned stupid decision not to stop and wait until conditions improved.

## 2. Black Friday's other blunder, October 7, 1977.

Everyone remembers this Phils-Dodgers playoff classic for other weird events. The way Phils fans booed Burt Hooton off the mound. Danny Ozark's brain fart that left Greg Luzinski in the field and defensive replacement Jerry Martin on the bench.

But do you remember the horrible call by umpire Bruce Froemming that hosed the Phils? It came in the ninth inning, as Phils closer Gene Garber was collapsing and just after Luzinski blundered Manny Mota's flyball into a three-base mistake. The Phils were still up, 5-4, with two outs, when Dodgers second baseman Davey Lopes hit a sharp grounder that ricocheted off Mike Schmidt's knee directly into Larry Bowa's glove. The Phils' shortstop deftly threw to first and seemed to get Lopes by a step.

Indeed, replays clearly showed the ball in first baseman Richie Hebner's glove as Lopes lead foot was still in the air approaching first base. But Froemming—in dark glasses and carrying a white cane—saw it differently. He flashed one of those overly emphatic "safe" signs that really means, "I'm not at all sure what I saw, so I'll try to sell it as hard as I can."

The play scored Mota, tying the game. A few pitches later Lopes went on to score. The next day they lost Game 4 and went home.

Blame Ozark. Blame Luzinski. Blame Garber.

Our bile is still aimed at Froemming.

## 1. Leon Stickle ruins a season, May 24, 1980.

Most hockey fans can't name a single official. But every Flyers loyalist remembers Leon Stickle and, in fact, recalls his middle name, which apparently rhymes with "Clucking."

The veteran lineman was working Game 6 in the Stanley Cup Finals between the Flyers and Islanders when New York winger Clark Gillies skated into the Flyers zone and dropped a pass for trailing center Butch Goring. The puck clearly crossed back over the blue line and into the center-ice zone before Goring picked it up and carried it over the line himself.

The Flyers on the ice eased up (foolishly in hindsight), waiting for the whistle. It didn't come. Stickle gave a "safe" signal—meaning no off-sides—and Goring saucered a pass to teammate Duane Sutter, who flipped a shot over Flyers goalie Pete Peeters.

Let us assure you: This wasn't one of those marginal calls where you're searching for that speck of white ice between the puck and blue line. This one was at least three feet past the line. Any Peewee League player would know this was offsides.

But Stickle wasn't as astute as a Peewee League player.

The Flyers lost the game and, thus, the series. Meanwhile, Stickle went on to work in the NHL for another 21 years.

Some things just aren't fair.

And one that really helped . . .

## 1. John LeClair scores through the side of the net, April 14, 2000.

The Flyers always had a tough time scoring on Dominik Hasek, the Buffalo Sabres' acrobatic goalie. But in Game 2 of the first round of the 2000 NHL playoffs, they came up with a shot that even Hasek couldn't stop.

With the Flyers down, 1-0, winger John LeClair skated in and wristed a steep angle shot—the kind that Hasek always handles with ease. The goalie hugged the post. But suddenly, the puck was in the net.

Hasek appeared shocked. The goal judge turned on the red light, and the two referees called for a center-ice faceoff. The video judges, whose job it is to review every goal, did not phone down a complaint.

After the next whistle, the confused Sabres skated over to their own net. Defenseman Dixon Ward discovered a huge hole in the mesh where LeClair's shot had gone through.

The Sabres screamed, but too late. Also, an ESPN replay aired later clearly proved that LeClair's shot had gone through—or perhaps created—the gap. No matter.

NHL rules state that once an ensuing faceoff takes place, a play can no longer be overturned. The goal counted.

The Flyers went on to win the game and the series. LeClair—never a big-time post-season producer—had to be grateful for the gift.

# Ten Things I Hate about SEPTA

**10. Why do I always get the seat next to the fat guy eating a hoagie with onions?**

**9. When a trolley can't get around a double-parked car.** And it always happens when you're late for work.

**8. Broken escalators at Suburban station.** A workout that Pat Croce wouldn't survive and one you certainly don't need at 7 a.m.

**7. That lovely aroma from the underground trolley stops.** Napalm smells better in the morning.

**6. Schedules? What schedules?** Andy Reid has better clock management.

**5. It's 70 degrees and the heat's on.** Where do they keep the thermostat? In Delaware?

**4. Having to leave a bar by midnight to catch the last train.** And it's always the same night that you might have actually gotten lucky with that gorgeous redhead.

**3. Trolleys that pass you because they're full.** Ever see those Vietnam movies where people are desperately trying to get out of Saigon? They're hanging on helicopters, jumping onto backs of trucks. That's the look on the faces of these poor souls when the trolley zooms by. (Of course it's great when it's you that has the seat.)

**2. Listening to someone's conversation on their cellphone.** Yeah, I just love hearing how you were stood up last night, you loser.

**1. That lovely soggy-sweatsock smell when you're crammed on the Broad Street subway car with 8,000 worn-out Eagles fans headed home after a game.**

## Philadelphia's Ultimate Pick-Up Team :: Sonny Hill

Note: Sonny Hill has been Mr. Basketball in Philadelphia as long as anyone can remember. He is the executive advisor to the 76ers and founder and director of the Sonny Hill Community Involvement Basketball League. He is also a respected broadcaster who has called NBA games on CBS, and currently hosts a popular Sunday morning show on WIP. In 2003, Sports Illustrated ranked Hill among the 101 most influential minorities in sports.

This is my all-time Philadelphia high school team of players from the Public and Catholic Leagues back in the heyday. I picked the players based on these criteria: You're in the schoolyard and, if you lose, you have to wait a long time before your next game. With these players, I don't plan to lose.

**F—Tom Gola, La Salle High.** You're talking about a player who was way ahead of his time. Tom was a big man for his era, and he did things in the 1950s that people just started doing in the past 10 years—put the ball on the floor, rebound, play defense. A great team player as well.

**F—Ray "Chink" Scott, West Philadelphia High.** Another quintessential player who was ahead of his time. He was one year behind Wilt in high school, and was Wilt's best competition back then. At six-foot-nine, he could dribble, shoot the long jumper, play the post; he could do it all.

**C—Wilt Chamberlain, Overbrook High.** You don't need any comments from me here. If you don't know, you don't know basketball.

**G—Guy Rodgers, Northeast High.** So many light years ahead of the game that the game still hasn't caught up. Just six feet tall, but he was Magic Johnson long before there was Magic Johnson. Averaged 35 points per game in high school and went on to become one of the best-ever players at Temple. He could shoot both left- and right-handed hook shots. Imagine that.

**G—John Chaney, Ben Franklin High.** A folk hero in city basketball. John played at a time when not everything was on TV or radio, but word still got out on the street about how great he was. John would dribble the ball and five guys couldn't get it away from him. His best skill was his tenacity. The same drive you saw in him as a coach at Temple, he had as a player. As close as John and I were—and still are—he used to say to me, "I don't come to play against you, I come to kill you."

**My other top players include:** Wayne Hightower, Overbrook High, Jackie Moore, Overbrook High, Walt Hazzard, Overbrook High, Andre McCarter, Overbrook High, Wali Jones, Overbrook High, Lewis Lloyd, Overbrook High, Hal Lear, Overbrook High, Gene Banks, West Catholic High, Ernie Beck, West Catholic High, Joe Belmont, Northeast High, James "Tee" Parham, Northeast High, Jimmy Baker, Olney High, Rasheed Wallace, Gratz High, Claude Gross, Ben Franklin High

"Ready to play?"

## Ten Big 5 Players Who Had Better Pro Careers than Expected

Now, this does not mean we thought they were inferior collegiate athletes. Obviously, any ballplayer that starts at the Division 1 level is on, well, another level. Anyone who has ever played pickup ball with someone who even played at a small college can immediately see how much better that guy is than most of us Joe Schmoes. So this list salutes those who had much more deep-inside than we gave them credit for.

### Villanova

Why the heck do the Wildcats have so many players on this list? Does it show that the Big East is such a great conference that it's difficult to shine there? Or is it that the NBA gives Villanova players a longer look than it would if they were in some other conference? Here are five that surprised us.

**5. Chris Ford.** We thought Chris would be your classic NBA "tweener," but he played 10 years in the NBA and averaged more than 15 points a game in '79. By the way, did you know Atlantic City's own Chris Ford made the first three-point shot in NBA history? He also had a forgettable stint as coach of the Sixers in 2004.

**4. Harold Pressley.** Another alleged "tweener." Great defensive stopper on the '85 NCAA Championship team, Harold got drafted in the first round (17th overall) by the Sacramento Kings, played four years in the NBA and made a great deal of money.

**3. Alvin Williams.** Can't say we're ever surprised when a six-foot-five guard makes it in the NBA, but who knew this Germantown Academy grad, after being selected 48th in the draft, would be in his ninth year in the NBA?

**2. Malik Allen.** This Shawnee High grad went undrafted after his final season at Nova in 2000. Got into the NBA two years later, and is still playing today. That's perseverance.

**1. Doug West.** Yet another "tweener," Doug was the 38th pick of the 1990 draft and went on to play 12 years in the NBA. You never heard anything about him; he was just always "there."

## LaSalle

**3. Rasual Butler.** Another second-round pick (53rd overall in 2002), this Roman grad excelled with a LaSalle program that not many people were paying much attention to. Fortunately for Rasual, the NBA was. It looks like Butler has is going to have a long career.

**2. Tim Legler.** Undrafted, this lights-out shooter played for six NBA teams in 10 years— starting a grand total of four games. Tim played a grand total of *five minutes* in three games for Utah in 1993. But he's carved out a nice little niche for himself as an NBA analyst. The only people who aren't surprised how well Tim has done for himself are Tim and anyone who ever ran with him down on the Jersey Shore courts of Avalon on Saturday and Sunday mornings.

**1. Doug Overton.** While Temple's Marc Macon got most of the accolades during Doug's collegiate years, the Dobbins Tech grad had the much longer pro career. He sure took the long way to do it. Drafted in the second round in 1991, Doug played for eight teams, including the Sixers and Clippers twice and the Nets three times. Anyone sure he's retired?

## Temple

**1. Rick Brunson.** Proves that a guard with some height who's not afraid to play some "D" will always have a spot in the NBA. Rick not only went undrafted, it took him three years to get into the NBA. He has bounced around with many teams, including playing for three different teams twice. We always think that says something for a player when teams think fondly enough to want him around a second time.

## Penn

**1. Matt Maloney.** While this Memorial High grad and son of Temple coach Jim Maloney certainly got his fair share of accolades during an outstanding career at Penn, it was teammate Jerome Allen who was expected to have a better chance at making it in the NBA. After going undrafted, Matt played six years and scored a nice contract or two.

**One last note:** Though we knew Overbrook's Malik Rose was an outstanding player, who knew he was going to carve out the NBA career that he did? Well, Drexel's Malik did, and that's all that counts. Mean tuba player also, and we're not kidding.

# Big 5 Players Who Did Less than Expected in the NBA

This is not a list of players who had their careers cut short by injuries, like LaSalle's Ken Durrett, Michael Brooks, and the "L Train," Lionel Simmons. Boy, that's weird, three Explorers. We apologize if we're unaware of other injuries that might have prevented anyone on this list from realizing his pro potential. And please remember, we think all of the players listed here were magnificent. Maybe it's our fault that we expected too much of them at the pro level. It's not like they let us down, it's just that, well, we're big fans.

## Villanova

Here we go again. Six Wildcats. SIX! Again, it says so much about the quality of the Big East and the Big 5.

**6. John Pinone.** To be honest, it wasn't like we were expecting John to be a great pro, though he did have a stellar career at 'Nova. He was the eleventh pick of the third round in the 1983 NBA draft. But seven games? That's how long his career lasted with the Atlanta Hawks. Seven. Remember, we're talking about a three-time Big 5 Player of the Year and a third-team All-American who was, in the eyes of many, one of the greatest players in Big 5 history.

**5. Michael Bradley.** Only played one year for the Cats (2000–01), but what a year. Such a complete game and at six-foot-ten, this first-round pick should have started more than 13 NBA games in his first five years.

**4. Bill Melchionni.** All-American and a Bishop Eustace grad, Billy only played two years in the NBA (but was a member of the Sixers' 1967 championship team) before he moved on to a long, fine career in the ABA. Maybe we just wanted more NBA years from such a great shooter.

**3. Ed Pinckney.** Final Four MVP from that glorious championship season. All-Big East, All-Big 5, plus too many other awards to list here. Tenth overall pick in the draft, Ed had a journeyman's 12-year career and made a lot of money. I guess we were unfairly hoping for a little more, based on the good times and the insanity that swirled around 1985. A great guy who will be a head coach some day.

**2. Tim Thomas.** After all that fuss over whether or not Thomas was going to skip college ball completely in 1996 and go directly to the NBA, he ended up underachieving at both levels.

**1. Howard Porter.** Another Final Four MVP in 1971 when Nova took UCLA to the NCAA title game. Three-time All-American. Numerous Big 5 awards, and one of the top five Big 5 players ever. Played seven unspectacular seasons in the NBA.
    By the way, all of Villanova's records from 1971 were erased when it was revealed that,

before the tournament began, Porter signed a contract with an agent in his hotel room. The agent was Richie Phillips, who became head of the Major League Baseball umpires union and later advised 57 umpires to resign in a labor dispute. That move cost many of those umps their jobs forever. One was our own Eric Gregg, who ended up as commissioner of Wing Bowl.

## Temple

**1. Mark Macon.** I know John Chaney would never admit to this, but is Macon his favorite and greatest player ever? The eighth player picked in the 1991 draft, Macon played just six seasons in the NBA. After his first two years, he started in only 10 games. We thought he would hang around longer simply as a defensive player.

## LaSalle

**1. Larry Cannon.** First-team All-Big 5 three times, this Lincoln High grad and all-time Big 5 favorite was the fifth player taken in the 1969 draft. He ended up going to the ABA, bouncing from team to team (although he had one magnificent season with the Denver Nuggets), before wrapping up his career playing 19 games for the Sixers in 1974.

## Penn

**1. Jerome Allen.** Three-time first-team All-Big 5, it was Jerome (and not Matt Maloney) who fans thought to be a lock for the NBA in 1995. Yet the Episcopal grad started only one game in a short two-year NBA career.

## St. Joe's

**1. Clifford Anderson.** Edison High grad Anderson was widely considered among the best Big 5 players of all time, yet barely played in his four years of ABA and NBA ball. Also finished his career with the Sixers, appearing in five games with them in 1971.

For every Moses (Malone) who leads us to the Promised Land, there are too many false prophets. Here are 10 of the most infamous.

**10. John Vanbiesbrouck.** Well, Bob Clarke thought so anyway. "Beezer" was hired as the answer to the gaping five-hole at goalie that had plagued the Flyers since Hextall Version 1.1. Damn, they should have signed Mike Richter as a free agent that summer.

**9. Von Hayes.** He's all over this book, so we needn't go into detail here. Suffice it to say, that "Ted Williams swing" may have been a bit of an exaggeration.

**8. Chris Gratton.** A fascinating case of an emerging young star who got the huge bucks and became a Shrinky Dink under the spotlight. Would have been terrific as a third-line center. But billed as "the next Lindros," he looked like the next Barney Fife.

**7. George McGinnis.** He came as an expatriate ABA superstar who was going to take the Sixers to a new level. They won 12 more games in 1975 than the previous season, but were quickly dismissed in the playoffs. McGinnis was part of the whole "We owe you one" campaign, but it wasn't until he left—and Moses Malone later came in—that the Sixers paid that debt.

**6. Roman Gabriel.** When he showed up in 1973 (replacing John Reaves), he was quickly nicknamed, "The Messiah." Gabriel predicted a championship within two years—and who was going to doubt a three-time Pro Bowler and former league MVP? Still, despite Gabriel's strong play (he returned to the Pro Bowl as an Eagle in 1973), the team never managed a winning record in his five seasons here.

**5. Lance Parrish.** Remember the cringe-inducing bumper stickers? "Lance us a pennant." Not only did they sound contrived, but the muscle-bound catcher, who was supposed to protect Mike Schmidt in the lineup, couldn't lance a boil, let alone a pennant during his two years in Philadelphia.

**4. Shawn Bradley.** Some basketball experts who we really respect predicted this seven-foot-six stick figure would "revolutionize" basketball. The only revolt going on took place in the Spectrum stands after fans got to see how little effort The Great White Nope put into his game.

**3. Jim Thome.** Not since Pete Rose in 1979 had the Phils signed a free agent as significant as this Paul Bunyan look-alike. The first season went great—47 homers, 131 RBIs and that tearful final stroll around the Vet with Mike Schmidt. Around midseason in Year Two, things started to go downhill—too many strikeouts, nagging injuries, and a sense that the $13-million-a-year man wanted no part of being a leader. By the time he shut it down in Year Three, we had already declared his replacement, Ryan Howard, as the next savior. Do we never learn?

**2. Terrell Owens.** You all know the story. We don't even want to talk about it. Next question.

**1. Eric Lindros.** His nickname, earned as a teen, was "The Next One." It was meant to place him in the continuum of the NHL's all-time legends: Richard, Howe, Orr, Gretzky, Lemieux. It's debatable whether Lindros really had the talent to earn a spot on that list. It's irrefutable that he didn't have the heart or the cranium.

**Glen's story:** I was among the first Philadelphians to see No. 88 play, traveling to Oshawa for the *Inquirer* to write a feature on the 17-year-old Junior sensation. I wrote these lines: "The question isn't whether Eric Lindros will eventually lead his future NHL employer to a Stanley Cup. The question is how many."

Boy, I'd like to have those words back.

**Lindros' Philadelphia career came to a crashing end with some help from Scott Stevens**

**5. Ed Van Impe**

**4. Keith Primeau**

**3. Barry Ashbee**

**2. Ron Hextall**

**1. Dave Poulin**

Note: The Flyers general manager declined to offer insight on his choices, saying he didn't "want to insult anyone." He also modestly left himself off the list.

Clearly, any roll call of franchise leaders starts with "Mr. Flyer," who has spent over three decades with the organization, including 15 as its greatest player and nine as the captain. Clarke's work ethic stemmed from his austere upbringing in Flin Flon, Manitoba. He knew as a young child that he had two options—play hockey or work in the copper mines. "There was no way I wanted to work in those mines," he recalls.

He fought diabetes (diagnosed when he was 15) and a physique that, despite a rigorous workout regimen, could best be described as scrawny. He had neither a great shot nor fast feet, but he mastered the elements of the game that reward hard work—he was a tenacious forechecker, a great face-off man, and always the nastiest guy on the ice.

Clarke infused the franchise with the credo that stood for decades: losing was worse than death. There were many nights when the Flyers, following his lead, won on sheer will.

Let's take our own look at the names on his list:

**5. Ed Van Impe** was the first tough guy in franchise history and the team's captain before Clarke's arrival as a player. He is best remembered for tossing elbows that would strike opponents like jackhammers, including one against Valeri Kharlamov that prompted the terrified Soviets to skate off the ice during their epic 1976 game with the Flyers. "A Flyer always gave more than he had," Van Impe used to say. "You did what you had to do to win, and did it every single game."

**4. Keith Primeau** overcame a lot to gain the respect of the fans and his teammates. Early in his career, he was labeled an underachiever, and his public posture during the Flyers' dismissal of coach Bill Barber demonstrated anything but leadership. But through hard work and maturity, Primeau won over his critics. His heroic play during the 2004 Eastern Conference Finals against Tampa Bay was the kind of gutsy stuff on which Clarke built his own career.

**3. Barry Ashbee** came to the Flyers in 1970 and was appalled by the expansion franchise's lack of dedication to winning. He barked at teammates who seemed willing to accept mediocrity, and led the way by playing on an assortment of broken bones and torn ligaments. His career was cut short by a slapshot that crushed his right eye in 1974. He died at age 37 of leukemia, rocking the franchise. "The essential thing in life," Clarke eulogized in 1977, "is not to have conquered, but to have fought well."

**2. Ron Hextall** was a unique NHL player—a goalie who could skate like a forward and intimidate like an enforcer. No netminder before (or since) would do what he did in the 1989 playoffs, when he avenged a cheap shot to a teammate by mugging Chris Chelios, one of the NHL's toughest players. But there was more to Hextall than his belligerence. As he matured and mellowed, he became a powerful force in the locker room. Goalies never become captains, but if ever one was made for the role, it was "Hexy."

**1. Dave Poulin** followed Clarke as captain in 1984 and held the post for six years. An undrafted, undersized, unheralded college player, Poulin thrived during a 13-year NHL career. He is most remembered for his clutch play and ability to tolerate pain. Need an example? Remember the legendary 1985 playoff goal he scored at the Spectrum with the Flyers playing two men short? What you probably don't recall is that he did it while skating with two cracked ribs.

**10. Jeremiah Trotter vs. Andy Reid.** Eventually it was resolved, but it prompted a Pro Bowl linebacker to leave the Eagles in 2002. We still have nightmares of Joe Jurevicius sprinting past Trotter's replacement, Barry Gardner, in the 2002 NFC Championship Game.

**9. Dick Allen vs. Frank Thomas.** It started with a few racial jabs and ended with Thomas clocking Allen's shoulder with a baseball bat. Too many fans, unfortunately, sided with Thomas on this one, which soured Allen on the city.

**8. Scott Rolen vs. Larry Bowa.** Rolen didn't like anyone in Phils' management, but especially not Bowa. Who will ever forget the spring training shouting match between these two hotheads, which was caught by local TV cameras? Another case of a great player skipping town over personality problems with the boss.

**7. Reggie White vs. Norman Braman.** And yet another such case. Remember the pep rally for Reggie? Why is it that the good guy had to go and Mr. Scrooge stayed on?

**6. Jim Fregosi vs. South Philly.** When you describe the residents of a part of our city as, shall we say, too fond of their sisters, you can't expect to be embraced by the populace. This one was good for a few laughs.

**5. Rollie Massimino vs. the Big 5.** Yes, the Big 5 has bounced back, but there are still many people who say it has never fully recovered from Rollie's perceived snubbing of the Big 5 after 'Nova won the NCAA title in 1985. One thing we know is how to hold a grudge.

**4. Harold Katz vs. Andrew Toney.** The Sixers' owner refused to believe that Toney's feet really were injured. It took several years and many medical reports to prove Katz wrong and he still never apologized.

**3. John Chaney vs. John Calipari.** "I'll kill you!" Always fun to catch on tape a physical altercation between two middle-aged men.

**2. Joe Frazier vs. Muhammad Ali.** Yep, we love Ali too, but how he painted Frazier to the press was cruel and petty. This feud went on for years. Although we want to believe they reconciled, we don't quite buy it.

**1. Bob Clarke vs. Eric Lindros.** The all-time mother of all feuds. And Lindros' mother was the all-time mother of all feuders.

**Note: Vai Sikahema was twice a Pro Bowler during his eight-year NFL career. He spent two seasons with the Eagles and then never left town—making his mark as a popular broadcaster for NBC 10.**

## 10. Ben Chapman vs. Jackie Robinson, 1947.

Chapman, the Phillies skipper, led his players in chanting the "N" word at Robinson from the dugout. When the league demanded Chapman apologize and provided the press with a photo op the following night, Chapman still refused to shake hands with the Dodgers rookie, so instead, the two men held a bat—never once making contact. Not a proud moment in Philly sports history.

## 9. Frank Thomas vs. Richie Allen, 1965.

During batting practice on July 3, Thomas needled young Richie a little bit too hard. Allen threw a punch at his teammate and then invited him to take his best shot. Thomas did—driving his Louisville Slugger into Allen's right shoulder. One day later, Allen was on the disabled list and Thomas was placed on waivers.

## 8. Darryl Dawkins vs. the Spectrum, 1977.

Chocolate Thunder berated his teammates for not backing him in a fight with the Portland Trailblazers' Maurice Lucas during the NBA Finals. When he still couldn't get a rise out of the other guys, the six-foot-eleven behemoth ripped the metal door off a bathroom in anger.

## 7. Buddy Ryan vs. Norman Braman, 1987.

The battle started during the NFL players' strike, when Buddy backed the union and Braman served as a leader for NFL management. It grew progressively uglier during Buddy's term here, which ended in 1990.

Buddy liked to tweak Braman, who spent summers on the Riviera, by referring to him as "that guy in France." He went a few steps further by handing general manager Harry Gamble a plastic "scab ring" during the 1987 strike, and labeling Gamble as "Braman's illegitimate son." Classic Buddy.

## 6. Jerome Brown vs. Dennis McKnight, 1991.

The two guys squared off during a practice at training camp. That kind of thing happens all the time; what doesn't happen so often is what occurred next. McKnight, a big guard, confronted Jerome in the showers. Jerome was completely lathered up in soap as they squared off. Cooler heads prevailed when someone yelled, "Who the hell is going to step in between you two naked 300 pounders to break this up?"

## 5. Erica Hopkins vs. Wes Hopkins' girlfriend, 1992.

Actually, many fans witnessed this Vet Stadium brawl, but very few realized what they were watching. Wes's wife, Erica, confronted his mistress in Section 121, where the players' wives sat. Eric Allen's wife, Lynn, held the woman while Erica made like Rocky on a side of beef. One rumor among the wives claimed that before it went down, Lynn Allen and Sara White (Reggie's wife) slipped cash to the security guards to disappear.

## 4. Herschel Walker vs. Mark McMillian, 1993.

McMillian, a little cornerback, was considered the fastest guy on the team. He kept challenging Herschel, telling the former Georgia track star that he was all just a bunch of hype. They finally met before practice and agreed on a 40-yard race. Teammates lined the field, bets were placed, and someone filmed it all. Herschel blew him away.

## 3. Tommy Jeter vs. Keith Millard, 1993.

Supposedly Millard made a pass at the Texas rookie's wife, and the fight was on between the two Eagles defensive linemen. A huge tureen of soup went flying across the locker-room, as did two coolers of Gatorade. It turned out to be the closest Rich Kotite ever came to getting a Gatorade shower.

## 2. Offensive coordinator Jon Gruden vs. RB Ricky Watters's girlfriend, 1996.

Ricky's girlfriend was a cute Asian woman who weighed no more than 100 lbs. Yet, she confronted Gruden outside the locker-room following a game, screaming, "Give Ricky the damn ball!"

Gruden, used to verbal sparring with huge men, didn't know how to respond and stood silent. Considering that Ricky had 353 carries that season, I'm not sure she had a gripe.

## 1. Terrell Owens vs. Hugh Douglas, 2005.

The ill will started during TO's rehab from a broken ankle in 2004. TO felt slighted by Douglas, Donovan McNabb, and countless others who said the Eagles could win the Super Bowl without him. So when Owens arrived at training camp in 2005, he refused to speak to McNabb or Douglas. Douglas and a few teammates were on the elevator one night when the doors opened—and there stood TO.

"Hello," said Douglas.

Owens ignored him.

"You know," said Douglas, "I could kick your ass if I wanted to."

Other players had to step in to separate the two men.

And, well, we all know what this one led to.

Within the team game, we've been treated to some terrific individual rivalries over the years. Here are ten of our favorites.

**10. Bobby Taylor vs. Michael Irvin.** When Ray Rhodes drafted the rangy Taylor in 1995, it was specifically with the idea of covering the six-foot-two Cowboys receiver. Good plan. Taking away Taylor's rookie season (which we'll call a learning experience), the two men matched up six times. Irvin had just 22 catches for 315 yards and a single touchdown.

**9. Andrew Toney vs. Dennis Johnson.** Another case of a team adding a player just to stop its rival's star. In this case, the Celtics traded for "DJ" in 1983 after Toney torched them throughout the Sixers championship season. Hey, they didn't call him "The Boston Strangler" for nothing.

**8. Steve Carlton vs. Johnny Bench.** This was one of those Hall of Fame match-ups of the 1970s that always caused you to stop what you were doing and intently listen to Harry Kalas describe each pitch. Unfortunately, Bench often got the best of Lefty. Twice, the Reds catcher hit three home runs in a game against Carlton.

**7. Reggie White vs. Erik Williams.** The Cowboys cheap-shot tackle used every dirty trick to throw Reggie off his game. And it worked. Reggie would too often get so caught up in getting even with Williams that he became ineffective at chasing down Troy Aikman.

**6. Tommy Hutton vs. Tom Seaver.** Go figure this one. Hutton was a .248 career hitter—but finished at .700 against a pitcher who could be called the greatest righty of his era. And of Hutton's 22 career home runs, four were against "Tom Terrific."

**5. Jon Runyan vs. Michael Strahan.** They matched up 13 times between 2000–05, and Strahan had 13 sacks. To be fair, Strahan dominated the rivalry early, but Runyan adjusted and came to hold his own (and the Giants' defensive end's jersey). Strahan described the matchup as "wrestling with a dancing bear."

**4. Chuck Bednarik vs. Chuck Noll.** The NFL was a nastier game back in the 1950s, and nothing was as intense as the hatred between Bednarik and Noll, then a guard for the Browns. One memorable contest ended with those two slugging it out on the 50-yard line as the network credits ran over them on the TV screens of America.

**3. Julius Erving vs. Larry Bird.** Of the dozens of times they met, all everyone remembers is the famous fight of 1984, with Doc's long fingers enveloping Bird's throat. Doc always said he was embarrassed by the incident—but Sixers fans loved it.

**2. Dave Schultz vs. Terry O'Reilly.** No one recorded how many times these two NHL heavyweights fought, but it seemed to occur every game between the Flyers and Boston Bruins—often more than once per. Says Schultz: "I'm not sure I can call any guy the toughest, but me and Terry went at it more than anyone else." Says O'Reilly: "Dave had Game Seven anger in him every night."

**1. Wilt Chamberlain vs. Bill Russell.** You expected anything else? This is probably the greatest one-on-one rivalry in the history of team sports. We love the stories of how the Celtics would play every Thanksgiving in Philadelphia—and Wilt would try to slow Russell down by loading him up with his mom's home cooking. Another great story was how Wilt signed a $100,000 contract in 1965—and Russell threatened to retire until the Celtics gave him $100,001. Unfortunately, you know how this ends: Russell's Celts won seven of their eight playoff series against Chamberlain's teams. They were 4-0 in seventh games.

Note: Bill Campbell, "The Dean of Philadelphia Sports," has a career in broadcasting that spans seven decades. He has been the play-by-play announcer for the Eagles, Phillies, and 76ers. He also helped invent sports-talk radio in this city. He has been honored by the Philadelphia Sports Hall of Fame and the Basketball Hall of Fame.

Beyond that, Bill Campbell personifies class and dignity. Here is his list of the classiest people he has dealt with over the years.

**15. Angelo Musi,** Temple and Warriors guard. He was the captain of the 1946 Warriors team that won the title. He became a great friend and still is today. He's my daughter's godfather, so I sure can't leave him off this list.

**14. Steve Mix,** Sixers guard and broadcaster. Steve played on a lot of bad teams, but that wasn't his fault. He wasn't the most talented player, but he made the most of what he had, even leading the league in steals once. Also, I broke him in as a broadcaster and still enjoy listening to him.

**13. Jack Ramsay,** St. Joseph's and Sixers coach. As Van Brocklin did in football, Jack helped teach me basketball. Once, I conceded to him that I couldn't tell the difference between a zone press and a man-to-man press. So Jack invited me to practice and had his team walk through both so that I could understand what I was trying to broadcast. Could you see any coaches doing that these days?

**12. Tom Gola,** La Salle and Warriors guard. He played with class. He was the essence of what I wish all basketball players could be on the court—hustle and smarts. He could play guard, forward, or center.

**11. Lee Thomas,** Phillies general manager. He ran the team during some good times and some bad times. He had a tough job and took crap from a lot of people. He took it and never tried to pass it off onto anyone else.

**10. Bob Clarke,** Flyers center and general manager. He's a real man, a genuine guy. What I always liked is that he wouldn't try to duck out of the blame when he made a mistake.

**9. Paul Arizin,** Villanova and Warriors forward. He was the greatest competitor I've ever seen in any sport. I remember him as a young kid, starting out at Nova. He would come to a Warriors game and study Joe Fulks, watching his great jump shot, to get better. Paul became a great college player and then a great pro.

**8. Mo Cheeks,** Sixers point guard and coach. As a player, he was such a good guy. He's the last one I would have projected to become a coach, because I thought he was too nice to be tough enough. Honestly, his success has surprised me.

**7. Tony Taylor,** Phillies second baseman. One of the first Latin players in town, which couldn't have been easy for him. But Tony fit in, and commanded everybody's respect. You never heard anyone say an unkind thing about him.

**6. John Vukovich,** Phillies infielder and coach. Just a good guy. I know what it has cost him emotionally not to coach third base anymore because he's really an on-field guy. But he has handled the change with dignity.

**5. Merrill Reese,** Eagles broadcaster. He follows the rule that was taught to me by Byrum Saam when I started with the Phils: You can't be a decent broadcaster if you don't prepare. Merrill does that and nobody deserves success more than he because he worked so hard to get it.

**4. Julius Erving,** Sixers forward. The most gracious and accommodating guy to the media and fans. With as much notoriety as he had, he was always open. And he was always great with kids.

**3. Connie Mack,** A's manager and owner. I was a 23-year-old kid coming out of the service when I met Mr. Mack. He always called everyone "Mister," even his players. You can't imagine what it was like having the patriarch of baseball, in his eighties, calling a punk kid like me "Mister."

**2. Norm Van Brocklin,** Eagles quarterback. I was broadcasting the Eagles when he came in 1958. We did a weekly TV show together and, in preparing it, he and I would listen to my play-by-play from the previous game. He'd listen to my work and say, "Bill, you're the worst damned broadcaster I've ever heard. Get the damn play right." It was kind of jarring at first, but after a while I learned from him.

One other thing about Dutch: He was at a party at my house once. He's talking to my daughter, Chris, who was about five, and asked her, "Little girl, why don't you have a dog?" "Because my Daddy won't let me get one," she said.

Months passed. We all forgot about it. Then, on the morning of July 24—her birthday—the doorbell rings at 7 a.m. I answer the door in my pajamas, and there's this big quarterback with a small puppy in his arms. Chrissy had that dog for years.

**1. Robin Roberts,** Phillies pitcher. He never changed. Even at the end of his career he was the same guy as when he started. No pretense, just a completely genuine guy. He still is to this day.

**10. Larry Bowa.** He was five-foot-ten and about 145 pounds of battery acid when he came up to the Phils. We recently dug out his 1971 baseball card, on which he looks like an escapee from the high-school junior-varsity team.

**9. Pelle Lindbergh.** The math doesn't compute—a five-foot-nine guy covering 24 square feet of open space—but the Swedish import did it masterfully. Lindbergh would work and sweat so hard in games that he often finished them 15 pounds less than his stated weight of 170. Ahh, what might have been.

**8. Charles Barkley.** Not small by regular-person standards, certainly. He was listed at six-foot-five, although that was at least one inch too generous. He makes this list by being the shortest man ever to lead the NBA in rebounds. Barkley did it through timing, sweat equity, and an ability to shove aside opponents with that condominium-sized derriere.

**7. Bobby Shantz.** Sportswriters of the day referred to him as "The Elfin Southpaw," or "The Little Sampson of the Mound." They sure don't write like that anymore. The five-foot-six, 140-pound lefty out of Pottstown won the 1952 American League MVP Award pitching for the Philadelphia A's. There are old heads who swear they saw a gust of wind blow him off the Shibe Park pitcher's mound.

**6. Smarty Jones.** How many times did you hear him called, "The little colt from Philadelphia?" Or, "The small horse with the big heart?" We'll always remember Smarty running away from Rock Hard Ten in the 2004 Preakness. It looked like a mouse scampering from a rhino.

**5. Jameer Nelson.** A six-foot-nothing point guard out of Chester High, Nelson was college basketball's top player in 2003–04. He left St. Joe's as the Hawks' all-time leader in points, assists, and—most importantly—wins.

**4. Wilbert Montgomery.** They listed him at five-foot-ten and 190 pounds, but who's kidding. He lasted to the 6th round of the NFL draft in 1977 because scouts thought he was too small to make it in the pros. He left nine seasons later as the Eagles' all-time leading rusher. And that doesn't even count the 194 yards he put up against the Cowboys in the 1980 NFC title game.

**3. Lenny Dykstra.** The perfect pesky lead-off hitter. He had a strong case of Napoleon Complex, which served him greatly as a player, but not so well off the field. Dykstra stood five-foot-nine and could fold up to create a strike zone the size of a tri-fold wallet. He drew 129 walks in 1993, a season for which he deserved the MVP but finished behind Barry Bonds.

**2. Tommy McDonald.** The smallest player in the Pro Football Hall of Fame. The amazing thing about McDonald—who stood five-foot-nine and weighed 170—was his durability. He missed just three games in his first 11 seasons. His 35-yard touchdown catch in the 1960 NFL Championship Game remains a highlight in Eagles history.

**1. Allen Iverson.** The ultimate little giant. Twenty years from now, our lingering memory of AI will be of that scrawny little body—all elbows and knees—yo-yoing a crossover dribble into the land of the giants and scooping a feathery layup just before some seven-footer pounded him to the ground. He always got up again.

**Left to right: Dikembe Mutombo, Tyrone Hill, A.I., and Eric Snow**

## The Five Greatest Receivers in Eagles History
## :: Tommy McDonald

Note: Tommy McDonald is the Eagles' only Hall of Fame receiver; he helped lead the team to the 1960 championship.

Quarterback Sonny Jurgenson (9) center Chuck Bednarik (60) and wide receiver Tommy McDonald (25) of the Philadelphia Eagles pose for a picture at training camp. October 29, 1959.

**5. Pete Retzlaff.** A great receiver, he just didn't get thrown to a lot. Back then if you got thrown to two or three times in a game, that was a lot. Plus, he agreed to play tight end, which cut down his receptions even more. Nowadays it's easier for somebody to catch a lot of balls. The game is different.

**4. Pete Pihos.** Well, I didn't get to see him play, but his stats speak for themselves. Almost 400 receptions and 61 touchdowns back in the early days of the NFL. For that era, those were great numbers.

**3. Mike Quick.** An unbelievably reliable receiver. He always got the job done. With Quick, you didn't hope he'd catch it. You knew he'd catch it.

**2. Tommy McDonald.** Hey, I scored 84 touchdowns myself (66 for the Eagles). In 1960, I only caught 39 balls but 13 of them went for touchdowns. Say this about me: God made me little, but he gave me a big heart.

**1. Harold Carmichael.** A receiver has one object, that's to get in the end zone. His 79 TDs are the most in franchise history. That says a lot to me. So big, so smooth. How could anyone cover him?

And what about Terrell Owens? Well, it's hard for me to grade him because he didn't spend very much of his career with the Eagles. But he's awesome. I'd put him up there with Marvin Harrison and Randy Moss as the best guys around today.

Well, Big Daddy is Irish and Glen is a true "Mac," so who better than us to deliver a fun "All-Mc" and "All-Mac" list you can refer to on that grandest of holidays, St. Patrick's Day.

**10. Lonnie McFarland.** Lonnie is on the all-time Catholic League second-team all-star team, and is the 29th leading scorer in St. Joe Hawks history. But he will always be most famous for that one extra pass he made to John Smith to defeat top-ranked DePaul in the second round of the NCAA Tournament in 1981. One of the greatest games in Big 5 history, it's the one that ended with teenaged Dei Lynam jumping into her father Jim's arms.

**9. Jim McMahon.** Do you realize he only played 21 games with the Birds? So much fun to have around that it seemed he was in town longer. Jim was with the Eagles when "X"—the Spike Lee movie about Malcolm X—came out, and many of the players started wearing baseball caps with an X on the front. Jim showed up with an "O" hat, and his teammates loved it.

**8. Craig MacTavish.** Last guy to play in the NHL without a helmet. That alone earns him a spot here.

**7. Aaron McKie.** Hometown hero to us. Played for Gratz High, Temple, and then the Sixers. Tell us that's not the dream of every Philly kid who ever threw up a jumper on an outdoor court with no net.

**6. Donovan McNabb.** Well, he comes from Chicago, where they dye the Chicago River green on St. Patty's Day. That puts him on this list, doesn't it?

## From this point on, this list is reserved for champions.

**5. Dwayne McClain.** April 1st, 1985. The greatest college basketball game ever played, for our money. Nova beats Georgetown, 66-64, for the NCAA Championship. This area's last championship. Guess who's the leading scorer in that game, with 17 points? The 18th leading scorer in Wildcats history, Dwayne went to the NCAA Elite Eight three out of his four years with Nova. And the man could slam.

**4. Bake McBride.** An oft-forgotten member of the World Champion 1980 Phillies, but not by us. Take Bake off those Phils and you can forget about the only championship that franchise ever won. A clutch, money rightfielder with a great 'fro to boot.

**3. Rick MacLeish.** Two Stanley Cup Championships, and who can forget the sight of Rick gliding down the ice with his long hair flowing? Damn, it was fun when they played without helmets, wasn't it? He leads all Flyers with 10 game-winning goals in the playoffs, and rightly earned a spot in the franchise's Hall of Fame. Rick stayed in the area and we often see him down the Shore hanging at the Deauville Inn in Strathmere. He's still got the sweet 'stache.

**2. Tommy McDonald.** Not only the top receiver on the Eagles 1960 Championship team, but a member of the NFL Hall of Fame. And a nicer, funnier guy you'll never meet. Remember playing touch football as a kid? You'd argue over who was going to be what player. "I'm Mike Quick." "I'm Wilbert Montgomery."

**Big Daddy Alert:** The first player that I wanted to be when I was going long was Tommy Mac. Telling McDonald about that many years later was a real thrill for me.

**1. Tug McGraw.** We don't know where to begin. He captured the hearts of this city, first as a World Champion pitcher, and years later while going through his courageous battle against a brain tumor. He stayed funny and engaging right to the very end. We miss you, Tugger. We know you're up there right now buying a round. So the next one's on Glen and Big Daddy and anyone who's reading this right now.

# The Best and Worst Free Agents in Philadelphia History

In truth, Terrell Owens could make both of these lists. His one-and-a-half-season career with the Eagles was spectacular—but the fallout was devastating. Give him an honorable mention for best (with Herschel Walker, Brian Mitchell, and Carlos Emmons), and a dishonorable mention for worst (with Gregg Jefferies and every other wide receiver Andy Reid ever signed).

## Best

**10. Peter Forsberg,** Flyers, 2005. Obviously, he could move way up this list—or off it—depending on what occurs in coming years. A *Sports Illustrated* poll of NHL players named him the best in the league in 2006. We were impressed when GM Bob Clarke stole him from Colorado.

**9. Jim Thome,** Phils, 2003. It ended after just 361 games, far earlier than was expected. Plus, he wasn't much of a leader on a team that expected guidance from a guy making $13 million a year. But Thome produced 89 homers and 236 RBIs in his first two seasons—the best stats since anyone named Schmidt. On a business level, he helped create an excitement for a franchise that had been moribund too long.

**8. George McGinnis,** Sixers, 1975. His three seasons here—in which he averaged 21.6 points and 11.6 rebounds per game—are kind of forgotten. But McGinnis and Doug Collins formed the foundation that helped the Sixers rise in the mid-70s, forming the bridge between the 9-73 era and the team that eventually won the title. The knock was that his scoring always went way down in the post-season. Eventually traded for Bobby Jones, which helped the franchise as well.

**7. Jeremy Roenick,** Flyers, 2001. One of the most engaging athletes ever to pass through Philadelphia. Roenick was on the downside of his Hall of Fame career when he joined the Flyers, but still led the club in scoring his first two seasons. He played through concussions and broken jaws. Among many classy guys on this list.

**6. Jim Eisenreich,** Phils, 1993. Speaking of classy. Eisenreich arrived as an unheralded pickup (earning just $675,000 in '93), and then hit .318 for the last Phillies team to make it to the World Series. Over four seasons in red pinstripes, he batted .324.
**Glen Alert:** More than once, I witnessed Eisenreich, who battled Tourette's syndrome, in pre-game meetings with youngsters coping with their own afflictions. He was always an inspiration and a gentleman.

**5. Ricky Watters,** Eagles, 1995. Yeah, we know, "For who? For what?" Some fans will remember Ricky only for those four foolish words. But you shouldn't forget the 3,794 rushing yards he put up from 1995–97. No running back in franchise history ever surpassed that total over three years. In fact, no one else in franchise history ever had three straight years surpassing 1,000 yards.

**4. Jon Runyan,** Eagles, 2000. A rock at right tackle who didn't miss a game in six seasons. Do you remember how it all started? Andy Reid was wooing Runyan at a Center City steakhouse, when Temple's John Chaney (who was dining separately), sprinted to their table and shouted, "Don't come here. Don't ever come here for these fans." Gee, thanks, Coach.

**3. Troy Vincent,** Eagles, 1996. Many people forget how good he was in his eight years in green. Vincent and the oft-maligned Bobby Taylor gave the Birds a pair of top-flight cornerbacks season after season. Vincent made five straight Pro Bowls as an Eagle. Just two players in franchise history—Reggie White and Pete Pihos—ever topped that streak.

**2. Pete Rose,** Phils, 1979. At the time, his $800,000 salary was so exorbitant that Phils ownership convinced Channel 29 to help foot the bill. At age 38, Rose arrived with one assignment: Convert a team of talented underachievers into a champion. In 1980, he delivered. Rose was not quite the white-hot talent that he was in his earlier years in Cincinnati. But there never would have been a parade without him.

**1. Moses Malone,** Sixers, 1982. Technically, a trade—but only after the 76ers signed him and the Houston Rockets exercised their right-of-first-refusal. No matter, Moses showed up and—like Rose—delivered the title. Not quite in "Fo', fo', fo'," but close enough. In 1982–83 he led the league in rebounds, free throws, salary ($1.3 million), was on the all-NBA team and all-defensive team, won the regular-season MVP award, and was the Finals MVP. Kind of hard to top that.

## Worst

**10. Dhani Jones,** Eagles, 2004. Just beats out Nate Wayne in Andy Reid's Bad Linebacker Sweepstakes. Jones is an intellectual, quotable guy who designed a line of bowties and plays classical guitar. None of this would have been so annoying if he actually could play.

**9. John Vanbiesbrouck,** Flyers, 1998. Not that he was terrible; in fact, he's got the third-best goals-against average in franchise history. It's just that there were so many better choices at the time (most notably Mike Richter), that it seemed general manager Bob Clarke was settling for something out of the scratch-and-dent aisle. By the 2000 playoffs, Beezer had lost his starting job to flash-in-the-pan Brian Boucher.

**8. Scott Williams,** Sixers, 1994. General manager John Lucas gave Williams a seven-year, $18 million deal, figuring that the six-foot-ten stiff had something to do with all those Chicago Bulls championships. Umm, maybe that was more because of guys named Jordan and Pippen. Over four-plus years here he averaged a lusty 5.3 points per game and 6.8 muscle pulls per month.

**7. Danny Tartabull,** Phils, 1997. He'd rank higher on this list if he had signed more than a one-year deal at the (relatively) cheap price of $2 million. Tartabull fouled a ball off his foot on Opening Day, struggled for three games (0-for-7), and then went on the disabled list—forever. Cost per at-bat: $285,714. Cost per hit: Infinity.

**6. Chris Boniol,** Eagles, 1997. When he came here, he boasted the highest field-goal percentage in NFL history. We snickered at stealing one from the Cowboys. The joke was on us. A more gutless player never wore Eagles green. Boniol couldn't kick outside of wind-shielded Texas Stadium, and he certainly couldn't perform under pressure. Our everlasting impression is of him scooping up the snap that Tommy Hutton botched against the Cowboys and dancing around like Barney Fife on crack.

**5. David Bell,** Phils, 2003. An Ed Wade special—old, slow, and overpaid. Bell was going to be part of the Phils' fiery reborn attitude as they headed into a new stadium. Problem was, he couldn't hit, couldn't field, couldn't run. A four-year, $18 million contract meant that the Phils kept running him out there, game after horrible game, year after declining year.

**4. Matt Geiger,** Sixers, 1998. Signed a six-year, $48 million contract and—within weeks—declared that "basketball doesn't mean that much to me." Also sniffed his annoyance at Philadelphia weather, whining that shoveling snow "hurts my back."

The "Vanilla Gorilla" had one great moment as a 76er, when he planted bratty Reggie Miller on his keister during the 2000 playoffs. Other than that, he mostly sat on the bench, nursing arthritic knees and styling in $1,200 sunglasses. We're not sure, but we think he comes off the Sixers cap around the same time that Halley's Comet next arrives.

**3. Doug Pederson,** Eagles, 1999. Andy Reid signed his old Green Bay buddy to a three-year, $5 million deal, ignoring available free agents like Rich Gannon and Trent Green. In fact, Pederson was just keeping the seat warm for Donovan McNabb, but Reid kept lying and telling us what a talented, smart player the career third-stringer was. If anything should have tipped us off about Reid's ability to lie without cracking a smile, this was it.

**2. Chris Gratton,** Flyers, 1997. If you can remember back, he really was a dynamic young player for a horrible Tampa team who was going to supplement (or perhaps replace) Eric Lindros at center. What no one knew was how much he would shrink in the spotlight of playing for a team that people actually noticed. He got a $9 million signing bonus, a $16 million contract and an immediate case of what Roberto Duran used to call "manos de piedras"—hands of stone. Technically a trade, because the Flyers tried to appease angry Tampa owners by sending back some draft picks. That only made this a worse move.

**1. Lance Parrish,** Phils, 1987. Do you remember those horrid bumper stickers: "Lance us a pennant?" Sounded stupid at the time; now it's laughable. But expectations were high when Bill Giles bucked other Major League owners in the Era of Collusion by signing the muscle-bound, strong-armed catcher away from the Tigers. Parrish had won three Gold Gloves and five Silver Slugger awards in Detroit. In the Vet, it all turned to rust. He raged at the fans, sulked through minor injuries and counted the days until he could escape back to the American League.

**10. Not working.** The fact that you're down the Shore to begin with means you're not working. Unless you work down the Shore—and who wouldn't want those days back?

**9. It's close.** I remember the first time I drove to Nags Head NC. I said to myself, "This is nice. Hmmm. There's a beach. Some waves." But why would I drive nine stinkin' hours to get to a beach area that has nothing more to offer than our Jersey Shore?

**8. The Wildwood Tramcar.** I once did a gig at the old Spectrum where I got 18,000 maniacs to scream "WATCH THE TRAMCAR, PLEASE" in unison. Does anyone know the official name of it? (It's "The Sightseer.")

**7. Lucy the Elephant.** Like the giant clothespin in downtown Philly, Margate's famous landmark is just . . . uh . . . odd. Try to explain either to an out-of-towner.

**6. The 50's-Style Motels in Wildwood Crest.** Take a ride at dusk to view some of the most incredible neon this side of Vegas. Bring a camera. And hurry up. They're not gonna last too much longer with the condo explosion.

**5. The Ocean City Boardwalk.** I know it doesn't have the thrill rides that the Wildwood Boardwalk has to offer, but it has a gentle quaintness to it that can't be matched. Is there a better kiddie-ride spot left on this planet than Wonderland?

**4. The Bridge between Sea Isle City and Avalon.** You could pick any bridge on Ocean Drive at sunset and the view would be gorgeous, but this one's particularly high up. Plus, this bridge is symbolic—it separates the working class from the Main Line.

**3. Hiding from the Beach Tag Police.** An art form I have mastered over the years. Various methods work. Flat out running away. Pretending to be asleep. Developing that air of invisibility. Or my favorite—slipping into the water until you can see they are gone. (Which, by the way, is where I first met Angelo Cataldi.)

**2. Drinking.** I've always said, "Show me a man who doesn't like the Jersey Shore and I'll show you a man who doesn't drink." And where else would you stand in line to pay a cover for the right to buy overpriced drinks in a nightclub where it takes you 40 minutes to fight through the stuffed crowd to get to the bathroom?

**1. Chicks.** Show me a Wawa in Philly where you wait in line to buy a Shortie Hoagie behind two chicks in bikinis buying cigarettes. They're everywhere!

**10. Shells.** Played the same way you would play horseshoes, except that it's for cheap bastards like Angelo Cataldi who won't spend the money to buy a real set of horseshoes. Of course, that means it's not nearly as fun to play. It is, however, fun if you're sitting in a comfy beach chair and watching chicks play it in bikinis. In fact, there's no game on this list that isn't infinitely more watchable when the bikini factor is in play. Keep that in mind as you read on.

**9. Paddleball.** Maybe the most ridiculous game of all. Two morons with oversized paddles hitting a red ball back and forth for no apparent reason. There's no winner, no loser. It's never played anywhere other than the beach. Why? You could play it in a park, couldn't you? What possesses us to do it on sand? The bikini factor must be the only reason.

**8. Wiffleball.** To tell the truth, I was never a big wiffleball fan. "Oldhead" in my neighborhood would kick your ass if you were caught playing it instead of stickball with a pimple ball. Wiffleball was strictly for kids—under the age of two, maybe. I could never throw the damned thing. So why play it on the beach where there's always a strong wind? I sit and watch people swing at that stupid ball all day long and never hit it. Hour after hour. Plus, you always eventually lose the ball. Where do all these balls go?

**7. Fishing.** May God strike me dead. I have been sitting on the beach all my life and have never seen one knucklehead catch a fish. Guys are way out in the water. They've got those little white plastic things to put their rods in. They've got the tackle box. And every single day they walk home with no fish. Maybe they get chicks with this scam. I don't know. Why would they do it?

**6. Nerf Football.** Have you ever, EVER, seen anyone throw around a Nerf football anywhere else BUT the beach? Get a real football!

**5. Frisbee.** I'll admit to being a hypocrite, since there's no winner or loser in a Frisbee toss, and you never see anyone play it anywhere else but the beach. But the fact is, I'm good at it, and I suck at paddleball. So sue me. Look for me on the 35th Street Beach in Sea Isle running and diving into the surf making one spectacular catch after another. Frisbee rocks.

**4. Handball.** Played with a real ball with a real goal: to win. You grab a shell with a sharp edge, you make boundary lines in packed sand, and you're off and running. Played with the rules of Ping-Pong, it's actually a workout if you play for real. And if your kid gets knocked on his ass for walking through while the game's on, tough turkey! I used to play it for money back when I worked on the Wildwood boardwalk.

**3. Volleyball.** A terrific game played anywhere; it's particularly spectacular with the bikini factor tossed into the mix. Best played coed style. There should be permanent nets on more Jersey beaches. Write to your local Congressman about it. Really, there can't be more pressing issues, can there?

**2. Bodysurfing.** Face it, how many of us can actually surf? And dragging that boogie board (particularly one big enough to handle your fat butt) back and forth to the water, well, who wants to do that? Bodysurfing requires nothing more than . . . you guessed it. Catch that wave and whoever gets closest to the beach wins. That simple. And remember, I AM THE GREATEST BODYSURFER IN THE WORLD. (Forget that fraud "Redman." He got me on a morning after I had polished off a bottle of Johnnie Walker Black and a sausage pizza the night before.)

**1. Checking out chicks without getting busted by your wife.** Here's the trick: Grab binoculars. As you gaze upon one hot babe after another, mutter innocuous comments like, "Gee, look at that Grady-White. That's gotta be a 25-footer." Or, "You ought to see this idiot trying to put up his beach umbrella." Play it with another buddy and use a stopwatch. See who goes the longest without getting smacked upside the head.

Note: Tommy Conwell—along with his group, the Young Rumblers—is a Philly bar band legend and one of the finest guitar players you would ever hear, anywhere.

## Lead

**5. Jimmy Page,** Led Zeppelin. Not the most rippin', but he still sets the standard for thoughtfully constructed guitar solos.

**4. Stevie Ray Vaughan.** He was not human. He was from Mars. And he played Hendrix better than Hendrix.

**3. Eddie Van Halen.** He spawned a zillion annoyingly bad imitators, but really did do something different with the guitar. The loosest, most fluid player ever.

**2. Angus Young,** AC-DC. He had the best shake (vibrato) in rock history. He hit his stride, tone-wise, on the *Back in Black* album. The solo on "You Shook Me All Night Long" is the best in rock history, in my opinion.

**1. Chuck Berry**. Everybody plays Chuck Berry. But nobody plays it better than Chuck Berry.

## Badasses

**5. Johnny Thunders** of the New York Dolls and the Heartbreakers. If you don't know, get the Heartbreakers album, L.A.M.F. You'll see.

**4. Pete Townshend.** A badass in every way. He invented the windmill, the rock guitar jump, stabbing your amp with your guitar, smashing your guitar onstage, and trashing hotel rooms (with Keith Moon).

**3. Keith Richards.** It's hard to say exactly what he does with a guitar, but it comes out the Rolling Stones.

**2. Johnny Ramone.** He didn't invent punk rock, but he invented punk rock guitar. All attitude and volume.

**1. George Thorogood.** If you've seen him play, I don't need to say a word. If you haven't seen him, go see him.

## Philly Guitarists

**5. Tommy Conwell.** Hey, it's my list. Plus, I couldn't let it be all paisans.

**4. Jimmy Bruno.** A genius who still holds court at Chris's Jazz Cafe at 15th and Sansom from time to time. He once told the Inquirer that I was the second-best jazz guitarist in Philly. I honestly think he meant it to insult all the other jazz guitar players more than anything else.

**3. Rick Di Fonzo** of the A's. A hot guitar player who outclassed everybody. He played a Les Paul and used to play with his left hand over the neck just for kicks.

**2. Pat Martino.** My all-time hero. I'm still just trying to play like Pat. He's from South Philly. Pat's where it's at.

**1. Eddy Lang** (real name Salvatore Massaro). A jazz guitar pioneer from South Philly.

# Big Daddy's Favorite Cover Bands

It's easy to salute the bands and artists who—through talent, perseverance and luck—manage to get a song or CD out on the national charts. But what about the great cover bands slugging it out in the trenches? Night after night, set after set, these bands truly reach the Philly-area masses.

Maybe they're never going to get on Letterman or MTV, but more people have danced and partied to these bands than to some one-hit wonders. Years from now, you'll be with your boys recalling some wonderful drunken night and the story could very well begin with "remember the night we were at the Springfield and. . . ."

The horrible thing about putting together a list like this is that there are worthy bands left off. I'm taking my life in my hands just putting them in order. So here's what I did. As best as I could remember—and believe me, there's a lot of Johnnie Walker Black running through what's left of my brain—I've included the bands I have seen the most. Although there are other factors such as proximity, club environment, gorgeous-woman ratio, and cover charge, there must have been something about these bands that kept me coming back.

Here are some talented musicians who didn't make it, not because they are not as good as the bands listed below, but for the reasons listed above: The Chatterband, Steamroller Picnic, Witness, Strange As Angels, The Rockets, LeCompt, the Rage Band, Split Decision, Pegasus, The Heartbeats, Squeeze, Dewey Street (OK, so I drummed with the band, sue me), and many more.

One last thing: There should be a special mention for Blackthorn—without a doubt, the premiere Irish music band not only in our area, but in the country. Great guys, great musicians with a huge following, and I only kept them off the list because I'm not enough of an Irish music fan to grab a whole evening of it.

**10. Secret Service.** Truth be told, they're really not a band, which is why I ranked them tenth. They're just a duo with a drum machine. But Dom and Craig always put a smile on my face when I see them, and I've seen them more than any band on this list. Of course it doesn't hurt that they play at the OD in Sea Isle and I've been able to walk to see them for 20 years. They're funny as hell, they always seem to play the right song at the right time, they involve the crowd, they drink while on stage (always a plus), and how they have any voices left whatsoever after 2,478,972 sets is beyond me.

**9. Jellyroll.** My sister Liz once sang with the band. So did my main man, the legendary Spins Nitely. Throw in the fact that Jelly's sax man played on my very own "Let's Call In Sick" and how the heck could I leave them off? Been playing in the area for over 25 years. Jellyroll doesn't do the club scene anymore (they do mostly weddings and such), but they gigged for years and I rarely missed a show. One of the first bands in the area with a horn section. I'm a sucker for horns.

**8. Mr. Greengenes.** Like others on this list, the guys in Mr. Greengenes think they still have a shot at being an "original material" band and cracking the big time. And maybe they will; their own stuff is really fine. In the meantime, they're out there slugging it out and they never disappoint. Bryan's a dynamic front man who really works the crowd and they're always updating their material.

**7. The Fabulous Greaseband.** If you never saw this legendary oldies band in the legendary Phil's Bongo Room in Avalon, well, I feel sorry for you. It was always a thousand degrees and the entire building would SHAKE. Costuming, skits, great chops—always a great time.

**6. The Flaming Caucasians.** The house band for Wing Bowl and the old live Morning Zoo shows. I first saw the Caucasians on a break between sets at the Comedy Factory Outlet and I've loved them ever since. They used to back me up (which I'm sure they would like to forget) for occasional live shows. Great, offbeat taste in song selection and a truly fantastic name for a band, eh?

**5. The Exceptions.** My favorite night at the Jersey shore at the moment is Thursday night with The Exceptions at the Springfield. Not one, not two, but three exceptional lead singers with a fantastic brass section. They're a real party. They were the band at Angelo Cataldi's daughter's wedding and uh, well, they're still waiting for that check to clear.

**4. Backstreets.** I usually don't like tribute bands, but the beautiful thing about being in a Springsteen tribute band is that there are no stupid costumes. Just a bunch of great musicians playing song after song by the greatest live rock act of all time. Drink enough, dance enough, sweat enough—it's the next best thing. I never miss them when I'm down the shore. Not from the area, but they've sure played it enough to qualify. They're called the "B Street Band" now.

**3. Bonehead.** Came along at just the right time for me. I was getting tired of the same old songs from mostly the same old era. Bonehead covered Nirvana, Pearl Jam, and the like. I saw them at the OD in Sea Isle 30 times or more and they were always ferocious and loud. One of the best area guitarists I ever heard in Kevin Hug. Plus they recorded an in-your-face BDG ditty that I am still playing on the air to this day.

**2. Johnny O and the Classic Dogs of Love.** What separated this band from many others was Johnny himself. Yes, the band was tight and had great chops that could handle any genre of music, but you just never knew what you were going to get from Johnny. He was the real deal, a real nut. Some nights it was true genius; other nights a train wreck. It was the unpredictability of it all that kept you coming back and back and back. Not even sure what he or the band are doing these days. Let's keep our fingers crossed.

**1. Love Seed Mama Jump.** Again, like Bonehead and others on this list, Love Seed's original songs are real gems and, on a given night, if they're in the mood, they'll sprinkle a set with a few. But as a cover band they are a true original. From a reggae version of Peter Gabriel's "In Your Eyes" to an almost punk version of "Take Me Home Country Roads," you just never have any idea what they're going to do. They are extremely funky, and I've never seen their lead singer Rick Arzt throw even one song away after years of gigging hard night after night after night. Not quite sure how it ever happened, but they were once the house band for the Washington Redskins.

## Five Philadelphia Athletes Who Cut Records
## :: Ukee Washington

Note: Ukee Washington has been a fixture on Philadelphia television since 1986. These days he anchors CBS 3's early morning news show, as well as Eyewitness News at noon. As a child, the West Philadelphia native was an original member of the elite Philadelphia Boys Choir. Trust us, he's got pipes.

**5. Dick Allen. "Echoes of November."** I guess since Dick didn't earn the nickname "Mr. October" (that belonged to Cheltenham's Reggie Jackson), he settled for "Echoes of November," sung with a backup doo-wop group called The Ebonistics. It's a lot closer to a double than a grand slam. To be honest, listening to the one-and-a-half minute song today— well, call it a swing and a miss! But you can tell that Dick enjoyed recording it. And rumor has it that he sang the tune live at a Sixers game and was not booed. For that alone, one of my childhood sports heroes earns an inside-the-park homer.

**4. Wilt Chamberlain. "Down by the River."** This was the Big Man's take on a popular, traditional Negro spiritual. Dippy always had a knack for making people say their prayers when they met on the court.

**3. Dave Schultz. "Penalty Box."** He recorded this at the height of the Broad Street Bullies' glory days. It seems the Flyers' (Stanley) Cup runneth over so much that the Hammer's tune beat out Elton John's "Philadelphia Freedom" in the charts. Well, the Delaware Valley charts, at least.

**2. Tim Brown. "I've Got a Secret."** The Eagles running back from the 1960s sure did have a secret. Not only did he have great moves on the field, but he was just as talented in the entertainment industry. Brown performed this song in the mid-sixties on the game show, "I've Got a Secret." They should have made it the theme song. He also had a brief film career.

**1. Joe Frazier. "My Way."** As the record states, the heavyweight champ really did take the blows and he really did it his way. Smokin' Joe changed the words to fit his profession (and we don't think Frank Sinatra peeped a complaint). His group, Joe Frazier and the Knockouts, recorded a number of songs—including a snappy jingle for Miller Lite beer— and, to be honest, it didn't really matter how they sounded. Certainly, for the majority of his career, Joe had the number of everyone he faced in the ring.

# The Best—and Worst—Renditions of the Pre-Game Anthems :: Lauren Hart

Note: Lauren Hart has beautifully sung the "National Anthem" (and sometimes "God Bless America" and "O Canada,") before Flyers games since 1997. The daughter of Hall of Fame Flyers broadcaster Gene Hart, her version of the Anthem was featured in the Disney movie "Miracle." The singer/songwriter has released three CDs of her own work. You can learn more about her at her website: www.laurenhart.com.

## The Best

**5. Marvin Gaye's "National Anthem"** at the 1983 NBA All-Star Game. A great day. Doctor J was the game's MVP, and Marvin actually made the anthem sound sexy.

**4. Jimi Hendrix's "National Anthem"** at Woodstock. Wailing, piercing music. No one who heard it will ever forget.

**3. Ray Charles' "America the Beautiful"**—whenever he sang it. It's the sweetest song of all, and his rendition was perfection. The land, the people, the soul—no one did it better than Ray.

**2. Kate Smith's "God Bless America"** at Flyers games, 1973–74. In one of the most unusual marriages ever, an aging radio and film star became a good-luck charm for one of the toughest teams ever—the Broad Street Bullies. Prior to 9/11, no anthem ever meant more to a team, a building, and a city.

**1. Whitney Houston's "National Anthem"** in Super Bowl XXV, 1991. Hands down, my favorite anthem performance ever. Powerful vocals, great arrangement, a beautiful performance. At the time, Whitney was still one of the greatest talents on the planet. That was then…

## The Worst

**4. Caroline Marcil's "National Anthem"** at the 2005 World Hockey Finals, USA vs. Canada, in Quebec. This is my worst nightmare. She has a great voice, but. . . . First, she forgot the words and left the ice. She came back for another try, forgot the words again, and left a second time. Returning a third time, she slipped and fell to the ice on her back. To her credit, she sang it beautifully the next day on national TV. Ouch, I feel your pain.

**3. John Michael Montgomery's "National Anthem"** at Nascar's Golden Corral 500 in 2005. Slurred, stumbling, off-key and he used a cheat sheet. Did he actually sing "Penzoil's red glare" during the song?

**2. Roseanne Barr's "National Anthem"** at a San Diego Padres game in 1990. Just gross.

**1. Carl Lewis' "National Anthem"** at a New York Nets game in 1993. Midway through the song, he actually promised it would get better. It never did. You can run, Carl, but you cannot hide—because this has to be the all-time worst-ever rendition.

# Ten Guys Who Knew How to Celebrate

This list does not include one-time performances—like Vai Sikahema KO-ing the goal stanchion at the Meadowlands, or Chuck Bednarik punching the air over a fallen Frank Gifford. Instead, it honors the guys who had the kind of signature moves that every 12-year-old loved to imitate.

**10. Koy Detmer.** Not much of a player, but he knew how to party. His "Whip It" dance—or, as he called it, "Spanking the Monkey"—was an emphatic flogging motion that bordered on obscene. It riled Brett Favre when Detmer unveiled it against the Packers in 1998. And it so angered Andy Reid that he almost pulled Detmer from what turned out to be his career game, a Monday night stunner against San Francisco in 2002.

**9. Bernie Parent.** The opposite of Detmer in temperament. After every spectacular save, Bernie would simply stand up and slowly sweep his goalie stick back and forth across the crease in an arc from post to post. The greater the save, the slower he swept. Very understated. Very cool.

**8. Tug McGraw.** What made Tugger so great was that he wasn't afraid to let fans see him react like a real person, with genuine emotion. He would charge off the mound, slapping his glove on his thigh at the end of an inning. And he would pat his chest with his glove after a potential home run curved just foul. "Who would do that in the heat of the battle?" asked teammate Larry Bowa. "But it showed he had no fear. He was loose. That's how he played the game."

**7. Andre Dupont.** He scored just 42 goals during his eight-year Flyers career, but each one was a production. The "Moose Shuffle" more resembled a dancing bear, with Dupont's knees pumping up near his massive chest. Coach Fred Shero hated it, but the 17,077 packing the Spectrum couldn't get enough.

**6. Danny Jackson.** In hindsight, a lot of these acts seem silly, but at the time, we were entertained. Jackson, during the Phils' magical summer of '93, would end each Phils' win by assuming a muscleman pose and tearing off his tee-shirt, a la Hulk Hogan. A rare self-deprecating act by a somewhat pudgy athlete.

**5. Freddie Mitchell.** The self-proclaimed "People's Champ" was far better at celebrating his rare successes than he was at creating them. Like so many athletes, Freddie was a professional wrestling fan—thus his routine of strapping on an imaginary title belt.

**4. Brian Propp.** He was the most unlikely of celebrators, given his low-key personality. But we loved how he punctuated goals with the "guffaw"—a snaking, left-to-right hand movement starting at the hip and ending with him pointing to the sky. In the late 1980s, every Peewee player in the Delaware Valley tried to perfect that little hand gesture.

**3. Willie Montanez.** The first athlete we ever heard called "Hot Dog"—he also brought the mustard, relish and chopped onions. His flip of the bat after home runs (which later became a flip after foul balls and eventually became a whole baton twirling act on his way to the plate) was the inspiration for an entire generation of show offs.

**2. Allen Iverson.** Perfected a great signature move—cupping his hand to his ear to get the fans to turn up the volume. Also could improvise with the best. Remember his mocking stomp over Tyronn Lue in the 2001 NBA Finals? For that moment, at least, he showed the Lakers who was the boss.

**1. Terrell Owens.** Just a 21-game career in Philadelphia but, oh, what a body of work. Which was your favorite touchdown celebration? The sit-ups in the end zone against Chicago? The towel-over-the-arm waiter bit against San Diego? Tearing down the signs in Cleveland? Our favorite was his gyrating imitation of Ray Lewis' squirrel dance against Baltimore. Whatever you may think of T.O. now, we're betting you enjoyed every taunting, mocking moment while he was here.

## And three we always hated:

**3. Dhani Jones.** The "guitar man" routine looked foolish when he would make a tackle nine yards downfield.

**2. Donovan McNabb.** There's nothing cool about styling yourself after Michael Jackson.

**1. James Thrash.** Pointing to the sky after every six-yard reception seemed excessive. And how come he never cited God when he dropped all those passes?

# Greatest Non-Flyers/Non-Sixers Sporting Events at the Spectrum :: Ike Richman

Note: Ike Richman has been the publicist for the Spectrum for close to 20 years—and began attending events there from the moment the building opened in 1967. He has been to thousands of games, concerts, and other events in what is now the city's oldest professional sports building. These are his favorite games that didn't involve the city's two winter sports franchises.

## 8. NHL All-Star Game—Prince of Wales Conference defeats Clarence Campbell Conference 7-5, January 20, 1976.

The two-time defending Stanley Cup Champion Flyers hosted the 1976 All-Star Game. In a thriller, Pete Mahovlich of the Montreal Canadiens was named the game's Most Valuable Player.

## 7. NBA All-Star Game—East defeats West 123-109, February 3, 1976.

In another Bicentennial year all-star highlight, Bob McAdoo and Kareem Abdul Jabbar led their teams with 22 points. But it was Dave Bing of the Washington Bullets who was named the game's Most Valuable Player after scoring 16 points and dishing off four assists.

How impressive was it to host both the NBA and NHL All-Star games at the Spectrum in the same year? Apparently not impressive enough; Major League Baseball's All-Star Game was also played in Philadelphia that summer.

## 6. Heavyweight Championship, Joe Frazier vs. Muhammed Ali—Closed Circuit Television, October 1, 1975.

Long before the days of pay-per-view, boxing fans crammed arenas to watch title fights on big, closed-circuit screens. This match—the third between them—marked the first time two fighters earned $1 million for a bout. Near the end of the second round, Ali rocked Frazier with a good punch. Before he could follow up, referee Tony Perez, believing he heard the bell ring, stepped between the fighters to signal the round's completion—even though there was time remaining. Ali won the "Thrilla in Manilla" when Frazier couldn't come out for the 15th round.

## 5. Olga Korbut Performs at the Spectrum, November 10, 1974.

After capturing the hearts of the world with her dazzling acrobatic display, and capturing three gold medals and a silver medal at the l972 Summer Olympic Games in Munich, Korbut and a team of Soviet Olympic Gymnasts toured the U.S. for the first time in '74. Only seven cities were selected, including Philadelphia.

## 4. Indiana vs. North Carolina—NCAA Basketball Championship, March 30, 1981.

Indiana guard Isiah Thomas was named Final Four MVP as Indiana defeated North Carolina, 63-50.

### 3. WWF Steel Cage Match, February 18, 1978.

A standing-room-only crowd of 19,500, and a closed-circuit audience watching on PRISM, saw former WWF Champion Bruno Sammartino enter the 15-foot-high steel cage to reclaim his title from Champion Superstar Billy Graham. After a grueling eight minutes, Sammartino signaled for the opening of the cage, but foolishly decided to drop one more kick on Graham. Sammartino accidentally kicked Graham right out of the cage, which made Graham the winner in front of a stunned crowd in South Philadelphia.

### 2. Indiana vs. Michigan—NCAA Basketball Championship, March 29, 1976.

Bringing a perfect 31-0 record to Philadelphia and a chance to be crowned National Champions, the Indiana Hoosiers and Coach Bobby Knight faced Big Ten rival Michigan— the first time in Tournament history that two teams from the same conference met in the title game.

Indiana's starting five featured two All-Americans—forward Scott May and center Kent Benson—along with Quinn Buckner, Tom Abernethy, and Bobby Wilkerson.

Things started out badly for Indiana when defensive ace Wilkerson sustained a concussion two minutes in. The beefy Wolverines took advantage of his absence and grabbed a 35-29 halftime lead.

But Indiana rallied, shooting 60 percent in the second half. With May scoring a game-high 26 and Benson 25, the Hoosiers rolled to an 86-68 victory. At 35, Knight had won his first national championship.

The 1975–76 Indiana team is the last NCAA champion to finish the season undefeated.

### 1. Duke vs. Kentucky—NCAA Men's East Regional Finals, March 28, 1992.

The Shot Heard 'Round the (College Basketball) World. With two seconds remaining in a tight game—and a chance to get to the Final Four—Kentucky's Sean Woods hit a bank shot to give the Wildcats a one-point lead. After a timeout, Duke's Grant Hill flung the inbounds pass 80 feet down the court to a leaping Christian Laettner, who was near the foul line with his back to the basket. The 6-foot-11 senior dribbled, faked right, turned to his left and calmly hit a 17-footer to give Duke a 104-103 victory and its fifth consecutive trip to the Big Dance.

## The 15 Most Unbelievable One-Game Performances by Philadelphia Athletes Not Named Wilt

**15. Tim Brown returns two kickoffs for touchdowns, November 6, 1966.** Aaron Martin of the Birds also returned a punt all the way in the same game. What made it extra sweet was that they occurred in an upset over the Cowboys. A year later, Dallas got its revenge by breaking Brown's jaw with a cheap shot.

**14. Joe Fulks scores 63 points for the Philadelphia Warriors, February 10, 1949.** "Jumping Joe," the first of the NBA's jump shooters, set a single-game scoring record against the Indianapolis Jets that stood for a decade. To this day, no Sixer or Warrior not named Wilt has scored more in one night.

**13. Tom Bladon registers eight points, December 11, 1977.** A player often booed by hometown fans for his inconsistent play, Bladon scored four goals and added four assists against the Cleveland Barons in an 11-1 throttling. Paul Coffey is the only other NHL defenseman to register as many points in one game.

**12. Rick Wise does it all, June 23, 1971.** Wise complained of the flu heading into the game at Cincinnati. It was the Reds who soon felt sick, as Wise tossed one of nine no-hitters in Phillies history and slammed two home runs. He remains the only pitcher in history to accomplish that feat.

**11. Donovan McNabb enjoys a landmark day, December 5, 2004.** Often ripped as inaccurate, McNabb broke Joe Montana's NFL record with 24 straight completions (10 from the previous game, 14 on this day), and set an Eagles record with 464 passing yards. He threw five touchdown passes in the first half as the Birds ran up a 35-3 lead against the Packers.

**10. Bill Mlkvy scores 73 against Wilkes College, March 3, 1951.** "The Owl Without a Vowel" put up the fourth-most points by a Division I Player during a 99-69 Temple victory. (Note: Villanova's Paul Arizin scored 85 in one game two years earlier. We don't list Arizin's feat here because it came in a 117-25 win over the Naval Air Material Center, a men's league squad of military workers who had no business challenging a Division I program.)

**9. Adrian Burk passes for seven touchdowns, October 17, 1954.** Take away this game and Burk's six-year totals as an Eagle: 48 touchdowns, 77 interceptions. But on this day he couldn't miss, in part because the Redskins kept expecting the Eagles to run the ball. Four of the TDs were nine yards or fewer; the longest was just 26 yards.

**8. Tim Kerr pops in four goals in one playoff period, April 13, 1985.** He single-handedly knocked the Rangers out of the playoffs. Kerr's hat-trick-plus-one tied an NHL record, as did his three power play goals in one period. Three of the goals came in three minutes and 27 seconds. As was Kerr's style, the four scores totaled about 13 feet.

**7. Allen Iverson drops 55 on New Orleans, April 20, 2003.** It came in Game One of the post-season, with AI scoring 21 in the fourth quarter to hold off a Hornets' rally. Only five other players have scored 55 or more in a playoff game—Chamberlain, Michael Jordan, Rick Barry, Charles Barkley, and Elgin Baylor. Pretty good company.

**6. Terrell Owens dominates Super Bowl XXXIX, February 6, 2005.** No matter how you may feel about him today, you should always cherish T.O.'s nine catches for 122 yards, especially coming off his return from an ankle injury. Had the Eagles won, he would have been the game's MVP. And, if so, hey, who knows how everything else would have turned out.

**5. Jim Bunning twirls a perfect game on Father's Day, 1964.** The father of six needed just 90 pitches and 2:19 to beat the Mets. It was the first National League perfect game since 1880. We knew it was a big deal when he appeared on Ed Sullivan that night.

**4. Reggie Leach connects five times in one playoff game, May 6, 1976.** The back story is that Leach was hung over and slept through morning practice before the Semifinals game against the Bruins. Coach Fred Shero had to be persuaded by "The Rifle's" team-mates to let him play. Leach scored on three backhanders and two forehanders to tie an NHL record.

**3. Mike Schmidt smacks four homers, April 17, 1976.** With the wind blowing out at Wrigley, the Phils rallied from a 13-2 deficit to beat the Cubs, 18-16, in 10 innings. Schmidt went 5-for-6 with eight RBIs, and became the first National Leaguer in modern history to hit four homers in a row. Two came off the Cubs' Rick Reuschel and the last off Reuschel's brother, Paul.

**2. Wilbert Montgomery buries the Cowboys, January 11, 1981.** There was concern before the NFC Championship Game that injuries might keep Montgomery from playing, at least at full tilt. He allayed that fear on the Eagles' second play from scrimmage, sprinting 42 yards for the first touchdown. On the day, Montgomery rushed for 194 yards.

**1. Steve Van Buren carries the Eagles to a title, December 18, 1949.** This one is a shade ahead of Montgomery's effort because, 1) Van Buren out-gained Wilbert by two yards, and 2) It was the league's title game. They played it in a torrential rainstorm in Los Angeles, and Van Buren slogged through the mud to destroy the Rams. His 196 rushing yards stood as a postseason record until the Redskins Timmy Smith rushed for 204 in the 1987 Super Bowl. For his record-setting effort, Van Buren received a $1,094 game check and a commemorative Zippo lighter.

**10. Deion Branch takes over Super Bowl XXXIX, February 6, 2005.** The most-recent pain, so we'll list it first. The Patriots' 5-foot-9 receiver had just 35 catches in the regular season. With the Eagles' strong secondary, who thought going into Jacksonville that he would be a problem?

Well, he was. Eleven catches and 133 yards later, Branch was the Super Bowl MVP. He even managed to outshine Terrell Owens.

**9. David Cone spoils Fan Appreciation Day, October 6, 1991.** Against a dreadful Phils team on the final day of the season, Cone pitched a three-hit shutout and struck out a National League-record 19 hitters (a mark since broken by Kerry Wood). Shortstop Kim Batiste (leading off!) whiffed all four times he faced Cone. A 24-year-old Phils catcher named Doug Lindsey, in his Major League debut, fanned in his first three at-bats. And the Mets got seven runs, which the fans did not appreciate.

**8. Rod Martin becomes Ron Jaworski's favorite receiver, January 25, 1981.** The Eagles won the coin flip in Super Bowl XV. They got the ball and Jaworski's first pass was picked off by outside linebacker Martin who returned it 17 yards, to the Philadelphia 30. A few minutes later, the Oakland Raiders scored to take the lead. Basically, repeat that sentence three times and you've got a sense of the game.

Martin's three interceptions remains a Super Bowl record. On the day, he was the Eagles' third-leading receiver.

**7. Wilt gives the Sixers a glimpse of the future, November 26, 1964.** Here's the amazing thing: Not only does Mr. Chamberlain own every scoring record for the franchise. He also owns nearly every scoring record against the franchise.

In 1964, after the Warriors had moved west—and before his return to his hometown—Chamberlain went off for 63 at the Convention Center. More than four decades later, it remains the highest-scoring game any opponent ever had against the Sixers.

If you include the franchise's tenure in Syracuse, the top-five scoring performances against the Sixers (nee Nationals) were all accomplished by Chamberlain.

**6. Emmitt Smith ruins Halloween, October 31, 1993.** On a cold, rainy day at the Vet, Smith sliced through the remnants of the Eagles' vaunted defense for 237 yards on 30 carries. The despised Cowboy rambled 62 yards in the fourth quarter for the clinching touchdown, outracing the entire secondary.

The game kept the two teams moving in opposite directions, giving Dallas its fifth straight win and Rich Kotite's Birds their third straight loss.

**Glen Alert:** I'll never forget the kid who showed up at my house that night, trick-or-treating in a Dallas Cowboys outfit. I stiffed him.

**5. Sandy Koufax inspires Jim Bunning, June 4, 1964.** Twenty-one pitchers—from Noodles Hahn to Pascual Perez—have tossed no-hitters at the Phillies since 1900. The most impressive performance, we think, was Sandy Koufax's 91-pitch, one-hour-55-minute gem at a packed Connie Mack Stadium. Why? Well, 12 strikeouts and just one walk, for starters. And the guy he walked, Richie Allen, was immediately erased on a double-play. Plus, the Phils were a terrific hitting team that season—at least until September.

Seventeen days later Jim Bunning one-upped the great Koufax, twirling his Father's Day perfect game at Shea Stadium.

## 4. Magic jumps center, May 16, 1980.
Certainly, you remember the story: The Sixers trailed three-games-to-two in the NBA Finals, but caught an apparent break when Lakers center Kareem Abdul-Jabbar went down with a sprained ankle. Twenty-year-old point guard Magic Johnson was chosen to replace Jabbar—a move that drew guffaws from Philadelphia fans and media, if not Sixers players.

Guess who got the last laugh. Magic sky-hooked the Lakers to victory with 42 points, 15 rebounds, 7 assists, and 3 steals. He became the first rookie to win the Finals MVP Award. Elsewhere, this is remembered as one of the great moments in NBA history. In Philadelphia, we just shake our heads in disgust.

## 3. Red Berenson's double hat trick, November 7, 1968.
Just more than 9,000 fans at the Spectrum watched "The Red Baron" tie an NHL record with six goals in the St. Louis Blues' 8-0 pasting of the Flyers. Berenson scored the game's first five goals, including four against Flyers goalie Doug Favell during a nine-minute span in the second period.

After the sixth goal, which came with 5:56 left in the game, Flyers fans gave Berenson a respectful ovation. Defenseman Ed Van Impe—who had been on the ice for all six goals—gave him a vicious slash across the back of the legs.

## 2. Joe Montana figures out the Eagles, September 24, 1989.
The Birds led 21-10 in the fourth quarter and were so dominant—sacking Montana eight times—that many expected Niners coach George Seifert to pull his starting quarterback.

And then Joe turned into Super Joe. In the fourth quarter, he was 11-for-12 for 227 yards and four touchdowns. Montana needed only 5 minutes 32 seconds to ring up those four touchdowns, using 18 plays to cover a total of 252 yards.

For the day, Montana was 25-for-34 for 428 yards and five touchdowns. Buddy Ryan's Eagles were humbled, to say the least. "You just need to stay cool," offered Joe Cool.

## 1. Mario flattens the Flyers, April 25, 1989.
Penguins star Mario Lemieux was questionable for Game Five of the Patrick Division Finals, after catching a shoulder to his head the previous game. His cobwebs cleared quickly enough for him to set or tie four NHL records.

He scored four goals in the first period alone, and didn't stop. By the end of the game—won 10-7 by Pittsburgh—Lemieux had five goals and three assists. "A snowball with number 66 on it," said Flyers Coach Paul Holmgren.

**Here's an interesting side note:** Lemieux's is the only performance on this list played in the enemy's building. The two Super Bowls, of course, were played on neutral territory, and the other seven feats were all accomplished in Philadelphia.

Note: Ray Didinger's coverage of the Eagles over the years has earned him a spot in the Pro Football Hall of Fame and the Philadelphia Sports Hall of Fame. Didinger wrote about football and other sports for the *Philadelphia Bulletin* and *Daily News* for 27 years. He is currently a senior producer for NFL Films and co-host, with Glen Macnow, of WIP's Saturday morning show. He is also the author of eight books on football, including the 2005 best-seller, *The Eagles Encyclopedia.*

"In writing *The Eagles Encyclopedia,* I went through thousands of pages of research dating back to the first season, 1933. In pouring over all that material, I developed a new appreciation for certain players. I wouldn't call them forgotten players because in most cases their names were familiar. But these were the 10 players who, upon further review, made me think: 'I knew he was good, but I did not realize he was this good.'"

**10. Jermane Mayberry,** guard, 1996–2004. He was done a disservice by the Eagles coaches who played him out of position early in his career. Once they moved him from tackle to guard, Mayberry developed into a Pro Bowler. His departure after 2004 was one of the main reasons the middle of the Eagles offensive line caved in around Donovan McNabb.

**9. John Bunting**, linebacker, 1972–82. He was underrated his entire career, beginning with his selection as a 10th round draft pick, but he was one of the most consistent performers on a defense that allowed the fewest points in the NFL from 1979 through '81. His jarring hit on Ron Springs on the first series set the tone for the Eagles' 20-7 win over Dallas in the 1980 NFC Championship game.

**8. Terry Hoage,** safety, 1986–90. He was not as physical as Wes Hopkins nor as intimidating as Andre Waters, so he was not as celebrated as he should have been playing in Buddy Ryan's defense. But Hoage had a keen instinct for finding the football and, in 1988, he led the team with eight interceptions. Ryan called him "a Gary Fencik with speed," comparing him to the Chicago Bears' All-Pro safety.

**7. Marion Campbell,** defensive end, 1956–61. Most Philadelphia fans only remember Campbell as the head coach who won just 17 games in three seasons after succeeding Dick Vermeil. The Swamp Fox is not given enough credit for what he accomplished as a player. He was the best defensive lineman on the '60 championship team and he played most of the season on a bad ankle.

**6. Ed Blaine,** offensive guard, 1963–66. Acquired from Green Bay, Blaine developed into one of the best linemen in the game. He played between two future Hall of Famers—center Jim Ringo and tackle Bob Brown—and graded out higher than both of them in 1966 when the Eagles went 9-5. Blaine retired after that season at the age of 26 to pursue a doctorate in zoology.

**5. Chuck Weber,** linebacker, 1959–61. To this day, most fans believe Chuck Bednarik was the middle linebacker on the 1960 championship team. Not so. Weber, the other Chuck, played the middle, Bednarik played outside. Weber, a West Chester State grad, also called the defensive signals and was second on the team with six interceptions. Weber also recovered the fumble after Bednarik's legendary hit on the Giants' Frank Gifford.

**4. Harold Jackson,** wide receiver, 1969–72. I was blown away when I looked back at Jackson's numbers. In four seasons with the Eagles, he led the NFL in receiving yardage twice—and that was with Norm Snead, Rick Arrington, Pete Liske, and John Reaves throwing the ball. He played 56 games with the Eagles and went over the 100-yard receiving mark 13 times. That averages out to 23.2 per cent of his starts, the highest ratio for any Eagles receiver prior to Terrell Owens.

**3. Norm "Wildman" Willey,** defensive end, 1950–57. Glen Macnow rolls his eyes when I talk about Willey having 17 sacks in one game against the New York Giants. It sounds far-fetched, but it did happen. Quoting a newspaper account from 1952: "Willey awed inhabitants of the Polo Grounds by dumping (quarterback) Charlie Conerly 17 times while he was attempting to pass." Sacks did not become an official statistic until 1982, so there is no mention of Willey in the record book and most fans never heard of him. But he was one of the best defensive players of his era.

**2. Tommy Thompson,** quarterback, 1941–42, 1945–50. Hall of Fame halfback Steve Van Buren was the star of the championship teams of 1948–49, but Thompson did a superb job running the T-formation. In 1948, a 12-game regular season, Thompson led the NFL with 25 touchdown passes. Sammy Baugh of Washington was second with 22. No other quarterback in the league had more than 14.

**1. Bobby Walston,** tight end and kicker, 1951–62. Walston still is the Eagles all-time leading scorer (881) more than 40 years after his retirement. He was overshadowed on the 1960 championship team by wide receivers Tommy McDonald and Pete Retzlaff, yet he averaged 18.8 yards per catch, outstanding for a tight end. Walston also provided one of the biggest plays of that season, kicking a 38-yard field goal in the final seconds to lift the Eagles to a 31-29 win over Cleveland. General manager Vince McNally called Walston "the best draft pick I ever made" and he selected more than 400 players in his 15 years with the Eagles.

Note: As a splendid wide receiver for the Eagles from 1982–90, Mike Quick got to compete against some of the NFL's best cover men each day in practice. And, since 1997, he has served as the Eagles radio color commentator.

**10. Bobby Taylor.** He was better than a lot of people give him credit for. Maybe not a great hitter, but he could tackle people around the knees and he had very good cover skills. He was talented at getting his hands on guys at the line of scrimmage and throwing them off their routes. Plus, with his long, rangy legs, not many teams could get the deep ball by Bobby.

**9. Michael Lewis.** He's still evolving, but he's already a great player. (Eagles defensive coordinator) Jim Johnson uses him the right way. He doesn't blitz a lot—although he has the ability to run blitz—he's more of a centerfield type with good cover skills. Still has the potential to get better.

**8. Herman Edwards.** He was the smartest player I've ever seen in the secondary. He would study tendencies and the plays that other teams would run from different formations. Right before the other offense snapped the ball, Herm would scream out what they were going to run. That's how he made it so long in the NFL. He wasn't the greatest athlete, but he was a smart and studious guy.

**6B. Andre Waters.** He's really tied with the next guy—I couldn't decide the order, so they're both No. 6. Andre was perfect for Buddy Ryan's 46 Defense. The Eagles needed a guy at safety who could cover tight ends or take on a pulling guard. Andre wasn't big, but he had a huge heart. He was fearless and, boy, could he hit.

**6A. Randy Logan.** A monster from Michigan who could hit like a linebacker. He also wasn't very big at all, but he knocked people out. He had no regard at all for his own body. What a huge impact player he was.

**5. Troy Vincent.** Great ability and great hands. What I always recall with Troy, was that even if a guy beat him with the first move, Troy had the speed to catch up and still make the play. No one could bump at the line of scrimmage like him and throw a receiver off his pattern.

**4. Wes Hopkins.** One of the most feared guys in football. He roamed the secondary, and opponents feared coming into his area. I remember talking to receivers on other teams, like Roy Green of the Cardinals, and they'd say, "How's Wes? Is he healthy? Is he playing?" They were scared. I was glad he was on my team because I never wanted to get hit by him.

**3. Roynell Young.** I had to go against him every day in practice. As a young guy it taught me a lot to ago against an All-Pro like that. Roynell had great cover skills, he was great with his hands, and he was mean as a snake.

**2. Eric Allen.** He was the best cover guy I ever saw on the Eagles. His great ability to stay with guys allowed the defensive coordinator freedom to do a lot of things, because you always knew that Eric could go one-on-one with the other team's best receiver and not get burned. It helped the team in so many ways.

**1. Brian Dawkins.** Both he and Eric Allen could be Hall of Famers some day. Brian tops my list because of his overall impact on the defense and the variety of ways you can use him. On one play he's blitzing, and on the next he can cover as well as any cornerback. Plus, he's a safety who hits like a linebacker.

With this town's deplorable history, we're leaving out hundreds of heartbreakers; including Villanova-North Carolina in 2005 on that despicable traveling call, and two particularly horrid Eagles losses to Dallas (do the names Chris Boniol and Roy Williams evoke any memories?). Even a horse named Smarty broke our hearts. So we'll spare you hours of gory details and cut to the chase.

**10. Devils 2, Flyers 1; May 26, 2000.** After losing two straight in the Eastern Conference Finals, the Flyers returned home for Game 7. No way they'd blow a 3-1 series lead to the stinkin' Devils. Not behind goaltender Brian Boucher. Not with Eric Lindros back on the ice. Well, Scott Stevens took care of No. 88 in the first period with a vicious—but clean—shoulder to the head. Patrick Elias scored two goals, and the Flyers' fans went home as stunned as Lindros.

**9. Nets 101, Sixers 98; April 26, 1984.** Fans were still on a high from the 1983 NBA championship. Granted, the Sixers fell from 65 regular-season wins to 52, but there seemed no way they could lose to New Jersey. IN THE FIRST ROUND! But they did, as Micheal Ray Richardson went nuts for the Nets. Even though Doc guaranteed a win in the deciding Game 5, it was not to be. Imagine how much more heartbreaking it would have been had we known the '83 title was to be the last were ever going to see.

**8. Celtics 91, Sixers 90; May 3, 1981.** The Julius Erving-led Sixers, in the midst of the five-year "We owe you one" campaign, got up 3-1 over the despised Celtics in the Eastern Conference Finals. Then they lost the next three games by a combined five points, including this one-point tearjerker. This was before Danny Ainge and Dennis Johnson showed up—the smirking Cornbread Maxwell and the towel-waving M.L. Carr were already there. Oh, woe is we.

**7. Bears 20, Eagles 12; December 31, 1988.** The Fog Bowl is so well-documented elsewhere in this book that I will add this one nugget: Mike Quick still recalls that, after the game, when the Eagles finally left the locker room, the fog was completely gone and had been replaced with bright, gorgeous sun. Maybe Stephen King isn't a Red Sox fan after all. He's a Bears fan. "Roll in the fog, we might lose!" Of course, the fact that the Bears had to play in the same fog is a factoid I choose to ignore.

**6. North Carolina 75, Temple 72; March 24, 1991.** With a trip to his first Final Four on the line for John Chaney, Mark Macon's three-pointer clanged off the rim and the Owls came home from the Meadowlands on this cloudy Sunday afternoon, denied one more time. Although Chaney would get to the Elite Eight in 1993, 1999, and 2001, he would never get this close to the Final Four again. This was before "Goongate" and John Calipari, back when the entire town wanted this win for Chaney in the worst way. A tremendous 31-point effort from Macon in his last game as an Owl was just not enough.

**5. Oklahoma State 64, St. Joe's 62; March 27, 2004.** Ten seconds. Three incredible mood swings. With a trip to the Final Four at stake, Pat Carroll hit a late three-pointer to put St. Joe's up by one. We were all booking flights to San Antonio. In a blink of an eye, John Lucas III (yes, the son of that former Sixers coach), who was 2-for-11 from the three-point line at that point, drilled a three. Then College Player of the Year Jameer Nelson got a good look, but his fade-away jumper ticked off the rim. The Hawks—undefeated in the regular season—went home empty. Absolutely crushing.

**4. Buccaneers 27, Eagles 10; January 10, 2003.** The Birds had beaten Tampa four straight times. The Bucs had never won a playoff game on the road, and their record with the temperature below 32 degrees was like 0-217. It was the last game ever at the Vet. Duce Staley scored a minute into the game. Who knew then that would be the Eagles' last lead of the game? All this with a trip to the Super Bowl on the line. By the way, it's a good thing it was the crummy old Vet's finale or Joe Jurevicius would still be down there avoiding Eagle tacklers. Rumor has it he repeats this run every summer in the parking lot.

**3. Panthers 14, Eagles 3; January 18, 2004.** No way they could lose three NFC Championship games in a row, could they? Not to a team from a town where the only sports that matter are college hoops and NASCAR. (If you even consider NASCAR a sport, which we don't.) We couldn't be denied again, could we? But we were. At home, no less. On a cold, damp, cloudy, miserable evening, the only thing lousier than the weather was the Eagles' offense. Carolina rookie cornerback Ricky Manning Jr. intercepted Donovan McNabb three times. Fans were less angry than stunned as they staggered out into the night.

**2. Dodgers 6, Phillies 5; October 7, 1977. "Black Friday."** Game 3 of a best-of-five NLCS against the Dodgers. The series was tied at a game apiece. The Phils had a 5-3 lead in the ninth with two outs and nobody on, and reliever Gene Garber on the mound. In every similar game situation that season, manager Danny Ozark replaced defensive liability Greg Luzinski with Jerry Martin. Not this night. Up came 41-year-old Vic Davalillo, who incredibly beat out a bunt. Then, 39-year-old Manny Mota lifted a flyball to left that Luzinski butchered, allowing Davillilo to score and—when Ted Sizemore messed up a relay—Mota moved to third. (Most fans have forgotten Sizemore's key error over the years). Davey Lopes then hit a smash that caromed off Mike Schmidt right to shortstop Larry Bowa, who quickly threw to first. Replays show that the throw beat Lopes, but umpire Bruce Froemming blew the call, allowing the tying run to score. Then Garber's pickoff attempt (what was he thinking?) eluded first baseman Richie Hebner, moving Lopes to second. He promptly scored on Bill Russell's single up the middle.

The Phils, of course, failed to score in the ninth. A day that started off with so much elation—as fans booed Dodgers pitcher Burt Hooton so loudly that he walked in three straight runs in the second—ended in another suicide alert for long-suffering Phillies fans.

**BDG Alert:** I was at this game and will always remember the 20-minute walk to the car with my brother, followed by a 40-minute ride to his apartment. Neither of us said one word to the other.

**1. Cardinals 11, Mets 5; October 4, 1964.** This is where it all begins. The decades of pessimism. The feeling that no matter how excited you get about your team, they're still going to lose in the end. Right here, this day. Look no further. Heck, this is where "Negadelphia" begins to spread like the virus that Agent Smith tells Morpheus about in *The Matrix.*

Everyone remembers the Phils' 10-game losing streak that blew the 6-1/2-game lead down the stretch. What's forgotten is that the Phils still could have tied for the pennant after finally beating the Reds on Friday night, October 2. All they needed was another win Sunday and for the Mets to somehow beat St. Louis. Behind a shutout performance by Jim Bunning, the Phils held up their end on Sunday, winning 10-0. (By the way, Chris Short won the Friday game, which somewhat vindicates Manager Gene Mauch, so criticized for overusing his two star pitchers down the stretch.) But the Mets, of course, failed to defeat the Cards. That was it, folks. Season over. The biggest collapse in sports history. Why us?

# The Best Names to Announce :: Dan Baker

Note: Dan Baker was raised in Southwest Philadelphia and Mount Ephraim, N.J. He works in athletic administration with Drexel University and the Big 5. But most fans know him through his two moonlighting gigs—he has been the on-site public address (PA) announcer for the Phillies since 1972 and the Eagles since 1985. When you cheer—or boo—a player upon introduction, the voice you are responding to is Dan Baker's.

"My favorite names tend to be those with multiple syllables," says Baker. "They just lend themselves to more melodic interpretations."

## Phillies

**7. Lenny Dykstra.** He was full of energy. I tried to capture that in announcing him and let the fans know what was coming—Lenny DYK-stra! How about the season Lenny had leading off in 1993? Few lead-off hitters have ever performed better than he did that year.

**6. Dick Allen.** He was one of my heroes growing up. I'll never forget the way the ball jumped off his bat when I watched him in the sixties as a fan at Connie Mack Stadium. By the time Dick returned to the Phillies I was doing the PA announcing. What a thrill it was for me just to say his name.

**5. Scott Rolen.** His name just came rolling off your lips—Scott Rolllllennn—no pun intended. I was heartbroken to see him go. What a great defensive third baseman.

**4. Greg Luzinski.** The Bull! Boy, could he energize a crowd with those Bull Blasts of his in the mid- to late-seventies. He played on some of the best Phillies teams of all time, and was one of the most exciting players we ever saw.

**3. Juan Samuel.** It must be something about second basemen. What an exciting player when he first came up. And what a nice guy.

**2. Ted Sizemore.** Ted once came back for an old-timers game and told me that he loved the way I said his name. "Let me hear it just one more time," he said. I was happy to oblige. You know: Siiiiizzzzzzemore!

**1. Mickey Morandini.** He played with a certain flair and always hustled. Philadelphia baseball fans admire guys who work hard, and Mickey sure did. You couldn't help but like him, and his name: Mickey Morandiiiiinnnnniiiii!

**Eagles**

**7. Duce Staley.** The workhorse. DUUUUUUUUUUCE! Enough said.

**6. Brian Westbrook.** He's some kind of football player. I really hit that "k" at the end for impact.

**5. N.D. Kalu.** You know, I give particular emphasis when a person uses initials instead of a first name—like J.D. Drew. But then, N.D. has a terrific two-syllable last name to go with the first. Kal-UUUU.

**4. Hollis Thomas.** Just like it is for second basemen in baseball, for some reason it seems like a lot of my favorite names in football belong to defensive linemen. For Hollis, it's the combination of all of those sibilant sounds at the end of his first and last names: HOL-LISSSS THOMASSSS!

**3. Hugh Douglas.** The fans would respond perfectly by echoing his first name when I announced him after he tackled somebody. HUUUUUUUGH DOUGLAS!

**2. Jerome Brown.** I loved to announce it when he recorded a sack. He could get to the quarterback in a hurry. His last name is perfect for elocutionists.

**1. Reggie White.** His name sounded majestic—just like he played. Simply the greatest defensive lineman ever.

## My Favorite Hockey Names to Call Out :: Lou Nolan

Note: Lou Nolan has been the in-house voice of the Flyers since 1972, calling thousands of games, including two Stanley Cup championships. He also served as PA announcer for the 2002 Winter Olympics in Salt Lake City, which he calls "the pinnacle for any broadcaster."

Here are his all-time favorite names:

**12. Simon Gagne**—See-moooan GANNN-yeaaaa. A ton of fun to draw the name out, and I'll continue to get to do so as he continues to use those great hands to score goals.

**11. Vincent Lecavalier**—Vin-san Le-cav-il-YEA. I know I called that name far too much in the 2003–04 season, because he kept scoring against the Flyers. Boy, is he good.

**10. Per Djoos**—Pear Juice. He had a short career for Detroit and the New York Rangers, but he was an announcer's dream. How could something from the shelf of your market not be a favorite?

**9. Gordie Howe.** I only got to say this name once, in an old-timers game as I recall. But I was very honored just for that opportunity.

**8. Rick MacLeish.** His goal won the Stanley Cup for the Flyers at home on May 19, 1974. Calling that one was my own personal crowning announcement.

**7. Rod Brind'Amour.** I always loved this name. Rod was definitely a favorite, and a great guy.

**6. Steve Yzerman**—EYE-zer-mann! A great player with a name that just rolls off your tongue. One day he scored a hat trick at the Spectrum. As I announced him as the first star, he skated over and handed me his stick. A very classy guy.

**5. Bobby Orr.** A thrill to just say his name. But much more than that, it was a great thrill to call the penalty against him as he pulled down Bobby Clarke at the end of the first Stanley Cup game and just about assured the Flyers victory.

**4. Vincent Damphousse.** I love the great French names. VIN-san Damm-FOOSE. I pronounced this name many times. It seems like Vinny was always on the board with points his entire career.

**3. Yvon Cournoyer.** The great Montreal Canadiens scorer. He's top three for sure. EE-von Corn-y-YAY. What a great name to get to say.

**2. Vyacheslav Solodukhin**—V-AAH-she-slav So-lo-DUKE-in. He played for the Soviets in that infamous 4-1 Flyers win back in 1976. The great Gene Hart helped me with Soviet pronunciations. It's really easy once you get it.

**1. Bobby Clarke.** He has to be #1. Know why? I called this name more than any other Flyer—both for scoring and getting sent to the sin bin.

## My Favorite Names to Announce :: Matt Cord

Note: Matt Cord, a longtime popular Philadelphia radio deejay and host, has been the Sixers' PA announcer since 1998.

**10. Raja Bell.** "RRRRRaaajjawww Bell." His name was fun to say, plus all the ladies would scream when he came in.

**9. Pepe Sanchez.** "Juan Pep-pay Sannchezz." Every time he got the ball, all you heard from the crowd was . . . "shoot!"

**8. Brian Skinner.** "Brian Skkinnnnnerr." My inflection on "Skinner" is said just like Superintendent Chalmers calls out the principal on The Simpsons.

**7. Todd McCulloch.** "Big Mac Maw-Cullaahh." On his trading card, it gives props to the Sixers PA announcer for the nickname "Big Mac." That's me, of course.

**6. Aaron McKie.** "Aaarrrrroonnn Mick-Keeeeeeeee." The building would always echo after the McKie part.

**5. Theo Ratliff.** "Theeeeooooooo Rattt-Lifff." I'd always used to see Iverson mouth the "Theeeooooo" part when I said his name.

**4. Kyle Korver—hitting a three-pointer.** "Double Kaayyyy for the Treyyy." It's got Korver's stamp of approval.

**3. Dikembe Mutombo.** "Dikkkeemmbbbayy Muuuuuu-Tuummm-bow." With all of his middle names, thank God I didn't have to announce his full name.

**2. Jumaine Jones.** "Juuuu-MAIN-Jones." Not a great player, but just about my all-time favorite to announce.

**1. Allen Iverson.** "Allllennnnn EYE-ver-son." Who else? Without a doubt, I've said this name the most during my nine-year career.

## Our Favorite Johnsons

As the adage goes, "You can't win without a Johnson." With all respect to the Birds' Albert, Alonzo, Bill, Chris, Don, Dwight, Eric, Gene, Jay, Jimmie, Kevin, Lee, Maurice (a Temple alum), Norm, Reggie, Ron, the other Ron, and Vaughn, well, sorry you didn't make the cut.

To the Phils' Charles, Darrell, Davey (yes, that Davey), Jerry, John (who names their kid John Johnson?), Ken, Si, Syl, and Tom—try again next year.

As for George, well, how is it you're the only Sixers' Johnson not to cut the mustard? We didn't focus on the Big 5 or any coaches (all apologies to the Eagles defensive coordinator, Jim) because, you know, we have lives. There's only so much time you can spend on a list, eh?

**10. Alvin Johnson.** According to many NFL websites, Alvin doesn't even exist. Study the Eagles media guide, however, and it appears that this Hardin-Simmons grad got in one game in the Championship year of 1948. He punted once for five yards. Yes, you read that right, five yards. Hmmm, wonder why he never punted again? Let's start an Alvin Johnson fan club.

**9. Reggie Johnson.** What a lucky Johnson. Got swapped to the Sixers at the trade deadline. Guess what year? You got it, the 1983 Championship year. This forward out of Tennessee, who was drafted in the first round by the Spurs two years earlier, played all of 32 minutes in the playoffs and still got a ring. A year later he was out of the league. Ask ringless Charles Barkley if life is always fair.

**8. Charles Johnson.** The skinny wide receiver arrived from Pittsburgh and caught 90 balls for eight touchdowns in two seasons with the Eagles. Fans never liked him and he quietly left town. His replacement, James Thrash, did no better, and it's because of these two mediocrities—along with a few others—that the fans started screaming for the Birds to sign "a true number one." This eventually led us to Terrell Owens, which leads us to . . . well, you know how that story ends.

**7. Jimmy Johnson.** Unless you want to count Kim Johnsson, and frankly we were tempted, Jimmy is the only Johnson to ever play for the Flyers. This center from Winnipeg played the first five seasons of the Flyers' existence from '68 to '72 and put up decent numbers. Damn, how many Jimmy Johnsons are there on this planet?

**6. Alex Johnson.** He had a fine 13-year career as a big-league outfielder, unfortunately just 140 games of it with the Phils. He broke in here in the infamous 1964 season, hitting .303 in 109 at bats. So he has to be included just for being on that team. He was hitting .294 the next year when the Phils sent him to St. Louis in a deal that brought future National League President Bill White and Bob Uecker.

**5. Deron Johnson.** This first-third baseman put up big home run and RBI numbers for the Phils from 1969 to 1972 (plus 12 games in '73). In 1971, the first year at the Vet, he slammed 34 homers and had 95 RBIs.

**4. Dirk Johnson.** Yes, we know, he's a punter. But he punted for the Birds in the Super Bowl, for crying out loud, and that counts for a lot in our book. Nothing spectacular, mind you, but no disaster either. And when you do anything at all in that game, it's magnified a hundredfold. Plus, he used to brand cattle in Colorado, so there's extra points for that.

**3. Ollie Johnson.** We're aware that this Southern High grad only played 66 games for the Sixers from 1980–82, but he's the only Johnson in the Big 5 Hall of Fame, where he starred for the Temple Owls.

**2. Clemon Johnson.** This 6-foot-10 backup center arrived just in time from Indiana in 1983 and was a big help to the Sixers as they drove to their last NBA Championship. He appeared in 12 playoff games, logging more than 200 minutes. This graduate of—get this—Florida Agricultural and Mechanical University, proved a point that, while one Johnson is good, two—Reggie and Clemon—will earn you a parade down Broad Street.

**1. Charlie Johnson.** Hands down, no Johnson had as great a career with a Philadelphia pro team as did this defensive lineman out of Colorado. (By the way, all three of the Eagles' Johnsons attended college in Colorado). In a five-year career with the Birds, Charlie went to three Pro Bowls (1979–81). Here's to you, Charlie. You're still Our Favorite Johnson.

**10. Jim Thome for Magarity Chevrolet.** "I came to Philadelphia for two reasons—to win a championship and Magarity Chevrolet." Funny, he forgot to mention the $13 million a year for six years.

**9. Eric Lindros and Bob Clarke for Ellio's frozen pizzas.** The acting is so wooden you can almost feel the splinters. At the end, Clarke swipes young Eric's slice fresh from the toaster oven. We can almost see Bonnie Lindros off camera, shrieking, "He's stealing from my baby!"

**8. Donovan McNabb and mom for Chunky Soup.** He's scrambling for his life in game action and she's telling him to eat more soup. It bothered us that one of the products they pushed—after the Super Bowl loss—was New England clam chowder. It bothered us more that the spots continued to run 6,400 times a day after McNabb got injured and the Birds suffered through a horrible 2005 season.

**7. Charles Barkley for Nike shoes.** "I am not your child's role model." Fine, Charles, then please don't try to hawk them overpriced sneakers carrying your name.

**6. Darren Jensen for Pro-Image Hair Centers.** The backup goalie played less than 1,800 minutes in net for the Flyers in the 1980s. Somehow, we've seen his head—before and after hair plugs—10 times that amount on late-night TV infomercials.

**5. Buddy Ryan for Super Million Hair Color.** Another guy trying to convince us bald men to feel inadequate. Poor Buddy, stuffed like a sausage into an ill-fitting sport jacket, looks baffled as the emcee sprays some sap's head with hair-in-a-can. Near as we could figure, it was Krylon Black No. 1602.

**4. Julius Erving for Chapstick.** "Look! It's Doctor J!" "No, I'm Dr. Chapstick." For a guy as cool as Doc, this ad was overwhelmingly nerdy. The only redeeming quality was Erving's foot-high afro.

**3. Phillies players for the new Citizens Bank Park.** In an incredibly embarrassing 2004 promo for "real grass," Randy Wolf frolics through a pasture and Jason Michaels puts a buttercup under his chin. Judging from their excitement, you'd think the players were smoking grass rather than playing on it. This tacky spot barely edges out the 2005 Phils promo, where a big-nosed teenage girl goes to a Phils game, takes a Bobby Abreu foul in the schnozz and comes away as a beauty. Yeah, that makes us want to buy tickets.

**2. Muhammad Ali and Joe Frazier for Vitalis.** This ad came out right before the 1971 fight at Madison Square Garden, so Ali boasts, "Joe Frazier, you're gonna be so messed up on March the 8th, even Vitalis won't help." We could be wrong here, but did it make much sense to have two black fighters promote a product used exclusively by white folks?

**1. Bobby Clarke and Roman Gabriel for Jack Lang Clothes.** Return with us now to the mid-70s era of long sideburns, platform shoes and pastel leisure suits. The Flyers captain and Eagles quarterback even try their hand (feet?) at a little disco dancing. Truly a humiliating moment for both.

**Honorable mention:** Angelo Cataldi and Al Morganti for Camera and TV Stop. We respect and admire our colleagues, but Angelo in that referee's uniform giving the "safe" sign—well, hold the Clio.

# Top 10 Golf Courses in the Delaware Valley
## :: Howard Eskin

Note: Howard Eskin, an original member of 610-*WIP* Sports-Talk Radio in 1986 and current afternoon drive-time host, is known as Philadelphia's "hardest-working sportscaster." He is an avid golfer and a fan of the pro game.

One thing I know will happen after I name my Top 10 golf courses in the Philadelphia area: Someone will be offended at my order or why I left a course off the list. I have played many other terrific tracks in this area, but it's not easy to get it down to 10.

You should know that my taste for golf courses is not the traditional layouts. I like to think a couple shots ahead and that's what I can do when a course is a different layout.

I actually shot rounds of 75 and 73 at two of my very favorites on this list. That's part of my affection with those two. Figure out which courses they may be. The answer comes later in the list.

**10. Golf Course at Glen Mills.** I had to include one public course in the Top 10. And this course clearly deserves to be in that mix. Most courses that are not private clubs are easy to move the ball around. Not Glen Mills. You would never know it's a public course.

**9. Ace Golf Club, Lafayette Hill.** One of the few new courses in the area. It was the old Eagle Lodge, but it's nothing like that course now. Every hole is different. I consider Ace one of the best in this area, with an amazingly beautiful clubhouse.

**8. Gulph Mills Golf Club, King of Prussia.** Beautiful clubhouse and golf course. But very difficult to score on this course.

**7. Applebrook Golf Club, Malvern.** Another course where the layout is far from traditional. This Malvern course is a challenge, but not a course I would say is unfair to most golfers. For me, it's an enjoyable round of golf.

**6. Stonewall Golf Club, Elverson.** Most holes at this Chester County course are wide open. But the elevated tees create some tough decisions on which club to use. Just like at Merion Golf Club, you better stay in or close to the fairway. If not you may be there a while. Another thinking man or woman's golf course.

**5. Aronimink Golf Club, Newtown Square.** This is probably the most traditional course on my list. I know many in the area rank this one no lower than third, but remember, I told you I'm not as much a fan of the traditional. History is gigantic at this one and it's very difficult. Plays long, and some holes are so difficult it sometimes makes you want to quit the game. One of my favorite memories is Arnold Palmer's last competitive round of golf in this area in the 2003 U.S. Senior PGA at Aronimink.

**4. Commonwealth National Golf Club, Horsham.** I know some people will say I ranked Commonwealth so high because it's my home course. The reason it's my home course is because I think it's a great course and one of the best in the area. It's the only non-traditional course Arnold Palmer has designed. There is almost no "breather" on any one hole. You better score well on the front nine because it only gets tougher on the back nine. You better not lose concentration on this course, and you're forced to think several shots ahead on most holes.

**3. Saucon Valley Country Club, Bethlehem.** Saucon is not just one great golf course and the home of some major championships—it's three great courses. The U.S. Seniors played their open on the "Old Course" at Saucon, but the one I like almost as much is the "Weyhill Course" at Saucon Valley.

**2. Merion Golf Club/The East Course, Ardmore.** All you need to do is see one of golf's most famous photos to feel the history of Merion. It's Ben Hogan hitting his second shot on the fairway at 18 in the 1950 U.S. Open Golf Championship. Merion almost always eats me up. I think it's tougher to score on than Pine Valley. Ranked seventh in the world and second for me in this area.

**1. Pine Valley Golf Club, Pine Valley, N.J.** This course is ranked number one in the world. So it would make no sense to rank Pine Valley anywhere but number one in this area. It's got a mystique about it. Most cannot even get a look if not invited by a member, and not any hole but the one you are playing can be seen from the other. Many greens are bigger than some cities, but they are tougher than any greens in the area. It's the dream of every golfer to play Pine Valley.

**By the way,** those two scores I mentioned I shot earlier were a 75 at Pine Valley and a 73 at the "Old Course" at Saucon Valley.

Boy, this isn't too daunting of a job, is it? Hundreds have been made over the years, which is weird because sports movies traditionally don't do well at the box office.

But even a mediocre sports movie, or a comedy sports movie, can hit us on some emotional level. Characters like Rocky Balboa and Roy Hobbs have left as much of an impression on some of us as Joe Frazier and Mike Schmidt.

We left out documentaries and made-for-TV movies, which eliminates great works like *Brian's Song, Hoop Dreams, When We Were Kings, Four Minutes, 61\**, and many others.

Some flicks—like the original *Heaven Can Wait*—are left off because there's just not enough sports in them. Others, like the classics *Breaking Away* and *The Hustler* don't get invited because, well, they're about cycling and pool. To tell you the truth, those movies use sports as a backdrop to tell a much bigger story anyway.

So, here's the standard we used: In the end, these are the 10 we like the most. Boy, that's scientific, isn't it?

**10. *Friday Night Lights,* 2004.** Based on Buzz Bissinger's heartbreaking book, it tells the story of the incredible pressure high school sports can put on kids. It also highlights the depressing reality that, for too many boys in this country, sports is not only their only way out but it's also the only way they know how to feel good about themselves. When Boobie Miles's season and life go down the drain from an injury, and he breaks down in his car, there's not a dry eye in the house. All the kids are credible as teenagers and athletes, and Billy Bob Thornton and Tim McGraw are excellent as the head coach and overbearing alcoholic father. The only reason this comes in as low as 10 is because it hasn't yet stood the test of time.

**9. *Bang The Drum Slowly,* 1973.** Heartbreaking tale of an incredible friendship between a Major League star pitcher (Michael Moriarty) and a green catcher (Robert DeNiro) who's desperately trying to make the team even as he's terminally ill. It accurately portrays spring training which is, for fans, a great season of hope, but for players, often a trying time. Vincent Gardenia is his usual great self as the manager. Look for Danny Aiello in a small role.

**8. *Caddyshack,* 1980.** Bill Murray and Rodney Dangerfield just destroy the world of snobbish golf—led by the perfectly cast Ted Knight—and in the process, destroy the audience with laughter. *Caddyshack* would also make our top 10 comedies. A true classic. Did you know that after the filming was over, director Harold Ramis realized that Murray and Chevy Chase didn't play one scene together? So the three of them met for lunch and wrote the classic scene where Ty Webb's ball crashes into Carl Spackler's shack and they end up sharing a bong and some thoughts on life—all filmed in one take. And whatever happened to "Lacy Underall?"

**7. *The Bad News Bears,* 1976.** As funny as *Bears* is, it's not far from the truth of what the world of Little League baseball is all about. The coaches, the kids, the parents—none of us are all that perfect, are we? For a little comedy, we would rank Walter Matthau's performance as grumpy, drinking coach Buttermaker with any performance of his career, which is saying a lot. Tatum O'Neal, Vic Morrow, Jackie Earle Haley, and Chris Barnes as "Tanner" lead a strong ensemble cast. Did you know that Buttermaker is never seen drinking the same brand of beer more than once? Next time you watch it see how many brands you can pick out.

**6. *Rudy,* 1993.** As corny as corny gets, but it all works because Sean Astin captures every undersized kid in America who ever had doors slammed in his face and still refuses to say no. Based on the true story of "Rudy" Ruettiger, who dreams of playing Notre Dame football but lacks both the physical attributes and the grades. That's a really fat Jon Favreau of *Swingers* fame playing Rudy's friend, and Charles S. Dutton bringing dignity to "Fortune," the janitor with an unfortunate past.

**5. *Over the Top,* 1987.** Sylvester Stallone as arm-wrestler Lincoln Hawk who . . . YEAH, RIGHT! JUST MAKING SURE YOU'RE PAYING ATTENTION.

**5. *Slapshot,* 1977.** Reggie Dunlop, the Hanson brothers, "Killer" Carlson, Ogie Ogilthorpe, "Dr. Hook" McCracken, the Sparkle Twins, OLD TIME HOCKEY! If Hollywood ever made a movie specifically for one group like *Slapshot* was made for us "Broad Street Bully" fans, this was it. Paul Newman leads as player/coach of the barely surviving Johnstown Jets, a small-town minor league hockey team. Hard to believe that this hilariously vulgar script was written by a woman, Nancy Dowd. When the driver of the Jets starts pummeling the team bus "because he's gotta make it look mean," we totally lose it. Al Pacino turned down Newman's role.

**4. *Rocky,* 1976.** Won the Oscar for picture of the year, and it tells the story of Sly Stallone the struggling actor as much as it tells the story of the down-on-his-luck two-bit fighter Rocky Balboa. Ultimately, however, it tells the story of you and I, doesn't it? Because of the sequels, people forget that Rocky loses the fight, and that's one of many cool touches of the film. It's about just hanging in there, believing in yourself, and getting a chance. Arguably the greatest score in movie history, it's only marred by the completely unbelievable fighting sequences. In real life, a penniless Stallone turned down $150,000 to sell the script because he knew that playing "Rocky" himself was his only chance of hitting the big time. Way to go, Rock!

**3. *The Natural,* 1984.** The greatest baseball movie ever made, period. Mythical. Magical. Majestic. "What do you want out of life, Roy?" "I want to walk down the street and have people say, there goes Roy Hobbs, the best there ever was." Do you know who used to say that all the time in real life? Ted Williams. Unlike a lot of other films on this list, this is no small film simply about "competing." This is about Babe Ruth, Michael Jordan, America itself. The best there ever was. Incredible cinematography, a grand score by Randy Newman, and a cast that includes Robert Redford, Robert Duvall, Kim Basinger, Darren McGavin, Glenn Close, Robert Prosky, Wilford Brimley, Barbara Hershey, Richard Farnsworth, Michael Madsen, and Joe Don Baker. Are you kidding me? Would be Number One if it was just 10 minutes shorter.

**2. *Hoosiers,* 1986.** Absolute perfection. A slight rip-off of *The Natural* in tone and style, but years after its release, who remembers that? Based on the 1954 Indiana State high school basketball champs, the Milan Indians. Starring the always-believable Gene Hackman as Coach Norman Dale, this movie is "for all the little schools who never got a chance to win the big one." That about sums it up, doesn't it? Funny how Dennis Hopper's performance as alcoholic assistant coach Shooter is his finest ever, even though he's not blowing up buses or killing anyone. Watch for the scene where Maris Valainis as Jimmy Chitwood makes shot after shot on an outdoor hoop while Hackman's talking to him. It was done in one take and Valainis is the only actor on the Hickory team never to actually play high school basketball.

**1. *Raging Bull,* 1980.** How else can you say this? Robert DeNiro's portrayal of psycho middleweight champion Jake LaMotta just might be the single greatest performance by an actor in the history of movies. They should have given him two Oscars—one for all the weight he put on to show LaMotta's downward spiral and another for the under-appreciated boxing shape he whipped himself into. It completely answered any question of whether an athlete brings his "work" home with him. Joe Pesci comes out of nowhere and Cathy Moriarty is old-school sexy. Sometimes it takes a real brute to rise to the top. Only *Slapshot* or *Scarface* curse like this baby, so please, NEVER watch this on network TV, where too much is edited out. The only black-and-white flick to make this list.

**Glen says:** I let Big Daddy handle this list because, quite frankly, he begged. Not a bad job, but I've got a few disagreements. First of all, *Rudy* is the most insipid, manipulative sports movie ever, so it's off. So is *Bad News Bears*—which is about kids, not sports—as well as a few others of his choices.

One interesting note is that both Big Daddy and I omit a movie that nearly every critic puts at the top of his list of sports movies—*Field of Dreams.* I always found it a little too reverential. Plus, it all builds up to the scene where Kevin Costner and his dad play catch—and then the dad throws like an eight-year-old girl. Destroyed it right there.

So, just to save the reader, here are the real Top Ten Sports Movies of All Time:

**10. *The Big Lebowski,* 1998.** Great movie about bowling, life, and being cool. Just edges out another great bowling movie, Kingpin.

**9. *Friday Night Lights,* 2004.** For the reasons stated by Big Daddy.

**8. *The Natural,* 1984.** I rank it lower than Big Daddy because I'm not as much of a sentimental sap as he. Still, has to make the list.

**7. *The Longest Yard,* 1974.** The original, of course, not the Adam Sandler rip-off. The 47-minute football scene is the greatest that football has ever been done in a movie. "I think I broke his #@%#*&% neck!"

**6. *Slapshot,* 1977.** How can I, as a hockey guy, rank this movie lower than Big Daddy? No offense, there are just a few others that I love even more. Make sure you read Flyers Coach Ken Hitchcock's take on this film on page 37.

**5. *Bull Durham,* 1988.** Like *Slapshot,* but about minor league baseball and the life of traveling town-to-town by bus in hopes of reaching "The Show." Susan Sarandon at her sexiest. This movie started the "sports-movie/chick-flick" genre (copied by *Jerry Maguire*) that actually produces date films you can enjoy.

**4. *Caddyshack,* 1980.** For reasons already stated. Rumor has it that 4,381 pounds of pot were smoked by the cast and crew during filming.

**3. *Raging Bull,* 1980.** I probably have it too low. A great, great film—just a little tough to watch.

**2. *Hoosiers,* 1986.** I've literally seen it hundreds of times, and know every single line of dialogue—and yet I never flip the channel when it comes on.

**1. *Rocky,* 1976.** The champ of sports movies, and it gets a special nod for being filmed here. Hundreds of sports movies have told the story of the downtrodden underdog getting his shot at the big time. Rocky did it the best. Probably deserves its own chapter in this book. Hmmmm. . . .

**10. Sylvester Stallone, inspired by the 1975 fight between Muhammad Ali and Chuck Wepner**—aka "the Bayonne Bleeder"—wrote the original screenplay for the movie in three days.

**9. When producers got the script, they had no idea who Stallone was.** An aide showed them a photo of the cast of *The Lords of Flatbush,* and their interest grew. Problem was, the producers had mistaken Stallone for another cast member—blond-haired, blue-eyed Perry King. When they later met Stallone, the producers almost backed out.

**8. Actresses considered for the role of Adrian included Susan Sarandon** (who did a screen test) and Bette Midler (who turned it down). Producer Irwin Winkler was so intent on not having Stallone star in the film that he offered the then-obscure actor $150,000 to let either James Caan or Ryan O'Neal play the lead role. Stallone declined, knowing it was his breakout role.

**7. Eventually, the studio agreed to cast Stallone as Rocky if he promised to keep the cost of production under $1 million.** He almost made it—the bottom-line cost ended up at $1.1 million. Since then, the movie has grossed more than $400 million in box office and rentals.

**6. *Rocky* was the first movie ever to use the Steadicam,** the Oscar-winning camera stabilizer invented by Philadelphian Garrett Brown. The device, unveiled in the boxing scenes, allows a cameraman to move around without the picture becoming jumpy. It is now a staple in nearly every feature movie, and is even available for home-video cameras.

**5. Stallone, a strong believer in method acting,** spent so much time punching the frozen sides of beef in the training scenes that his knuckles were permanently disfigured.

**4. The entire movie was shot in 28 days.** The two scenes of Rocky running up the museum steps—failing and then succeeding—were filmed two hours apart, before and after sunrise.

**3. Several improvised moments made the final cut.** The scene where Gazzo the mobster pulls out an inhaler occurred only because actor Joe Spinell started having an asthma attack during filming. And the scene in Rocky's kitchen where Adrian shies away from a kiss, came about because actress Talia Shire had the flu and instinctively pulled away, trying to prevent Stallone from getting sick.

**2. Stallone was so nervous about the night-before-the-fight scene** where he admits his inner fears to Adrian—and so nervous about director John Avildsen's threats to cut it out—that he got drunk before filming it and nailed it in one take.

**1. For reasons no one has ever explained, the fight between Rocky and Apollo Creed was filmed in reverse order.** The actors started—in heavy makeup—with Round 15 and went backwards to Round 1. Many credit this as the reason *Rocky* won the Oscar for best editing.

**10. Jimmie Dykes.** He was hired by the Athletics in 1951 to take over for Connie Mack, who had managed a mere 50 years. Dykes lasted three seasons, never finishing higher than fourth. In fact, he holds the Major League record for managing 21 years without once getting to the post-season.

**9. Bo McMillin.** Also replaced a coaching legend in 1951, when Hall of Famer Greasy Neale was fired after a blowup with Eagles ownership. McMillin won his first two games as head coach and then stepped down after a stunning announcement that he had incurable cancer. His replacement, Wayne Millner, lost eight of the final 10 games.

**8. Jumbo Huzvar.** Steve Van Buren retired as holder of seven NFL records and the best running back of the league's first 30 years. His replacement as the Eagles' primary ball-carrier was Huzvar—a six-foot-four, 247-pound mastodon from Hershey—who rushed for 349 yards and a 3.3-yard average in 1952. Since World War II, no one has had fewer rushing yards and still led the Eagles for a season.

**7. Bobby Del Greco.** When Richie Ashburn was traded to the Cubs in 1960, Del Greco took over as the primary centerfielder (the Phils actually tried six players there that season). Del Greco was a 27-year-old journeyman (the Phils were his fifth club), who managed 10 homers but just 26 RBIs in 300 at-bats. By 1961, he had moved onto his sixth club.

**6. Darrell Imhoff.** The defender who gave up Wilt's 100 points later came here in exchange for The Dipper. Averaged 9.2 points and 9.7 rebounds as the Sixers' center in 1968–69—a decline of a mere 15.1 points and 14.1 rebounds from Mr. Chamberlain.

**5. Pete Peeters.** He was the top goalie prospect in the Flyers' system when Bernie Parent's eye injury ended his career in 1979. A year later, Peeters and Phil Myre shared the nets during the Flyers record 35-game unbeaten streak. Probably the most successful name on this list, he is also its surliest, most miserable character.

**4. Mel Bridgman.** Became Flyers captain in 1979 when Bobby Clarke gave up the "C" after seven seasons to become a player/assistant coach. Bridgman's own production declined (16 goals, down from 24 the previous season), but the team got to the Stanley Cup Finals. He lost his captaincy in 1981 after a contract dispute.

**3. Charlie Hayes.** Two weeks after Mike Schmidt retired in 1989, Hayes came from the Giants to take over. Schmidt was making $2.25 million his last season; Hayes earned $68,000. He lasted three seasons with the Phils, 14 overall in the majors, but isn't remembered for much beyond making a throwing error to cost Terry Mulholland a perfect game in 1990.

**2. Steve Lappas.** Cranky old Rollie Massimino may have left Villanova on bad terms in 1992, but he also departed with 357 career wins and a national title. In fact, Nova had seen just three men's basketball coaches since 1936 (Al Severance, Jack Kraft, and Rollie), who combined for 1,008 wins. You could argue that Lappas had high standards to meet. He never did, failing to go far in the NCAA tournament or win-over the snooty alum. The biggest surprise is that he lasted nine seasons.

**1. Mike Flores.** When Reggie White left as a free agent in 1993, Flores—an 11th round pick out of Louisville—stepped in as the Eagles' left defensive end. "We'll be just fine at that position," predicted Coach Rich Kotite. White had averaged 15.5 sacks a season over the prior eight years. Flores managed three.

So many records, so little space to cover them all. And we're not even going to bring up the 20,000 women Wilt supposedly bedded. (OK, I guess we just did.) In later years, Wilt said that the number was taken out of context and that it was nothing to be proud of. (Really?) Before we get started, let's ring up another cool Wilt number. He always carried at least $5,000 cash on him because, he said, "Who's gonna rob me?"

**10. Wilt scored at least 65 points in a game 15 times.** Everyone else in NBA history has combined to do this six times.

**9. Wilt led the NBA in assists in 1967–68.** To this day, he is the only center in history to lead the league in assists. Plus, get ready for this, he averaged 24.3 points per game and 23.8 rebounds a game that same season. To quote Tom McGinnis, "Are you kidding me?"

**8. For 10 straight years Wilt averaged at least 20 points and 20 rebounds per game.** Ten years. Everyone else combined has pulled this off a total of three times in league history.

**7. On November 24, 1960, Wilt pulled down 55 rebounds in one NBA game.** Against Bill Russell, no less. And the Warriors lost.

**6. In Wilt's very first NBA game, in 1959, he scored 43 points and pulled down 28 boards.** How's that for bringing the rookie along easily? In fact, he averaged 37.6 points and 27 rebounds his first season.

**5. Okie dokie, how do these numbers grab you? In 1,045 NBA games, Wilt never fouled out.** Not once. Ever. Because of his amazing stamina and conditioning, Wilt actually averaged 48.5 minutes per game in the 1961–62 season. In fact, if it wasn't for one measly six-minute breather he took in one stinking game, he would have played every single minute (including overtimes) of the entire season.

**4. When Wilt was playing for Overbrook High, he once scored 60 points in 10 minutes against Roxborough High.** SIXTY IN 10 MINUTES. He scored 90 points in the game. Wilt's Overbook High teams went 56-3 and won two City Championships.
Big Daddy Alert: My alumni brothers, West Catholic, of 1953, actually beat Wilt and Overbrook for the City Title after practicing all week by shooting around a guy standing on a chair.

**3. And while we're talking T-E-A-M here, Wilt's 1971–72 Lakers team won 33 straight games on its way to an NBA Championship.** A record, like most here, that stands to this day. A forgotten fact is that Elgin Baylor retired the game before this streak started.

**2. In 1961–62, Wilt averaged 50.4 points per game for the season.** Is that just ridiculous or what? That's every game. Night in, night out. Guess that kind of blows the old, "Let's let Wilt score and concentrate on stopping the other guys" strategy, doesn't it? For the record, Wilt averaged 30.1 points and 22.9 rebounds per game for his career. We're getting tired just writing all this.

**1. On March 2, 1962, in front of 237,469 fans in Hershey, Pennsylvania (must have been a big arena, eh?), Wilt scored 100 points in a game against the New York Knickerbockers and then hitched a ride back to his pad in New York with a couple of Knicks.** He shot 36-for-63 from the field, and 28-for-32 from the charity line. He pulled down 25 ribbies. He broke nine records in one game. There's a book dedicated to just this one game—*Wilt,* 1962 by Gary Pomerantz. The 100 points is the mother of all records. Never to be broken.

**Big Daddy Alert:** My first game of any kind—professional or collegiate—came when my Dad took me to see Wilt and the Warriors play at the late, great Convention Hall in 1960. I don't remember who they played or whether they won or lost. But I remember this: The teams walked down giant ramps next to the side of the legendary stage that hosted many conventions and legendary artists like the Beatles. Before the game, my Dad took me down to one of these ramps (no elaborate security back in those days) to stand there so I could see Wilt walk by. And boy, did he ever. I could have reached out and touched him, he was so close. A giant in every way. Everything about him shouted, "Take a good look at me, lad, because you'll never see the likes of me again."

And we never will.

Note: Buzz Bissinger is a contributing editor at *Vanity Fair* and the author of several best-selling books, including *Friday Night Lights, Three Nights in August,* and *A Prayer for the City*. He lives in Philadelphia and formerly was an investigative and political reporter for *The Inquirer* from 1981 to 1988.

**9. *The Inquirer* sports page.** Without Bill Lyon, what's the point?

**8. Dick Vermeil.** Wah, wah, wah. Probably crying as he reads this. Get a grip, Dick. Just get a damn grip.

**7. Larry Bowa.** Bombast + Arrogance + A World Series Ring = a lousy manager who made too many decisions by the seat of his butt. Makes Don Knotts (Charlie Manuel) look like Tony La Russa.

**6. Larry Brown.** Great coach. Treacherous and traitorous man. Makes Al a study in character. Brings new meaning to the phrase cut and run.

**5. Stephen A. Smith.** Shooting all sorts of bricks with that tired rip-off Cosellian schtick—and you know what I'm talking about, Angelo. In a heated race with Mitch Albom for the Guinness World Record on most columns in a row written without ever actually attending a single sporting event.

**4. Eric Lindros.** All that supposed talent and what will he be remembered for? The only person in sports to get a concussion while sleeping.

**3. Jim Thome.** The king of the incidental home run. Responsible for bringing Don Knotts to the Phillies. Then he goes to the World Champion White Sox. Baseball is a stupid game.

**2. Andy Reid.** No Super Bowl ring. Too little of a clue on game day. Where's the beef? Still inside your diminished but copious gut. Bill Cowher wins games he shouldn't. You never do. Given the way you handle press conferences by never saying anything, you do have a future—as a spokesman for the Bush Administration.

**1. Donovan McNabb.** Get rid of the goofy smile, stop vomiting in the final two minutes, shed a few pounds because you're not an offensive tackle, set a personal goal of completing two timing patterns against the New Orleans Saints, and take lessons from your mother in personality over a bowl of Campbell's Soup.

**10. John Felske, Phillies.** Showed all the mental acuity of Homer Simpson during his two-plus-year stint in the 1980s. The good news for Felske: We think he's just holding down this tenth spot until Charlie Manuel (aka Elmer Befuddled) gets fully vested.

**9. John Lucas, Sixers.** The first of four 76ers coaches to earn a spot on this list, which tells you something. Lucas was a reformed addict who saw it as his life's mission to rescue troubled souls. That may be a great idea for a soup kitchen, but troubled souls do not make for a successful NBA franchise.

**8. Wayne Cashman, Flyers.** He was a competent assistant coach who got the big job in 1997. Demonstrated all the leadership skills of FEMA director Mike Brown. You could actually see the sweat drenching through his shirt on your TV. He stepped down on his own to become an assistant again. Give Cashman this; unlike many of us, he knew his own limitations.

**7. Joe Kuharich, Eagles.** Not the only "worst" list he makes in this book. Before coming to the Eagles, Kuharich was most known for being the only losing coach in the history of Notre Dame. Between 1961 and 1975, the Eagles head coaches were Nick Skorich, Kuharich, Jerry Williams, hailstorms, poisoned cattle, Ed Khayat, Mike McCormack, locusts, and raining frogs. Fortunately, Dick Vermeil got here before the plagues took each Philadelphian's firstborn son.

**6. Terry Francona, Phillies.** What bothered us most is that Francona spent his four seasons here constantly trying to lower expectations. Actually, what bothered us most is that he wound up in Boston and won a World Series.

**5. Johnny Davis, Sixers.** Trusting him with a $200 million NBA franchise was like trusting a pimply 15-year-old with the family sedan. What Pat Croce and Ed Snider saw in him defies description.

**Glen note:** The day he was named, I was on WIP blasting the choice. A furious Snider called me and compared Davis to Fred Shero in terms of being an unknown who would come in and prove his genius. "The name of the game is to win," said Snider. "W-I-N."

Not in Davis's case. Enduring memory: Davis calling a timeout in the final seconds of a blowout loss so that rookie Allen Iverson could continue his late-season streak of 40-plus-point games.

**4. Art Fletcher, Phillies.** Yeah, we never heard of him either, so go ask your grandfather about the guy who ran the Phils for four dreadful seasons in the 1920s. Here's what our research found: There are 187 guys in history who managed as many Major League games (623) as Fletcher. Just one ever did worse than Fletcher's .382 winning percentage. You could look it up.

**3. Rich Kotite, Eagles.** The only guy on this list who actually won a post-season game—but who's kidding, that was Buddy Ryan's players and Bud Carson's defense. Kotite was perceived by fans as a confused buffoon, by players as a puppet of ownership, by media as a flop-sweating ignoramus. After losing the final seven games of 1994, Kotite was fired by Jeff Lurie. He was quickly hired by the Jets, and many in the New York media suggested that Kotite had gotten a raw deal in Philadelphia. Kotite rewarded their faith by going 4-28 over two seasons.

**2. Doug Moe, Sixers.** At one point he was considered a competent—even innovative—NBA coach. That wasn't in Philadelphia. Moe had the work ethic of a Florida retiree, he just neglected to tell that to Harold Katz before signing a five-year contract in 1992. And, yes, it really is true that Moe sometimes whistled an early end to practice so he could get to a movie matinee.

But, rather than us rip the guy, we'll give you two of Moe's own quotes to sum him up:

"The passing game is basically doing whatever the hell you want. But what coach is going to say, 'We're a freelance team?' It sounds like you're not coaching. Hey, if a coach gets some sort of thrill when the team runs a play right, that's good. I just happen to think differently."

"Somebody said to me, 'It's Friday the 13th, are you going to be jinxed?' I said, 'Bleep, you can't jinx us. We stink.'"

**1. Roy Rubin, Sixers.** When he was hired to coach the Sixers in 1972, Rubin was asked how he felt about coaching Hal Greer, a future Hall of Famer entering his fifteenth season. "Who?" he responded.

Rubin came to the Sixers from Long Island University, which, near as we can tell, has never seriously challenged for the NCAA title. He predicted the Sixers would be "neck-and-neck" with the Celtics in 1972–73. They fell just 59 games short. He got fired with a 4-47 record. By then, the Sixers had acquired the nickname "The Universal Health Spa," because they made all the other sick teams well.

Note: Michael Barkann is the popular host of *Daily News Live,* on Comcast SportsNet, as well as host of the station's post-game show for all four pro sports teams. He has also worked for CBS Sports and the USA Network covering the Olympics and U.S. Open Tennis Tournament. He does not like to discuss his brief term broadcasting the XFL.

### 10. Clarke Drops the A-word on TV—Bob Clarke, Wachovia Center, March 16, 2000.

The Eric Lindros era had reached Its low ebb in Philadelphia during the spring of 2000. On March 4, Lindros suffered a concussion in Boston on a hit from defenseman Hal Gill. Afterward, Lindros' parents accused the Flyers' training staff of ignoring the warning signs of a concussion and letting him play four more games before he was pulled from the lineup with severe headaches.

Between periods of a home game against the Canadiens, Clarke held an impromptu session with the media in the Wachovia Center press box. He denied the allegations and told reporters they could have gotten their own answers from the Flyers trainers.

"But you don't let us talk to the trainers," protested *The Inquirer's* Tim Panaccio.

"Sure I do," Clarke said. "They just won't talk to you, because you're an asshole."
His words were broadcast live on Comcast SportsNet. No seven-second delay. No "bleep." And no subsequent apology from Clarke.

### 9. Made in the Shade(s)—Jim McMahon, Veterans Stadium, July 17, 1990.

The Eagles had just signed veteran quarterback Jim McMahon to back up Randall Cunningham. The media packed into the small pressroom on the fourth floor of the Vet, waiting to talk to Jimmy Mac.

As a joke, the Eagles' media relations department handed out sunglasses to everyone in attendance. The purpose was to have a little fun with McMahon, who always wore shades and was himself a perennial prankster—and media hater. McMahon walked in, took a look around, answered all the questions, and never once acknowledged everyone wearing the sunglasses!

Finally, a reporter asked McMahon what he thought about everyone's shades. He peered out at everyone with a look of indifference, as if to say, "I don't get it, and I don't want to get it."

### 8. Pull the Choke! Pull the Choke!—Terry Murray, Joe Louis Arena, Detroit, June 6, 1997.

"Many teams have been through these problems before. Basically, it's a choking situation for our team right now."

With those words, Flyers Coach Terry Murray basically pushed his team from three-games-to-none down to the golf course for the summer.

One day after the Flyers had lost, 6-1, at Detroit, Murray told reporters that the Flyers were on the brink of a choke against the Wings in the Stanley Cup Finals. He told the team as much in a meeting and then repeated it to reporters.

What were captain Eric Lindros' thoughts on hearing Murray's remarks? No one knew at the time—Lindros skipped out on the media, sneaking through the stands of Joe Louis arena. Later that day, Detroit swept the Flyers with a 2-1 win in Game Four. A choke? Or were the Flyers simply overmatched? It was probably the latter, but no matter—one week later Terry Murray was fired.

## 7. The Coach Burns Out—Dick Vermeil, Veterans Stadium, January 10, 1983.

Dick Vermeil was the best coach the Eagles had seen since Buck Shaw, and the first coach to take them to the Super Bowl. But, after seven seasons, Vermeil had reached his end. After a crushing 1982 season, in which NFL players struck for seven games and the Birds finished 3-6, Vermeil decided he had nothing left to give. The first sign, he later said, was that tension had made his neck so tight he couldn't turn his head from side to side. Some players feared he was nearing a nervous breakdown. So he called everyone to the Vet two weeks after the season.

"I'm just burned out," he announced. He talked of spending too many nights sleeping on his office couch and too many 6 a.m. mornings breaking down the film one more time. With red-rimmed eyes and a quavering voice, the coach's coach stepped down.

"I'm my own worst enemy," he said. "Far too intense, far too emotional. . . . My problem is the highs don't last long enough and the lows linger for days. It gnaws at your insides."

Vermeil spent the next 14 years as a TV football analyst. In 1997 he became the head coach of the St. Louis Rams and, three years later, led them to a Super Bowl win. He retired after that, but returned to coach the Kansas City Chiefs for five strong years.

## 6. Carlton the Door, Man—Bill Giles, Veterans Stadium, June 25, 1986.

Nearly three months into the 1986 season, Steve Carlton was struggling big time. For 14-plus seasons, Lefty had pitched his heart out for the Phillies. He was—and still is—the second-winningest left-hander ever. But he had pitched horribly the first three months of the season and twice had to meet with Bill Giles to convince the Phillies owner he could still pitch. Finally, Giles made the tough decision to cut Lefty loose.

At a hastily called news conference, Giles tearfully announced that the Phillies had released Lefty. Asked for Carlton's reaction upon hearing the news, Giles said, "He didn't say a whole lot other than 'I can still pitch.'"

## 5. Who Let the Dogs Out?—Mike McCormack, Veterans Stadium, September 29, 1975.

McCormack was in his third season as coach of the Eagles. The Birds had gone 7-7 in 1974, and things seemed to be taking shape. But the Birds lost their first two games of 1975 and, at the regular Monday news conference, reporter Tom Brookshier asked the coach, "Mike, how many dogs do you have on the roster?"

To everyone's surprise, McCormack answered: "If you're talking about real mutts, I'd say two."

The next week, as the Eagles hosted the Redskins, fans at the Vet tossed a huge inflatable dog bone around the stands, and chanted, "Al-po, Al-po."

Then, at season's end, they waved goodbye to Mike McCormack and hello to . . . Dick Vermeil.

**4. Deep Schmidt—Mike Schmidt, Jack Murphy Stadium, San Diego, May 29, 1989.**
"I feel like I could easily ask, uh, the Phillies to make me a part-time player, and to hang around for a couple years, to add to my, uh, statistical totals. However, my respect for the game, my teammates, the fans, won't allow me to do that. For these reasons, I've decided to retire as an active player."

For 17-plus seasons, Mike Schmidt played third base for the Phillies. He was the town's greatest enigma. Fans loved him. They hated him. They stood for him. They booed him. He won it all. He couldn't catch a break. He once said Philadelphia was the only town where a player could "experience the thrill of victory, and the agony of reading about it the next day." One thing Phillies fans knew for certain was Schmidt's place in history. No one ever played third base any better. He was a Hall of Fame lock.

At age 39, Schmidt knew his skills were abandoning him. He had allowed a costly error the night before at San Francisco. So, on a Monday afternoon at Jack Murphy Stadium, just two hours before the Phils were to play the Padres, he said goodbye to baseball. Actually, he cried goodbye to baseball. It was a site to behold coming from a man who almost never displayed any public emotion at all.

"Some 18 years ago, I left Dayton, Ohio, with two very bad knees and a dream to become a major-league baseball player . . . and . . . uh. . . . ."

He began to cry.

"I thank God the dream came true. . . ."

Sobbing, he stopped speaking. After Schmidt was unable to compose himself for about a minute, Phillies president Bill Giles took over the microphone. He eloquently thanked Schmidt for "over 7,000 hours of baseball in a Phillies uniform," and for the work ethic that never accepted mediocrity.

At his most vulnerable moment, Schmidt was the man. He truly was.

**3. "I'll Kick Your Ass!"—John Chaney, Amherst, MA., February 13, 1994.**
After Temple's one-point loss at U Mass, head coach John Chaney interrupted Minuteman coach John Calipari's news conference, pointing a finger and shouting, "Next time I see you, I'll kick your ass!"

Calipari had confronted two of the referees following the game. Chaney thought he should have been present during any post-game meeting with the refs and blew the roof off Calipari's newser. Beautiful. Come on now, didn't you want to see what would have happened had Coach reached his destination and gotten his hands on a little Calipari booty?

**2. "Next Question!"—Terrell Owens/Drew Rosenhaus, Moorestown, N.J., November 8, 2005.**
One sunny day in South Jersey, Terrell Owens vainly tried to save his Eagles career. He had been suspended for remarks he made about quarterback Donovan McNabb in a nationally telecast interview on ESPN. TO said that had Brett Favre been quarterbacking the Eagles, the team would be undefeated.

Owens had already been given two chances to apologize, and failed to do so. The first time, in a media gathering at the Eagles practice facility, he expressed regret to everyone but McNabb. A day later, he was given the chance to apologize to the whole team, and refused. Coach Andy Reid suspended Owens for the Eagles' Sunday Night game at Washington, which the Birds lost 17-10. Following the game, the Eagles lengthened

Owens's suspension to four weeks, which had him singing a different tune—in front of his house.

So, that Tuesday, TO declared his respect for his quarterback—oh, it was beautiful—and apologized up and down and back and forth. The *piece de resistance,* however, came from his agent, Drew Rosenhaus—who undid any chance Owens had of reinstatement by acting like a buffoon.

Rosenhaus read a statement calling Owens a "great person" and said, "He is here again today to make sure that everyone understands that he is making an apology."

But when asked specifically about his client's plight, Rosenhaus could only reply, "Next question!" Thirteen times.

### 1. Practice Makes Perfect—Allen Iverson, Wachovia Center, May 7, 2002.

This has to be the all-timer. Allen Iverson—tortured by his coach, the media, and the Sixers' first-round playoff loss to the Celtics—was incredulous that anyone would wonder about his workout habits. When asked about how much time he actually put in practicing, AI couldn't take it any more and delivered this soliloquy:

"I'm supposed to be the franchise player, and we're in here talking about practice. I mean, listen, we're talking about practice. Not a game. Not a game. Not a game. We're talking about practice. Not a game. Not the game that I go out there and die for and play every game like it's my last. Not the game. We're talking about practice, man. I mean how silly is that? And we're talking about practice."

I don't think any player ever put his insides on the outside like AI.

## What if . . .

Philadelphia sports fans are always left to wonder, "What if we had drafted this guy over that guy?" Or, "What if the superstar hadn't been injured that season?" Or, "What if our clubs' owners weren't such a band of blithering idiots?"

We are left with too few championships. Instead, we live in the Land of What Might Have Been.

Ahh, what might have been. We've assembled a list here of 20 of the biggest "what ifs" in Philadelphia sports history—each of which would have dramatically affected our sports lives.

What if . . .

**20. The Phillies—and not the A's—had packed up and left town back in 1954?** For the first half of this century, this was a two-team city. Both losers, by the way. The A's went on to 14 post-season appearances and four world championships since moving on. The Phils . . . well, not so successful. Not that the A's would have enjoyed all that success if they'd stayed here. We're just saying.

**19. Vince Lombardi had taken the Eagles head coaching job when it was offered in 1958?** Lombardi was a New York assistant at the time, and Giants owner Wellington Mara talked him out of coming here by saying the Eagles were a second-rate organization. The irony is that the Eagles hired Buck Shaw who—two years later—beat Lombardi's Green Bay Packers in the NFL title game. Still, for the long term, who wouldn't want Lombardi?

**18. The Cuban Missile Crisis had never occurred?** Huh? What's the sports connection, you ask? Well, here's the story: In October 1962, the three Kennedy brothers—President John, Attorney General Bobby, and future Senator Teddy—were chatting about what they might do after Jack was finished in the White House. Teddy noted that Eagles owner Jim Clark had just died and the team was up for sale. The President ordered him to immediately meet with team management. Alas, the next day—moments before Ted Kennedy was to board a train for Philadelphia—American spy planes revealed the presence of Soviet missiles in Cuba. The football plan got sidetracked and never was revisited.

**17. Phils pitcher Art Mahaffey hadn't been spooked by the sight of Reds rookie Chico Ruiz insanely breaking for home in the sixth inning of a scoreless game that September afternoon in 1964?** Mahaffey threw the ball away, the Phils lost the game, 1-0, and the great swoon was on. Did Ruiz's steal of home lead to every other mistake that created the infamous 10-game losing streak? Had Mahaffey's throw hit catcher Clay Dalrymple's glove, would the Phils have kept their 6-1/2 game lead?

**16. The 1968–69 La Salle basketball team hadn't been on probation and, thus, ineligible to play in the NCAA Tournament?** The Explorers finished 23-1 that season under new coach Tom Gola, but had to stay home because of violations under former coach Jim Harding. They were ranked No. 2 at the end of the regular season. Could they have challenged Lew Alcindor and his powerhouse UCLA squad?

**15. The Phillies had recognized that Dallas Green knew their farm system pretty damn well when—**as the Cubs new general manager in 1982—he insisted that the Larry Bowa-for-Ivan DeJesus trade be sweetened by including a minor-league third baseman whose path here was blocked by Mike Schmidt? Green moved the kid to second base and Ryne Sandberg went on the have a Hall of Fame career in Chicago.

**14. The NCAA Men's Basketball Tournament had started using the shot clock one year earlier?** The Villanova Wildcats took just 10 second-half shots in their brilliant win over Georgetown in 1985. It was the last season without the clock, and there's no way Nova could have frozen the ball under the new rules. Taking things one step further: 1985 was also the first year the Tournament expanded from 48 to 64 teams. Nova—an eight seed—probably would have been left out under the old setup. Sometimes, timing is everything, eh Rollie?

**13. Leonard Tose had actually moved the Eagles to Phoenix in 1985?** Would we have quickly gotten a replacement team? Would it have been called the Eagles? Could we have ever gotten used to dressing in different colors, say purple and black, and heading down to the Vet to chant out P-R-E-T-Z-E-L-S . . . Pretzels!?!?

**12. Someone had the common sense to take away Pelle Lindbergh's car keys that night back in 1985?**

**11. Harold Katz hadn't concluded that Brad Daugherty was "soft" after working him out at Katz's Villanova home back in 1986?** Katz's not-so-temporary insanity led to two of the all-time worst trades, both on draft day that year: Sending the first-overall pick (which became Daugherty) to Cleveland for journeyman Roy Hinson and—even worse—trading Moses Malone, Terry Catledge, and two first-rounders to Washington for Cliff Robinson (who spent the next three seasons being intimidated by Charles Barkley) and Jeff Ruland (whose lower leg seemed to fall off every time he got up from a chair).

**10. Cris Carter had been able to get clean before Buddy Ryan had to cut him in 1990?** Carter caught 89 passes as an Eagle—and 1,012 after Ryan released him. Carter cleaned up and the Vikings signed him. Shouldn't we have benefited from that greatness?

**9. The Phils had recognized Jeff Jackson as nothing more than a good high school player on draft day in 1989?** They picked Jackson with the fourth overall pick, passing up an Auburn first baseman named Frank Thomas. Jackson never reached the bigs; Thomas went on to have 10 seasons with 100-plus RBIs.

**8. The Flyers had believed in scouting Eastern Europe a little earlier—say 1990?** That's the year they spent the fourth overall pick of the draft on an Ontario plugger named Mike Ricci, bypassing Czech sensation Jaromir Jagr.

**7. Green Bay's Bryce Paup hadn't cut through the line in the first quarter of the first game in 1991, injuring Randall Cunningham's leg?** The Eagles' defense was so dominant that season that they went 10-6 with the likes of Brad Goebel and Jeff Kemp at quarterback. Imagine what they might have done with the Ultimate Weapon.

**6. NHL arbitrator Larry Bertuzzi had ruled Eric Lindros property of the Rangers—not the Flyers—back in 1992?** Peter Forsberg (part of the deal that brought No. 88 here) would have played out his brilliant career in Philadelphia. The Flyers also would have kept Ron Hextall, two first-round draft picks, Chris Simon, Ricci, and a few other muckers. Would the two Stanley Cups Forsberg won in Colorado instead have been paraded down Broad Street?

**5. Jim Fregosi had left Larry Andersen in to pitch the ninth inning of Game 6 in the 1993 World Series?** Hell, the fans all knew that Mitch Williams was shot—how come Fregosi didn't see it? "Touch 'em all, Joe. You'll never hit a bigger home run."

**4. Eagles owner Jeff Lurie had fired Ray Rhodes when he should have—after the 1997 season—and promoted offensive coordinator Jon Gruden to head coach?** Instead, Gruden became head coach in Oakland and then Tampa Bay, where his Bucs beat the Birds in the 2002 NFC Championship game—on their way to a Super Bowl win.

**3. Matt Geiger had waived his no-trade clause back in the summer of 2000?** A complicated four-team trade that July would have sent Geiger—and Allen Iverson (!)—to Detroit, bringing Glen Rice and Eddie Jones to the Sixers. But Geiger refused to give up a $5 million trade kicker and the Pistons, unable to add that much to their salary cap, backed out. Given a reprieve, Iverson won the scoring title in 2000–01, leading the Sixers to the NBA Finals. Iverson won the MVP that season, although, looking back, maybe the true MVP was Geiger—just for his selfishness.

**2. Blaine Bishop had the common sense to tell Andy Reid that his pulled groin muscle kept him from running in the 2002 NFC Championship Game against the Tampa Bay Bucs?** Instead, Bishop kept his mouth shut and Joe Jurevicius caught a short crossing pass that he easily took 71 yards down the field while Bishop chased after him like Fred Sanford. Bishop said afterwards that he worried teammates would question his guts if he signaled to have rookie Michael Lewis replace him in the Eagles secondary. Instead, we'll forever question his brains.

**1. Big Daddy's wife hadn't picked Smarty Jones in the 2004 Belmont Stakes pool down at the Deauville Inn in Strathmere.** We're still convinced that had Debby pulled another slip out of the hat, Philadelphia's favorite horse wouldn't have blown that lead down the stretch and would have captured the Triple Crown.

# Our 10 Favorite Gambling Movies

Sports and gambling have gone together since the days some Roman bet on how quickly the lion would devour the Christian. Just tell it to Pete Rose, Paul Hornung, Jeremy Roenick, Rick Tocchet, and many more.

Hollywood figured out this allure a long time ago. Movie makers deduced how much we love to gamble and, thus, enjoy watching other people gamble.

With due respect to *Hard Eight, The Grifters, House Of Games, Bad Lieutenant, The Odd Couple, Lock, Stock and Two Smoking Barrels, Easy Money, The Pope Of Greenwich Village, Boiler Room* and *Guys and Dolls* . . . here are ten of the best.

**10. *Casino*, 1995.** When this movie first came out, it felt like a lame rip-off of *Goodfellas*, released five years earlier and also directed by Martin Scorsese. It's certainly not as good, but it captures the mindset and irresistibility of gambling well. Plus, it has fine performances from Sharon Stone and Don Rickles—and how often can you say that about a flick?

**9. *Ocean's 11*, 1960 & 2001.** Again, we're not saying either of these movies should win an Oscar (they didn't), but they're a lot of fun because of great casts and engaging capers. Frank Sinatra, George Clooney, Dean Martin, Brad Pitt, Sammy Davis Jr., Julia Roberts, Don Cheadle, Angie Dickinson (who appears in both), Matt Damon, and many others.

**8. *Let It Ride*, 1989.** A critical and box-office dud that still manages to get mentioned in half the movie topics we bring up on WIP. Rarely on cable, not on any most-rented list, but it made one hell of an impression on the handful of people who saw it—including us. Richard Dreyfuss is a lot of laughs as the racetrack degenerate. David Johansen's goofy performance as his sidekick makes you wonder what happened to his acting career. And Michelle Phillips and Jennifer Tilly make for good eye candy. Plus you get Teri Garr in her usual performance as a nagging housewife. Co-written by Nancy Dowd, who gave us the immortal *Slapshot*.

**7. *The Cooler*, 2003.** What we love about *The Cooler* is that it addresses the fact that no matter how hard you try to play an angle, or count cards, or try to outsmart your opponent, sometimes winning and losing comes down to just pure luck. William H. Macy plays a "cooler," a casino employee who cools off winning casino gamblers simply by sitting next to them. Maria Bello, Alec Baldwin, Paul Sorvino, Ron Livingston, and N'sync's Joey Fatone round out an excellent cast. Okay, well maybe not Fatone.

**6. *Atlantic City*, 1980.** Two of the glamorous attractions of gambling are the false sense that you are a big shot going for the score, and the sense that you're doing something a little "bad." Nothing captures this better than *Atlantic City*. Burt Lancaster, in a note-perfect performance, portrays an elderly mobster wannabe who has been around Atlantic City long enough to remember when gambling was illegal there. Nice shots of the town, and of Susan Sarandon in an unforgettable scene with lemons. That's the fruit and her, uh, own lemons.

**5. *Rounders*, 1998.** This movie helped start the national poker obsession of today's high school and college generation. Although the usually reliable Matt Damon is miscast as the baby-faced phenom, Edward Norton and John Malkovich are dead-on perfect. It's just one of those flicks that's impossible to pass while channel surfing. The excellent cast is rounded out by John Turturro, Famke Janssen, and the great Martin Landau.

**4. *The Sting*, 1973.** Refreshingly, this is the only film on this list that doesn't attempt to "look into the soul" of what makes a gambler tick—other than Paul Newman and Robert Redford knowing that Robert Shaw can't walk away from a bet that he perceives as being a sure thing. The only picture on this list to win the Oscar for Best Picture. Jack Nicholson turned down the Redford part.

**3. *The Hustler*, 1961.** Hmm, back-to-back Paul Newman films—and they couldn't be more different. Dark and depressing from beginning to end, with Newman giving an incredible performance as "Fast Eddie" Felson. The only thing that keeps *The Hustler* from topping this list is that we're not sure it's not more about being willing to stop at nothing to be the best than it is about the allure of actually winning the money. Most gamblers who play at casinos and racetracks know they're never going to be the tops at anything. They're just gamblers. Newman, in *The Hustler,* is after more. All four principal actors—George C. Scott, Jackie Gleason, Piper Laurie, and Newman—were nominated for Oscars and none of them won. Newman won years later reprising the role in the overrated *The Color of Money.*

**2. *The Gambler,* 1974.** We're sure many of you know at least one guy who, despite having lost everything to gambling (and we mean everything), just can't stop himself. James Caan is dynamite as the out-of-control, self-loathing degenerate Axel Freed. A brooding film with a weird ending, it's not to be missed. Paul Sorvino is exceptional as the bookie, and look for James Woods in a tiny role. By the way, how can a household name like Caan still be underrated?

**1. *California Split,* 1974.** We guess '74 was the year of neglected gambling films, eh? George Segal and Elliott Gould play degenerate gamblers who couldn't be more different in every way but one: They just can't live without the "juice" that only gambling can provide. Segal plays the shy, reflective type and Gould is a fun-loving free spirit who sees nothing but the instant gratification that gambling provides and feels no guilt about it. Cards, racetracks, pro and college games, pick-up basketball—these two will bet on anything. It's sexy, hilarious, and actually suspenseful at the end. Trust us, and seek this film out on DVD.

# Ten Extremely Lucky Philadelphia Athletes

Since the day Joey Caveman threw a rock further than Felix Caveman, it was Joey that was gonna score the awesome-looking babes. Chicks dig the "long ball." They dig the uniform, the money, the fame, the whole nine yards. You think Marilyn Monroe would have looked at Joe DiMaggio if he was just another San Francisco fisherman like his Dad? We think not. Here are some local jocks you won't see perusing the local classifieds the next time they need a date. By the way, this is a really impressive list.

**10. Randall Cunningham and Whitney Houston.** Before Randall tied the knot, rumor had it that he had the hots for Bobby Brown's future "better" half. Anyone who has seen Whitney's act on *Being Bobby Brown* knows that Randall could have married Janet Reno and made out better. Whitney is bats.

**9. Cole Hamels and Heidi Strobel.** When Cole was brought up to the Majors he said he called his girlfriend first, then his parents. Well, we can certainly understand that. This beauty was a contestant on *Survivor: The Amazon* and lasted 33 days on that show—but not before she stripped to get some Oreo cookies. (Who wouldn't?) This led to a cover shot on *Playboy.* Thanks, Cole, for making it easier to be a Phillies fan.

**8. Bo Belinsky and Mamie Van Doren.** This Phils pitcher once threw a no-hitter for the Angels, but that was the highlight of his short 28-51 career. Bo had a much better record with the ladies, dating many playmates and Hollywood starlets, including blonde bombshell Mamie. She did well herself, bedding luminaries such as Elvis Presley, Warren Beatty, Steve McQueen, and Broadway Joe Namath.

**7. Petr Nedved and Veronika Verekova.** Sure, the Flyers improved by adding Nedved, but so did the overall look of the crowd with the addition of his *Sports Illustrated* swimsuit model wife.

**6. Rodney Peete and Holly Robinson.** If you were married to this gorgeous TV star, you'd be smiling all the time too.

**5. Charles Barkley and Madonna.** It was Madonna's legendary appearance on the Letterman show on March 31st, 1994, when she strongly hinted that she had "known" Sir Charles intimately. It's the same Letterman show where Madonna drops the F-bomb 13 times in a 20-minute appearance, a network television record at the time.

**4. A.J. Feeley and Heather Mitts.** We can't help it. We're old school. When we see a beautiful woman, we expect her to be dating the absolute cream of the crop. It kills us when we see a great-looking dish on the arms of some dork. And when you're as spectacular looking as Heather and one of the world's premiere female athletes, former Eagles quarterback A.J. qualifies as a dork. He's barely a backup for crying out loud. We were backups!

**3. Kobe and Vanessa Bryant.** If you think there is a chance you would have never heard of our $4 million rock-wearing girl, then think again. Kobe discovered her while she was dancing in a video for Snoop Dogg (when she was 17), and you know the Dogg just doesn't use Alpo for his videos.

**2. Chris Webber and Tyra Banks.** Maybe Chris's game wasn't quite what it once was when he came to the Sixers, but we can only pray that this "on-again-off-again" relationship with maybe the most beautiful model of all time is ON ON ON!

**1. Alexander Daigle and Pamela Anderson.** We don't care if it was only one date. This is Pamela Anderson we're talking about! How did this underachieving hockey player do it? We wish the Flyers had realized this left-winger was a dud as quickly as Pam did.

## Best Mustaches in Philadelphia :: Lou Tilley

Note: Seven-time Emmy Award winner Lou Tilley is the host of CN8's Out of Bounds, a nightly look at the issues shaping the sports world. The Philadelphia native has been a staple on local television for more than 20 years.

## Special Awards

**Coaches' Division:** Temple basketball coach Fran Dunphy leads a strong field. Who knows how many back-door plays Fran keeps stored inside that broom? Andy Reid is a close second; former Eagles assistant Jeff Fisher had a great one; and Fred (The Fog) Shero seemed so lost in thought he may never have known that he even wore one.

**The Intimidators:** All Phillies relievers. Jose Mesa's was bandito mean and snarly. Sparky Lyle's was long, waxed, and a little gnarly. Mitch Williams' needed some spackle.

**Media:** I give myself the nod here; I thought it defined me. On my recent 20th anniversary in Philly, I shaved it, hoping to take back a decade. Retired WIP host Steve Fredericks is forever young in his. Jim Gardner of Channel 6 has the last of the great tubers, and we suspect that radio veteran John DeBella would be a soprano without his.

**Broad Brush Bullies:** Rick MacLeish tops the list, with Dave Schultz, Bob Kelly, Don Saleski, Orest Kindrachuk, and Bernie Parent all wearing facial hair for the orange-and-black. Do you see the connection to the intimidating relievers?

## And Now, the Top 10

**10. Lou Tilley.** Pardon my indulgence. I kept it for 28 years. I was bucking the recent clean-shaven trend, until ESPN's Dan Patrick referred to it (on my show) as "a leftover from the Ron Jeremy, bad-porn era." End of era. End of 'stache.

**9. Reggie Jackson** (Philly native). His growth was so lush that Sports Illustrated put him on the cover of its 1972 baseball issue. There was history here. Did you know that, before Reggie, the last Major League player with a mustache was Philadelphia A's catcher Wally Schang, way back in 1914? Look it up.

**8. Julius Erving.** Most people remember the great 'Fro. But, while Doc trimmed the head, he left the lip intact. Struggled with gray strands in later days.

**7. Mike Quick.** For African-American guys, the mustache is often standard issue (see Arthur Fennell, Ukee Washington), but for Mike it was more than the usual pencil-thin growth. Set the local standard.

**6. Ron Jaworski.** Like his nickname, it revolves around his mouth. Started out with the full beard, pulled back to the mustache, and then, like yours truly, tried to trim years by trimming the remains.

**5. Rick MacLeish.** A personal all-time favorite. He's still wearing it. It still has desired effect. Here was one Broad Street Bully who almost never dropped the gloves. He never had to. The look said it all.

**4. Mike Schmidt.** He said it was because of some skin problems. My personal suspicion: trying to hide behind it. Nicely groomed. Consistent coloring. Think of Schmitty, you see the 'stache.

**3. Cris Carter.** Took it to the extreme. Runaway winner in the Groucho Marx division.

**2. Tim Rossovich.** Surprise! A standout for God-awful "Joe Must Go" Eagles team. So tough he ate glass—literally. A Pro Bowl linebacker who also played defensive end at 225 pounds. The mustache, it was believed, was an extension of his chest hair.

**1. Fran Dunphy.** There may be no face, no voice, no att-tee-tude that better exemplifies a native Philadelphia jock. Quiet? Shy? Withdrawn? Don't believe it. Understated, passive? You'd better not "D-up" this former La Salle guard with those thoughts. The mustache serves as cover for the genius—and the snarl.

We can be sports fans for the next 50 years, and here are 10 things we're fairly certain that we'll never see again.

**10. The likes of Karl Wallenda's high-wire stunts at the Vet.** Given the cost of liability insurance these days, no team would take the chance of allowing a 67-year-old circus act to perform headstands 200 feet above the paying customers on a tightrope.

**9. An arena closed because the roof blew off.** It happened at the Spectrum on March 1, 1968, during a matinee performance of the Ice Capades. The Sixers finished their season at Convention Hall; the Flyers moved their home games to Quebec City.

**8. A 30-year-old Eagles season-ticket holder make the team as a walk-on.** Vince Papale—who never even played college football—did it in 1976. He stayed with the club for three years as a hard-nosed special-teams player. Disney ended up making a movie of his life, called *Invincible*.

**7. A hockey game cancelled for a president's speech.** Nine days after September 11, 2001, a preseason contest between the Flyers and New York Rangers was delayed before the third period so that President Bush's address to the nation could be broadcast on the Wachovia Center's Jumbotron screen. When it came time to resume the game, players on both sides agreed that—given the magnitude of the president's words—it would be inappropriate to resume playing hockey. They shook hands and skated off as 14,000 fans applauded in agreement.

**6. A team president actually solicit the opinions of the fans.** When Pat Croce recognized in 1997 that his 76ers had an image problem with the customers, he invited all the season-ticket holders down to the arena for a gripe session. And he really listened to their ideas. Sadly, we don't expect any other local sports owner to follow Croce's lead.

**5. A goalie lose sight of a puck in the sun.** It happened the last game of the 1969–70 season, when the glare coming through an open window at the Spectrum caused Bernie Parent to lose track of a fluttering shot from center ice and give up a rare cheap goal. The 1-0 loss cost the Flyers a playoff berth.

**4. A barefoot kicker.** By most accounts, there have been just four in the history of the NFL. Two of them—Tony Franklin and Paul McFadden—played for the Eagles in the 1980s. Since there hasn't been another since 1990, we're pretty sure we've seen the last of the shoeless ones.

**3. A baseball game that ends at 4:45 a.m. or starts at 1:25 a.m.** On July 2-3, 1993, six hours of rain delays turned a twi-night double-header between the Phils and San Diego Padres into an all-night event at the Vet. When Mitch Williams finally ended the marathon with a run-scoring single, it was the morning rush hour that fans had to worry about.

**2. A middle-aged physician picked in the NBA draft.** Sixers owner Harold Katz was pretty bored toward the end of the 1983 draft. When the 10th round finally rolled around, he used the team's choice to select Norman Horvitz from Philadelphia Pharmaceutical College. Horvitz happened to be a 50-ish doctor who worked for Katz's Nutri-Systems, Inc. (The pick was later deemed ineligible.)

**1. Players switch teams in the middle of an NBA game.** It started on November 8, 1978 and ended four months later, as the Sixers beat the New Jersey Nets in a contest that featured three players suiting up for both sides.
Here's the story behind the story: The game initially ended with the Sixers winning in double-overtime and the Nets protesting some highly questionable calls by the referees. NBA Commissioner Larry O'Brien upheld the Nets' protest and ordered the game resumed with six minutes left in the third quarter—the time of the refs' mistakes. The teams were told to finish the game March 23, 1979, before another scheduled Sixers-Nets contest at the Spectrum.
Except there was one further complication. On Feb. 7, 1979, the Sixers traded Harvey Catchings and Ralph Simpson to the Nets for Eric Money. The league ruminated, then decided to let all the players participate in the game for their new teams. So the three men appear on both sides of the box score.
Oh, and the Sixers won the suspended game. Again. They also took the second game of the faux double-header.

They come, they go, they come back again—as players, coaches, broadcasters, or executives. Here are some of the best—and worst—second acts in Philadelphia sports history. A couple of names—say Bill Barber and Larry Bowa—could arguably make either list. Here's hoping that Mo Cheeks changes the luck of prodigal sons returning as coaches.

## Best

**10. Ron Hextall.** He wasn't as brilliant coming back after a two-year exile as he was as the angry young goalie breaking in back in 1986. Still, Hexy was a key part of the Flyers rise in the mid-90s and a guy whose level of play always improved in the playoffs (yeah, you don't have to tell us about Claude Lemieux). Won 130 games in his first tour; 110 in his second. Not too shabby.

**9. Aaron McKie.** With Eddie Jones, he formed the best 1-2 combo in Temple history back in the early 1990s. Kicked around the NBA for three-plus seasons before joining the Sixers in December 1997. Immediately stepped up his game and became a key cog in Larry Brown's squad that made it to the 2001 Finals. For seven-and-a-half seasons, McKie again graced his hometown with dignity.

**8. Bobby/Bob Clarke.** As a player, "Bobby" was the best in franchise history. We don't need to tell you that. As a general manager—in two distinct tours—"Bob" has had his ups and downs. But the franchise, under his direction, is always at the top of the standings.

**7. Jeremiah Trotter.** Let's see, he came to the Eagles as a third-round pick in 1998, worked his way to Pro Bowl status, and left in a messy divorce after the 2001 season. Signed a huge free agent contract with Washington, where he went through two seasons injured and unhappy. Made up with Andy Reid in 2004 and came home—where he worked his way from the special teams back to the Pro Bowl. A leader and a class act.

**6. Dallas Green.** He was a hard-living relief pitcher who went 20-22 for the Phillies in four seasons in the early 1960s. Came back to manage in 1979 and, the following year, led the Phils to the only World Series win in their 120-plus-year history. They say that mediocre players make the best managers. Mr. Green is walking proof.

**5. Tom Gola.** In the 1940s, he starred at La Salle High. In the 1950s, he led La Salle College to the NCAA title. Had a nice pro playing career with the Philadelphia (and San Francisco) Warriors, helping win the 1956 NBA championship. Then he went back to La Salle to coach the 1968–69 squad that went 23-1. Finished it up with a successful local political career. Not much question why they named La Salle's arena after him, eh?

**4. Wilt Chamberlain.** There's simply no way that Act II with the Sixers could match Act I with the Warriors (or even, to those who may remember, the prequel career at Overbrook High). Still, Wilt averaged 27.6 points per game during his four-year return and we needn't remind you of his role on the 1966–67 team that went 68-13 and cruised to an NBA title.

**3. Billy Cunningham.** A three-act play, actually. In the first scene, the Kangaroo Kid plays sixth-man and rising star on that great Sixers team centered by Chamberlain. Then he departs for the ABA (remember the Carolina Cougars?). In the second scene, Cunningham returns to Philadelphia in 1974, only to have his career end two years later with a serious knee injury. Scene three—the finale—has Billy C. as the greatest coach in Sixers history, winning 520 games and the 1982–83 NBA Title. We're still lobbying for another encore.

**2. Bernie Parent.** What, you didn't know? Yes, Bernie did two tours of duty—the so-so and the outstanding. The first time around, from 1967–71, he was decent, nothing more. The Flyers traded him to Toronto for some scoring punch (getting Rick MacLeish in a turnaround trade to Boston), and Parent eventually ended up in the fledgling WHA. In 1973 he returned to the Flyers. When he did, Bernie became the most important cog on the team that won two Stanley Cups. In 1984 he became the first Flyer elected to the Hockey Hall of Fame.

**1. Richie Ashburn.** There are two groups of "Whitey" fans. The Old Heads who recall him as a fleet-as-a-deer center-fielder, and the Almost-as-Old Heads who grew up listening to him marvelously describe Phillies games on radio and TV. Both groups are privileged. Ashburn spent 12 years roaming Shibe Park and slapping his way to a .311 batting average. He left for three seasons to play out the string, before returning in 1963 to try his hand in broadcasting. The second career lasted 35 years—including 27 in which he and partner Harry Kalas made up the most beloved broadcasting team in city history.

## Worst:

**10. Pete Retzlaff.** As a player, "The Baron" was probably the most popular Eagle in the early- and mid-60s. He was the prototype of today's pass-catching NFL tight ends—blocking down on a defensive end on one play and snatching a long gainer on the next. His 1965 stats (66 receptions, 1,190 yards, 10 TDs) were astounding for the era. Not so astounding was Retzlaff's work as Eagles general manager from 1969–72. He resigned after a four-year record of 15-37-4. The fans who cheered Retzlaff the player booed Retzlaff the GM.

**9. Jim Bunning.** A Hall of Famer who won 74 games in four seasons (1964–67) for the Phils, each year finishing in the top five on the National League ERA list. And, of course, there was that perfect game. He moved on to Pittsburgh and Los Angeles before coming back in 1970 at the tender age of 38. In two more seasons, on two hideous Phils squads, he went 15-27. A frustrating ending of a great career.

**8. Tim Perry.** Had a real nice career at Temple in the mid-80s. Did you know that only Shaquille O'Neal, David Robinson, and Shawn Bradley ever blocked more shots in an NCAA Tournament game than Perry's eight against Lehigh in 1988? Was the seventh-overall pick in 1988, going to Phoenix, and we would have liked him fine there. But Perry came back in 1992 in the infamous trade that sent Charles Barkley to the Suns. For the next three-plus seasons we watched him ring up 7 points per game and wondered how Charles was doing out West.

**7. Kenny Jackson.** The Eagles selected this Penn State star with the fourth pick in the 1984 NFL draft (to be fair, it was a stinker of a class), and he averaged just 29 catches and three TDs in four seasons. So we all said goodbye. Somehow he ended up returning in 1990 to serve no apparent role beyond being Randall Cunningham's personal Mini-Me. Rumor had it that Buddy Ryan kept him around because the coach so enjoyed the honey-baked chicken from Jackson's Camden restaurant.

**6. Moses Malone.** If you look back at their history, the Sixers made a habit of bringing back once-great players long after their productive days were gone. Remember Wali Jones? Certainly, Malone's first four years here were brilliant and led to this city's last major sports championship. But when he wandered back in 1993, he was just some fat old CYO League refugee stuffed into that Number 2 jersey pretending to be the Great Moses. Kind of Sad.

**5. Pete Peeters.** In his first tenure with the Flyers, Peeters was a miserable guy, but a pretty good goalie, who was a big part of that 35-game unbeaten streak in 1979–80. In his second term, which ran from 1989–91, he was still a miserable guy—and a miserable goalie. One season he played in 24 games for the Flyers, and won exactly one.

**4. Derrick Coleman.** We hated him from the start, even though getting him in 1995 meant dumping Shawn Bradley. When the poison moved along to Charlotte in 1998, Sixers President Pat Croce vowed he would never have him back. Alas, Croce was gone from the franchise in October 2001 when Coach Larry Brown demanded a reunion with the lazy slug. In three more seasons there were occasional moments of motivation, lost among the general apathy that was DC.

**3. Marion Campbell.** He was an All-Pro defensive end who was critical to the Eagles 1960 NFL Championship. And he was a clever coordinator who ran the defense for Dick Vermeil's 1980 NFC Championship team. Too bad it didn't end there. Campbell became coach when Vermeil left in 1983. He rang up a three-year record of 17-29-1. To be fair, a lot of it wasn't Campbell's fault. But when you hear Eagles fans wax about the good old days of Vermeil or Buddy, they rarely recall that golden era of the "Swamp Fox."

**2. Andy Ashby.** One of those highly regarded prospects whom the local franchise always seems to let go, Ashby was twice an all-star after being drafted away from the Phils in '93. "What if he had stayed?" we always asked. We found out when he came back in 2000 (in a trade for Adam Eaton, another of those young prospects). He blended into Philadelphia like the Ayatollah, running up a 5.68 ERA by mid-season and going 1-6 at the Vet. He punctuated his final appearance by grabbing his crotch and inviting the local fans to get to know him more personally.

**1. Jim O'Brien.** This one will always be a mystery to us. How does a hometown guy—from Roman Catholic High and St. Joe's University—manage to take a city ready to embrace him and turn it against him so quickly? O'Brien did just that, through a coaching style that seemed to ignore logic and defense, and a cryptic manner that caused him to ponder every question as if it came from someone covered in dog poop. A less "Philly guy" you'll never meet.

# The Best Chants Emerging from the Seats in Philadelphia
## :: Larry Mendte

Note: Larry Mendte anchors CBS 3's *Eyewitness News* at 6 and 11 p.m. A native of Lansdowne, he began his news career delivering the *Evening Bulletin* as a boy. He is a graduate of Monsignor Bonner High School and West Chester University.

**10. "Dallas Sucks!"** Chanted by Eagles fans—sometimes without reason—as if all are afflicted with a strange epidemic of Tourette's. "Kobe Sucks!" is the Philadelphia pro basketball fans' cover of the same chant. (It almost brought Kobe to tears when the NBA All-Star game was played here in 2002.) And, of course, there is the very popular "Howard Sucks!" that seems to break out anytime Howard Eskin shows his face.

**9. "You're not Phil-ly!"** Here's a good one. In 2006, as Villanova was about to easily beat arch-rival Saint Joseph's in men's basketball—and clinch the Big 5 championship—the Wildcats' faithful started chanting, "We own Phil-ly, We own Phil-ly." To which Hawk fans reminded the fans from the Main Line that, "You're not Phil-ly, You're not Phil-ly!"

**8. "Over-rated."** Usually chanted when an underdog beats a nationally ranked team. But Philly fans are a different breed. When a mediocre Drexel team stayed with top-rated Duke in 2005 at a tournament in Madison Square Garden, Drexel fans started the chant, even though they lost by 10. Duke coach Mike Krzyzewski had to defend his team after the game. That's Philadelphia for you—we'll taunt you even when you are beating us.

**7. "Five For One."** The greeting Phillies fans gave Von Hayes when he arrived in 1983 after a trade with Cleveland for Manny Trillo, Julio Franco, George Vukovich, Jay Baller, and Jerry Willard. Hayes went on to have a decent career for the Phillies, but never lived down the chant that became his nickname.

**6. "Joe Must Go."** Sixty-thousand strong would scream this at Eagles Coach Joe Kuharich during every game of the 1968 season. A banner plane trailing the message even flew over Franklin Field. After 1968 Joe did go and was never heard from again.
A great variation on this came in 1992, during inept Giants Coach Ray Handley's last visit to the Vet. Knowing that Handley would soon face the ax, Eagles fans chanted, "Ray must stay."

**5. "T-O, T-O, T-O, T-O . . . T-O, T-O. "** It was music to Terrell Owens' ears and it is a reminder of how much this city loved T.O.—before we hated him. Sung to the tune of the European cheer, "Ole, Ole, Ole," Owens wanted the song played at Lincoln Financial Field every time he scored. The Eagles refused, but couldn't quiet the fans, who showered Owens with his favorite song whenever he crossed the goal line.

**4. "Booor-ing! Booor-ing!"** Penn students would recite this during painfully slow games with their archrival, Princeton. Before the 35-second shot clock was implemented, the Tigers used a slow-down offense. As in slooowwww-down. To be fair, it was boring.

**3. "That's alright, that's okay, you're going to work for us someday."** Saint Joe's Prep students would repeat this at basketball games when they lost to a team they felt was academically inferior.

**2. "We smell B-O-n-n-e-r."** Students from schools playing my alma mater in basketball chanted this during games. And Bonner fans would respond with, "It's your mother!" At least until the good Augustinian priests jumped off the bench and threatened "jug," a Bonner penance.

**1. "E-A-G-L-E-S . . . Eagles!!"** Such a common chant in this town, "Eagles" is the first word that most children here learn to spell. Practically a constant chant at the Linc, it is also used with a real Philly attitude at other sporting events. For instance, I remember one night, with the Phillies down 5-1, watching Larry Bowa pull Terry Adams for Rheal Cormier. Spontaneously the 400 Level started chanting, "E-A-G-L-E-S, EAGLES!" Now that is Philly!

# Great Players Who Came Here to Play Out the String

A lot of Hall of Famers played in Philadelphia—unfortunately too many of them earned their credentials elsewhere.

**9. Keith Millard.** A two-time Pro Bowler who set the NFL record for sacks by a defensive tackle (18) in 1989. Came here in 1993 to tag-team with William "Refrigerator" Perry (yes, "The Fridge" played two years in Philly) in the broken-down defensive linemen competition. His most notable deed was getting in a legendary locker-room fight with teammate Tommy Jeter.

**8. Tom Chambers.** What was this about? He averaged over 18 points per game during a 16-year career. Showed up at the Sixers in 1997, played one game (six points), and promptly retired. Was Larry Brown that unbearable?

**7. Dale Hawerchuk.** Scored 502 goals but remained somewhat unknown because he played in obscure outposts like Winnipeg and Buffalo. Landed in Philadelphia in 1995 for his moment in the limelight. Too late. Just 16 more goals in one-and-a-half seasons here.

**6. Andy Van Slyke.** Almost as big a star as Barry Bonds on the early-90's Pirates. Won five Gold Gloves and two Silver Slugger Awards his first 12 seasons. Came here in 1995, hit .243, and was most remembered for injuring a teenage girl dressed as Bert from Sesame Street because he thought it would be funny to punch a mascot in the face.

**5. Art Monk, James Lofton, Carlos Carson.** In the late '80s and early '90s, the Eagles kept trying to replace receivers Mike Quick and Cris Carter with once-great pass catchers residing on the scrap heap. Collectively, these three guys had 2,037 catches before getting to Vet Stadium—and just 20 while they were here.

**4. Paul Coffey.** Sixteen great seasons before he arrived in 1996 for a two-year gig as a turnstile. Flyers fans didn't boo him out of respect for his Hall of Fame career.

**3. Dale Murphy.** What a pleasure it was to watch this power-hitting outfielder and class act—at least during his years in Atlanta. When he came to the Phils in 1990, he still had the class—but none of the power . . . or bat speed . . . or foot speed.

**2. Bob McAdoo.** A Hall of Fame player, league MVP, and five-time NBA all-star who came here in his 14th—and final—season with two bad knees and no more energy left to tap. What we recall most from 1985 were the fans in the upper reaches of the Spectrum who used to pass a joint down the row and chant, "McAdoooooooooo."

**1. Danny Tartabull.** The all-time champ. In Kansas City he got votes for MVP. In various years, he led the American League in slugging percentage and highest salary. Hell, he even looked good on that episode of Seinfeld—remember him eating a donut with a knife and fork? Came to the Phils in 1997, went 0-for-7 in three games. Then he fouled a ball off his foot and never played again. Danny, we hardly knew ye.

# Big Daddy's Winter Olympics

If Philadelphia hosted the Winter Olympics, it would start with the lighting of the Official Olympic Trashcan down at the Italian Market. And Philadelphians would certainly take the gold in the following sports:

**10. Making obscene snowmen.** You know where to stick that carrot, don't you?

**9. Ice fishing in Cobbs Creek.** Terrific if you're trying to catch a car battery or an A&P shopping cart—since a fish ain't lived in that stream in over 100 years.

**8. Sledding on trash can lids.** No bobsleds, skeletons, or luges permitted. Who had money for sleds? My favorite winter wonderland scene was watching four guys (or better yet, one guy—preferably me—and three babes) come down a hill in a ripped-up refrigerator box.

**7. King of the Hill.** An awesome game to begin with, but truly Olympian in the slushy white stuff.

**6. Sticking your tongue on a flagpole.** There are plenty of flagpoles outside our sports venues. See whose tongue stays on the longest without calling an ambulance.

**5. Car bumper riding.** Not to be done on I-95 or the Schuylkill unless you're truly a professional. Best done on a small side street. You wait till a car stops at a red light, sneak behind it, grab the rear bumper, sit your ass down in the snow and have yourself a free ride. Particularly fun in pairs.

**4. Throwing snowballs at opposing coaches from upper levels of the Linc.** Governor Rendell can throw out the first snowball. Can we bring back former Cowboys coach Jimmy Johnson as the target for the inaugural toss?

**3. Shoveling a car out of the snow.** Let's see who gets his car out first before the city snow truck plows it back in.

**2. Drinking beer on the corner with only one glove.** Now we separate the men from the boys. Either we always lost our gloves or never had them to begin with, but facts are facts—I never drank Schmidt's on a street corner with the boys where we all had gloves. So you shared. One of the sad facts of getting older is that you keep losing gloves, but the art of sharing those toast devils has gone the way of hitchhiking. Gone. Forever.

**1. Throwing snowballs at Catholic schoolgirls.** Only the good-looking ones, of course. This event is open only to guys under age 20, like that "Flying Tomato" guy from the 2006 Winter Olympics. It would look downright kinky if Glen and I did it.

Note: Will Bunch writes and edits "Attytood," the *Daily News'* blog, which bills itself as "covering Philly and the world like Cheese Whiz." Bunch previously covered politics for the *Daily News* and spends his free time searching for the world's greatest jukebox.

When it comes to politics, Philly is widely praised as the nation's blogging capital. When it comes to sports blogs . . . well, the record is better than our championship-starved franchises, but there's also still room to move up in the standings. That said, here's a guide to 10 sports blogs that you should check out daily.

### 10. Deadspin—www.deadspin.com.
This property from the growing (and money-making) Gawker Media empire of blogs covers the nation—not just Philly—but it's the place to go for a mixture of mainstream sports news and offbeat stories you otherwise would have missed.

A typical screen of Deadspin posts covers everything from Roger Clemens brushing back his pregnant wife in backyard batting practice to a Peanuts comic strip about the 1962 World Series. Updated frequently, it's the best way to kill time on your office computer that (probably) won't get you fired.

### 9. The Good Phight—www.thegoodphight.com.
From its cracked Liberty Bell to its blood-red hue to that corny "Ph," The Good Phight is a good introduction to the world of "Phlogs"—Phillies-oriented sites that rule the sports blogosphere around here.

With several contributors, The Good Phight touches all the bases, giving "phans"—er, fans—a chance to vote on a question of the day and analyzing the current Phils line-up with a sprinkling of optimism that you're more likely to find on the Web than on, ahem, certain popular sports-talk stations.

### 8. Nest of Death—www.nestofdeath.com.
Philly's a football town, so you'd think we'd have a ton of Eagles blogs. But you'd think wrong. What the Eagles have on the Web is a bunch of message boards. Makes sense when you think about it—blogs and baseball are more about ego, whereas football is a little more faceless and a lot more about community.

The Nest of Death—the name outlived its gritty namesake, the Vet—draws more traffic during football season than most local sports blogs, averaging 130,000 hits per day. That could be for the lively discussion board, or maybe it's the healthy dose of Eagles cheerleader shots.

### 7. Phillies Nation—www.philliesnation.com.
This is another of those red-toned "phlogs" that bills itself as "the most comprehensive" Phillies blog. Host Brian Michael delivers on that promise with a regularly updated site offering riffs on everything from the metaphysical musings of ex-Phillie Darren Daulton to an honest-to-God line graph mapping the progress of pitcher Cory Lidle.

### 6. Flyers Fan Central—www.flyersfancentral.com.
It used to be said that there were only 17,310 hockey fans in Philadelphia, who just happened to sell out the Spectrum

40-50 nights a year. The new building's shown there are few more than that, but you wouldn't know it from the paltry amount of local blogs devoted to the NHL.

That said, PhillyFanCentral.com has a chance of filling the void. It's regularly updated with the latest news and notes about the Fly guys, and has nooks and crannies devoted to hockey chat. For all 17,310 of you.

**5. Shallow Center—www.shallowcenter.com.** The name may sound like a tribute to Doug Glanville, but host Tom Durso is a Philly guy who takes his favorite "shallow" subjects—from our sometimes-beloved baseball franchise to TV's *Lost*—and takes them deep. Thus, you'll find a review of *The Wedding Crashers* next to an essay on ugly american skier Bode Miller. No matter—the center holds.

**4. Balls, Sticks & Stuff—www.ballssticksstuff.com.** How's that for an aggressively male name? In an Internet feel-good story, blogger Tom G. started the site in Virginia because of homesickness for his native Philly, then moved back here in 2005. His site is one of the better produced, with actual interviews, lots of links—even a sense of humor.

**3. A Citizen's Blog—www.philliesblog.blogspot.com.** You might think that Michael Berquist has two strikes against him, since a) he's a lawyer and b) lives in Pittsburgh. That said, Berquist was one of the first Phillies bloggers, and one of the best, with a knack for analyzing stats in a hardcore, Bill James kind of style. Berquist is a Philly two-fer, since he also authors a blog about the Eagles, The Bird Blog—www.thebirdblog.blogspot.com.

**2. The 700 Level—www.the700level.com.** Nobody matches Enrico when it comes to covering the wide world of Philadelphia sports, including the holes—like Sixers and college hoops—that don't get enough coverage elsewhere. He's also more aggressive about linking to other sports blogs, so it's a good jumping-off point for the sports blogosphere. Besides, if there wasn't a Web site named The 700 Level, someone would have to invent one.

**1. Beer Leaguer—www.beerleaguer.typepad.com.** With its old-timey yet slick graphics, and its Reading attytood, Jason Weitzel's Beer Leaguer sets a standard for most other Philly sports blogs. You can always expect timely analysis of the foibles of the Phillies front office, as well as up-close-and-personal looks at future prospects that makes Beer Leaguer a daily read for many "phans."

Note: Daniel Rubin writes the compelling "Blinq" column for *The Philadelphia Inquirer*, a snarky blog covering all things Philadelphia and beyond. Rubin has been a reporter at the *Inquirer* since 1988, except for three years as an international correspondent based in Berlin.

It's hard saying these are the best Philly blogs, because the list changes with the tide, and sometimes people you never heard of come up with brilliant stuff. But these are the 10 that I bookmark in a category called "Blinq Essentials," the ones to read when I'm far away and longing for the sights, sounds, smells, and sweet and sourness of Philadelphia.

**10. Phillyist—www.phillyist.com.** It's a little fey with that mauve background, and sometimes it edges into what *Philadelphia Magazine* might be if it had a blog, but this local edition of a national chain of "ists" has its nose to the ground, scouts bargains, and sports a great sex writer.

**9. Citizen Mom—www.quinnchannel.typepad.com.** Amy Quinn was a newspaperwoman before a blessed event chained her to her Manayunk rowhouse. This is our gain. She writes of whatever's on her mind or on her CD player as her son grows and the chances of landing George Clooney further recede.

**8. Philly—www.dragonballyee.blogs.com.** Albert Yee, aka Dragonball Yee, writes this part-photo, part-lefty politics, part-this-is-what-I-spent-on-these-cool-new-boots blog with the fiery idealism of youth. A youth who moved here and thinks the city rocks.

**7. Philadelphia Will Do—www.willdo.philadelphiaweekly.com.** Written for *Philadelphia Weekly* by the Northeast-bred, Penn-schooled son of a *Daily News* sports copy editor. Daniel McQuade, aka D-Mac, is a prolific prodigy who saves you time by finding the looniest Craigslist postings and *Northeast Times* headlines along with occasional photos of puppies. Why puppies?

**6. This Urban Life—www.thisurbanlife.blogspot.com.** This is Inky shooter Eric Mencher's well-stocked photo blog, the sorts of wild visions he can't always get into the newspaper. Gorgeous.

**5. Things Thrown Five Minutes Ago—www.throwingthings.blogspot.com.** Some of the contributors are from other cities, but most are from here, a group of over-educated wiseasses devoted to such popular cultural confections as *American Idol* and *Lost*. A recent post: "Weezer's abstemious Rivers Cuomo is back at Harvard."

**4. Some Velvet Blog—www.somevelvetblog.blogspot.com.** When WXPN-FM program manager Bruce Warren isn't tinkering with the mix of singer-songwriters at the AAA public radio station, he is writing about and sharing some of the wildest-ass and most interesting music you've never heard of.

**3. Philebrity—www.philebrity.com.** The ironically named "deepest dish," written by Joey Sweeney, a piss-ant with a pea shooter. But a sniper I read a couple times a day. His headlines are illegal.

**2. The Philly Wire—www.phillyfuture.org/aggregator.** It's not one blog—it's a couple hundred of them gathered at Philly Future and excerpted chronologically, so you can taste in one place the full range of political discourse, private rantings, and strange obsessions of some of the area's best blog talent.

**1. Attytood—www.pnionline.com/dnblog/attytood.** Will Bunch writes and blogs wickedly for *The Daily News* and has his finger on the pulse of the lunchpail parts of this metropolis—which is quite a trick for a damned Ivy-Leagued suburban New Yorker.

# Ten Sports "Things" that Philadelphia Could Really Use

We think this is the greatest sports city in America. Still, there are entities that Philadelphia is missing that would make our fandom even better. We realize some items on this wish list are unlikely or impossible. We're just saying. . . .

**10. The Super Bowl.** We're not calling for a domed stadium here. We just don't think there's anything wrong with a Super Bowl played in the real elements.

**9. Better participatory sports.** Take some of those fields in Fairmount Park and let's build a world-class toboggan run. Or how about a body-surfing-friendly wave pool? Hell, there are 9,200 acres in America's largest intra-city public park. Let's use a few of them for something different.

**8. An annual stop on the PGA Tour.** The Delaware Valley has some of the greatest golf courses in America (see Howard Eskin's list on page 218). So how come dippy towns like Milwaukee and Blanc Rapids get annual visits and we don't?

**7. Outdoor hockey.** Ever since the Edmonton Oilers hosted the Montreal Canadiens in 2003, playing shinny in the great outdoors has become trendy. It's been tried in college games in Michigan and Wisconsin, and in the movies (see Mystery, Alaska). Here's our proposal: Once a season, the Flyers host the hated New Jersey Devils in a pond hockey match played in a flooded Citizens Bank Park. We guarantee it would sell out and become a highlight of the annual sports calendar.

**6. Summer Olympics.** Yes, it's the ultimate pipe dream. But there actually are local chamber of commerce and tourism types working on bringing the Games here in 2016. Crew on the Schuylkill. Beach volleyball at the Shore. A marathon that circles Kelly and West River Drives. Hey, if we can host the Republican Convention and Live Eight, we can host anything. Let's show the world how world-class this city truly can be.

**5. Nightlife near the sports complex.** So you leave a Phils, or Flyers, or Sixers game, and you want to hang with your boys to bust balls and relive the highlights. Well, you can head to Chickie's and Pete's and, uh . . . well that's about it. How come, with more than 400 events a year taking place around Broad and Pattison, no other smart business people have added something for post-game (or post-concert) nightlife? A few restaurants, bars, batting cages, mini-golf, anything? Seems to us there's a fortune to be made there.

**4. A Grand Prix event.** We'll be honest and tell you that we're not fans of auto racing. Still, there's something about Formula One cars driven by guys with names like Jarno, Fernando, and Ruebens zipping around actual city streets that draws in even us. Imagine them trying to negotiate past the fountains on the Ben Franklin Parkway. Cities like Detroit, Cleveland, and Indianapolis have hosted American Grand Prix races. We want to be next.

**3. A local college basketball tourney.** Run it at the start of the season. Invite the Big 5 schools, plus Drexel, plus, perhaps, Pitt and Penn State. Call it the Liberty Bell Challenge. Preliminary games at the Palestra and the title contest at the Wachovia Center. We guarantee it would become the toughest ticket of the year.

**2. An American League baseball team.** Yeah, we know—over David Montgomery's dead body. But did you know that Philadelphia is the largest media market in America with just one Major League team? If the Athletics, who left after 1954, don't want to return to 21st and Lehigh, we'll settle for the Royals, who followed the A's in Kansas City. Long-suffering baseball fans in this town deserve choice. And who knows, maybe some competition would spur the Phils to work harder toward making an occasional post-season.

**1. Real college football.** Philadelphia might be the worst college football town of any big city in America. Why? Because Happy Valley is three hours away and the putrid product that Temple runs out there attracts fewer fans than the WNBA (and, no, we're not calling for adding that product to town). Imagine how different autumn would be here if we could all rally around Local U every Saturday afternoon.

# My Favorite Phillies Memories :: Harry Kalas

Note: Since 1971, Harry Kalas has been the voice of the Phillies. In 2002, he was inducted into the Baseball Hall of Fame in Cooperstown, N.Y.

**10. I'll start with the opening of Citizens Bank Park in 2004.** It was my third stadium opening—I started with the Astros in '65, the same year they opened the Astrodome. Then I started with the Phils in 1971, the same year the Vet opened. Citizens Bank Park is a beautiful place, and a great place to work. And I was truly honored to have a restaurant named after me. I'm thinking this is the last stadium opening I'll be a part of.

**9. It isn't a Phils memory, but it was a thrill to meet my boyhood hero, Mickey Vernon,** who lives in Delaware County. I was 10 years old when my dad took me to my first game, in Chicago, to see the White Sox against the Washington Senators. We sat behind the Washington dugout. During a rain delay, Vernon picked me out of the stands and sat me on the Senators' bench. He talked to me and even gave me a ball. I became a fan for life, so it was great to meet him again all those years later.

**8. Any game Steve Carlton pitched was special for me.** I always had an extra bounce in my step when Lefty had the ball. He was a joy to watch at work. You knew the games were going to be quicker—he didn't waste a lot of time or pitches. I got along famously with Lefty. He was a good friend and would talk baseball with me until the cows came home. It helped that I didn't carry a notebook.

**7. The closing of the Vet was, of course, a special day for me.** I was there from the beginning in 1971 to the end in 2003. Sure, it had seen better days, but I still have so many fond memories of the old place. It was special to be honored as the person they asked to pull down the final number counting down the days on the outfield wall.

**6. Rick Wise pitched a no-hitter against the Reds in 1971.** I was 35 years old and it was the first Major League no-hitter I got to call, in my first year with the Phils. Wise also hit two home runs in that game—can you believe that? What a fun way for me to break in.

**5. I didn't get to call it, but Tug McGraw's final pitch to strike out Willie Wilson in the 1980 World Series was so special.** Back then, the hometown announcers didn't get to be part of the World Series. After 1980, Phils fans made such a fuss about it that baseball changed the rule, so I got to call the '83 Series. Tug was such a positive guy, always smiling, always appreciative of the fact that he had a chance to do what he did. I loved him.

**4. Michael Jack Schmidt's 500th home run, April 18, 1987, against Don Robinson of the Pirates at Three Rivers Stadium in Pittsburgh.** Out of Michael Jack's 548 homers, I probably called all but a handful. What a privilege to call his Hall of Fame career. I was told that they played my call for Mike after the game and he choked up. I'm flattered.

**3. The 1993 club, from Day One, has to be next.** Not much was expected from that crew and yet they took us to the World Series. What a cast of characters—Krukker, The Dude, my current partner, Larry Andersen, and the best team leader ever, Dutch Daulton. What a fun bunch to be around. And what a great team, in the real sense of team. So many come-from-behind wins.

**2. The 1980 National League Championship Series against the Houston Astros was unforgettable.** Remember, it was a best-of-five series, and four of those games went into extra innings. Imagine being down 5-2 to Nolan Ryan in Game 5 and coming back to win against a Hall of Fame pitcher. When we won that one, I knew we'd win the World Series.

**1. Undoubtedly, the top is my 27 years alongside Whitey Ashburn.** There was a combination of things making it special—his friendship, his expertise, his sense of humor. We spent every night together in the booth and on the road, and it never stopped being fun. I still think about His Whiteness every single day.

**If I can add one more,** it was a special moment for me, of course, when I was inducted into the Baseball Hall of Fame in 2002. It was just a breathtaking weekend, the ultimate honor from the game I love. You know what was most special about it? The huge number of Phillies fans who came to Cooperstown for the weekend. It was a sea of red hats.

No book like this would be complete without our take on the greatest athletes ever. We started with a list of 10, expanded it to 25 and then, well, kept asking ourselves, "How can we leave off *this* guy?"

Obviously, it's tough to compare the magnitude of Eagles and Phillies with that of boxers and Olympians. But we tried to spread the wealth. Heck, we even have three women represented.

Actually, the list's title is a lie. In this case, "all-time" means the last 60 years. Our starting point is the end of World War II—so don't think we hosed Jimmy Foxx. And we required that team-sports athletes played college or pro ball here—not just high school—so all apologies to guys like Reggie Jackson. And the individual-sports athletes also had to hang around a little during their competitive years. See you later, Carl Lewis.

One more guideline: Only those years in a local uniform count. So those Curt Schilling World Series moments in Arizona and Boston? They never happened. At least not for our purposes.

Like many lists in this book, this one will certainly promote debate. And if you think we snubbed Randall Cunningham, or overrated Allen Iverson—well, that's your opinion. Here's our opinion, and we don't mind if it gets you all riled up. In fact, we hope it does.

**100. Tug McGraw.** Leaped off the mound as the Phils won their only World Series in 1980. Five post-season saves in the red pinstripes.

**99. Jerry Sisemore and Stan Walters.** It's a bit of a cheat listing them together, but we didn't want to leave off either granite-like tackle of the Vermeil-era Eagles.

**98. Scott Rolen.** Ah, what might have been. Rookie of the Year in 1997. Three-time Gold Glover as a Phillie. A first-class jerk, but a great player.

**97. Bob Brown.** Nicknamed "Boomer" because that's the sound he made hitting opponents. Spent five seasons with the Eagles, eventually making the Hall of Fame. Weighed 285 in an era (1964–68) when most linemen weighed 40 pounds less. One of three Eagles named "Brown" on this list; can you guess the others?

**96. Dave Poulin.** Considered by many to be the best Flyers captain this side of Bobby Clarke. Never a great scorer (31 goals was his max during seven seasons here), but a key component to many winning teams.

**95. Harold Johnson.** Much-underrated Manayunk fighter won the light-heavyweight title in 1961 at age 34, and held it for seven defenses. Career record of 76-11, with 32 knockouts. Member of the Boxing Hall of Fame.

**94. Lisa Raymond.** The Wayne native was an NCAA tennis champion. Professionally, she ranked as high as No. 1 in doubles and No. 15 in singles.

**93. George McGinnis.** He played just three seasons with the Sixers (1976–78), but averaged 21.6 points per game and gave this city's hoops fans someone worth watching until Doc showed up.

**92. Lenny Dykstra.** The offensive sparkplug behind the '93 Phils. He got on base 325 times that season, and scored 143 runs.

**91. Marty Liquori.** Qualified for the Olympics (1,500 meters) as a 19-year-old Villanova freshman. Won three NCAA one-mile titles and beat world-record holder Jim Ryun in the "Dream Mile" in 1971. Set four American distance records within 11 days in 1977.

**90. Paul Palmer.** Owls tailback finished second (to Vinny Testaverde) in the 1986 Heisman Trophy balloting, a season in which he rushed for 1,866 yards. Proof that football actually existed at one point at Temple University.

**89. Clyde Simmons.** The "other" defensive end in Buddy Ryan's system. Led the NFL with 19 sacks in 1992. His 76.5 sacks as an Eagle rank second in franchise history, behind someone whose name will show up later on this list.

**88. Doug Collins.** A four-time all-star whose Sixers career was cut short by injury. His career field-goal percentage (.501) and free-throw percentage (.833) both rank near the top in franchise history.

**87. Vicki Huber**. Dominated NCAA middle-distance events as an undergrad at Nova in the late '80s. Named America's top female college athlete in 1989. Injuries derailed her goal of Olympic gold.

**86. Bob Boone.** Much-overlooked backbone of Dallas Green's title team. Two Gold Gloves and three all-star appearances as a Phil. Really knew how to handle pitchers and block the plate.

**85. Chris Short.** Fourteen seasons in a Phils uniform. Between 1963–67, his ERA was an impressive 2.82. His 132 wins are fourth all-time for the franchise. On a separate note, he holds about every career pitching record by a native Delawarean.

**84. Tim Brown.** An exciting, elusive runner during his eight seasons with the Eagles. In 1963, he set an NFL record with 2,425 combined yards (rushing, receiving, returns). In 1966, he became the first player to return two kickoffs for touchdowns in the same game. Against Dallas. Thank you.

**83. Curt Schilling.** Another name that makes you wonder what might have been had he stayed. Most valuable player of the 1993 NLCS, in which he bewitched the Braves. Five times during his Phils career he finished in the NL top 10 in ERA.

**82. Bobby Abreu.** Not exactly Pete Rose in the hustle department, or Reggie Jackson in the clutch. Still, Mr. Stats has to be respected for his .412 on-base percentage. Entering 2006, he ranked seventh all-time in stolen bases for the Phils, fifth in extra-base hits.

**81. Joe Verdeur.** La Salle grad won the gold medal and set an Olympic record in the 200-meter breaststroke in the 1948 London games. In his career, he set 19 world records in swimming.

**80. Seth Joyner.** A terrific playmaking linebacker who deserved to make more than the two Pro Bowls in which he represented the Eagles. Leader on the field and in the locker room.

**79. Bill Bradley.** Holds the Eagles records for interceptions in a season (11) and career (34). An outstanding safety who never played for a winning team during his eight seasons here.

**78. Reds Bagnell.** All-American running back for Penn in 1950, a year in which he finished third in the Heisman voting. His 490 offensive yards in one game against Dartmouth ranked as a national record for years.

**77. Jim Bunning.** Came from Detroit in 1964 and anchored a pitching staff that kept the Phils in the race until, oh, you know the story. Won 19 games in each of his first three seasons with the Phils. Usually gave the team 40-plus starts and 300 innings a season.

**76. Rod Brind'Amour.** This teen heartthrob could kill penalties, shadow other teams' scorers, and run a power play. Scored 235 goals in eight-plus years as a Flyer. He was the team's top playoff performer (13 goals) in the 1997 run to the Stanley Cup Finals.

**75. Joey Giardello.** South Philly Hall of Famer won the 160-pound world title at age 33. Career record: 100 wins, 25 losses, 32 knockouts.

**74. Rick Tocchet.** A triple threat who could score, pass, and fight for the Flyers. Scored as many as 45 goals in a season and registered as many as 299 penalty minutes. A truly unique player.

**73. Troy Vincent.** Played in five straight Pro Bowls for the Eagles; only Reggie White and Pete Pihos topped that streak. What a great secondary the Eagles had in the early 2000s, with Vincent, Bobby Taylor, Brian Dawkins and, uh . . . Damon Moore.

**72. Jim Furyk.** West Chester native had 10 PGA Tournament wins through 2005, including the 2003 U.S. Open. Career earnings: $24,232,739.

**71. Ferris Fain.** The only guy on this list from the A's, for whom he won batting titles in 1951 and '52. His career on-base percentage (.424) is among the 15 best in Major League history.

**70. Eamonn Coghlan.** Irish runner starred for Jumbo Elliott's Villanova teams in the 1970s. His 3:49:78 mile at the Meadowlands in 1983 remains the American indoor record and stood as the world record for 14 years.

**69. Johnny Callison.** Three-time all-star and, of course, MVP of the 1964 All-Star Game, which he won with a walk-off homer. Played the entire decade of the 1960s for the Phils.

**68. Bobby Jones.** Six-time NBA all-defense first-teamer as a Sixer. Others scored; he did the dirty work. When he did shoot, he did it well—note the .550 field-goal percentage.

**67. Brian Westbrook.** Another Nova guy, who's here more for his college career than his fine work as an Eagle to date. Set five NCAA records, including 9,885 career all-purpose yards. Has a real chance to move up this list in coming years.

**66. Pelle Lindbergh.** The NHL's first great European goalie, he won the 1985 Vezina Trophy and established himself as a fan favorite in his three-plus seasons. Everyone's heart was broken on November 12, 1985.

**65. Vic Seixas.** Tennis Hall of Famer won the 1953 Wimbledon singles title and the 1954 U.S. Open singles title. Played in more U.S. Opens than anyone ever and more Davis Cup matches than any American this side of John McEnroe.

**64. Andrew Toney.** "The Boston Strangler" tormented the Celtics and thrilled Sixers fans through the 1980s. Shot exactly .500 for his career. Very few guards today ever approach that percentage.

**63. Dawn Staley.** Dobbins Tech star was two-time USA Basketball Female Athlete of the Year. A fixture on national teams from 1989–2004. Played in three Olympics, and won three gold medals. Chosen to carry the American flag at the opening ceremonies of the 2004 games in Athens.

**62. Mark Recchi.** Bet you didn't remember that he holds the Flyers record for points in a season—123—in 1992–93. In two tours of duty, he totaled 232 goals and 395 assists, both in the franchise's top 10.

**61. Jerome Brown.** In just five seasons he established himself as an all-time favorite of Eagles fans. Big defensive tackle was the soul of the Eagles' Gang Green defense. Made two Pro Bowls before dying in car accident at age 27.

**60. Tom Brookshier.** One of the ultimate "Philly guys" on this list, although he comes from New Mexico. A slow cornerback—even in the days before the NFL was a track meet—but made up for it with toughness. The Eagles were 18-3 (including the 1960 title win) in his last 21 games.

**59. Larry Bowa.** Slap hitter who parlayed a fiery temper and great hands into five All-Star appearances. Just two players—Hall of Famers Schmidt and Ashburn—played more games in a Phillies uniform.

**58. Willie Mosconi.** Considered the greatest pool player of all time. He won 18 U.S. Championships and 13 World Championships in an era when pool was front-page sports news. Once ran 526 consecutive balls. Big Daddy once ran four.

**57. Eric Allen.** Intercepted 34 passes in his seven Eagles seasons, returning five for touchdowns. His 94-yard TD return against the Jets in 1993 is among the most exciting plays in franchise history. Five-time Pro Bowler in Philadelphia.

**56. Jameer Nelson.** St. Joe's point guard put up lofty career stats—2,094 points, 713 assists. He was the 2004 NCAA National Player of the Year when he and Delonte West led the Hawks to a 27-0 regular-season record.

**55. Ron Jaworski.** A blue-collar quarterback who withstood the fans' booing to set most of the Eagles' career passing records. NFL's Player of the Year in 1980, when he took the Birds to the Super Bowl.

**54. Al Wistert.** Captain of the Eagles' 1948–49 championship teams. A five-time All-Pro, the 215-pound two-way tackle opened holes on offense and stuffed the run on defense. Cited by historians as the best defensive lineman of the post-World War II era.

**53. Lionel Simmons.** The Big 5's all-time scoring leader with 3,217 points in four seasons at La Salle. The Explorers finished 30-2 his senior season and registered their last NCAA Tournament win. National Player of the Year in 1990. His seven-year NBA career was hindered by injuries.

**52. John LeClair.** Scored 50-plus goals in three straight seasons as left winger on the "Legion of Doom." Twice led the NHL in plus/minus, and twice was named first-team all-star. He'd rank higher on this list but for his mediocre post-season performances.

**51. Greg Luzinski.** Finished second in NL MVP voting in both 1975 and 1977. Averaged 32 homers and 112 RBIs per season between 1975–78. His 223 parabolic "Bull Blasts" thrilled Phils fans.

**50. Reggie Leach.** "The Rifle" combined a 100-mile-per-hour shot with a quick release to rack up 306 regular-season goals for the Flyers. His 19 in the 1976 playoffs earned him the Conn Smythe Trophy. His career was shortened by alcoholism, which he later overcame.

**49. Bill Bergey.** Rough, big (250 pounds) middle linebacker who, unfortunately, spent most of his career on those bad Eagles teams of the mid-70s. Final game of his career was the 1980 Super Bowl. Three-time Eagles MVP, he registered 1,200 tackles in his seven seasons here.

**48. Rick MacLeish.** Graceful, occasionally lackadaisical winger amassed the sixth-most goals (328) and fourth-most points (697) in Flyers history. He was the NHL's leading playoff scorer in both of the title years of 1974–75. Scored the lone goal in the 1-0 Cup-clinching victory over the Bruins in 1974.

**47. Matthew Saad Muhammad.** South Philly native won the light heavyweight belt in 1979 and defended it eight times during a Hall of Fame career. Twenty-nine KOs among his 39 pro wins.

**46. Del Ennis.** Underrated and underappreciated Phillie who got MVP votes in seven separate seasons—mostly playing for bad teams. Between 1949–55 he knocked in 780 runs, behind only Duke Snider and Gil Hodges among National Leaguers.

**45. Cliff Anderson.** Six-foot-four center averaged 20.6 points and 14.6 rebounds in his three-year St. Joe's career. All-American in 1967. His 1,228 rebounds remain a Hawks career record.

**44. Ron Hextall.** The ultimate Flyer, he guarded the nets with anger and bravado. His 240 regular-season wins are a franchise record and his Conn Smythe performance against Gretzky's Oilers in the 1987 Finals was one of the greatest ever. First goalie in NHL history to directly score a goal.

**43. Brian Dawkins.** Ferocious, emotional free safety is, pound-for-pound, one of the hardest hitters in Eagles history. A tremendous combination of skills—as 28 interceptions and 17 sacks through 2005 would attest.

**42. Joe Fulks.** "Jumping Joe" was basketball's first jump shooter. Led the Basketball Association of America (the NBA's forerunner) in scoring in 1946, its first season. His 63 points in a 1949 game was the NBA record for a decade. Named to NBA's Silver Anniversary team in 1971.

**41. Norm Van Brocklin.** "The Dutchman" spent just three seasons as an Eagle but led the team from last place to the NFL title. In 1960—at age 34—he threw for 24 touchdowns as the Eagles went 10-2. One of the great on-field leaders in Philadelphia history.

**40. Neil Johnston.** During an eight-year Warriors career (1951–59), he led the NBA in scoring three times and was named a first-team all-star four times. Six-foot-eight hook-shot artist started as a pitcher in the Phillies system; he turned to hoops only after an arm injury. Member of the Basketball Hall of Fame.

**39. Eric Lindros.** MVP in 1995, a year he tied for the NHL scoring title. Totaled 659 points in 486 games, the best point-per-game ratio in Flyers history. But, let's face it; this was the nastiest divorce in local sports history. Whoever's to blame, it was a colossal disappointment.

**38. Guy Rodgers.** Consensus All-American at Temple in 1957 and 1958, the year in which he led the Owls to the Final Four. A prototype of the modern-day point guard. Three-time Big 5 MVP.

**37. Mark Howe.** More goals (138) and assists (342) than any defenseman in Flyers history. His plus/minus was an amazing plus-85 in 1985–86. An underrated talent who belongs in hockey's Hall of Fame.

**36. Randall Cunningham.** "The Ultimate Weapon." An electric, sometimes infuriating QB who could pass, run, and—yes—even kick. In 11 seasons as an Eagle he emerged as the second leading all-time passer and fourth leading all-time rusher. NFL Player of the Year in 1990.

**35. Harold Carmichael.** Eagles all-time leader in receptions (589), yards (8,978), and TDs (79). A six-foot-eight target with good hands. Once held the NFL record by catching a pass in 127 straight games.

**34. Richie Allen.** NL's Rookie of the Year in 1964, when he led the league in runs and extra-base hits. His 42-ounce bat slugged the most-monstrous homers in Phillies history. Batted over .300 each of first four seasons.

**33. Donovan McNabb.** Career .682 winning percentage going into 2006 among NFL's best ever. Only QB in history to throw more than 30 TDs and fewer than 10 interceptions in the same season. Has been known to disappoint in big games. Best chance of anyone on this list to move up.

**32. Tim Kerr.** Only Flyer to top 50 goals four times. Scored 34 power play goals in 1985–86. Tough as nails and a class act, he played through personal setbacks and serious injuries, which ultimately shortened his career.

**31. Maurice Cheeks.** Mo holds Sixers records for steals (1,942) and assists (6,212). Spent his career making many others on this list look good. Hallmark moment was his exclamation-point slam-dunk against the Lakers in the 1983 Finals. Why is he not in the Hall of Fame?

**30. Brian Propp.** Second all-time in goals (369) and assists (480) for Flyers. Scored winning goal in his first NHL game. Registered 28 points in 1987 playoffs. Always a bridesmaid, he played in five Cup Finals—three with the Flyers—without ever winning.

**29. Pete Retzlaff.** Played 11 seasons for the Eagles, making five Pro Bowls—two as a wide receiver, three as a tight end. Key member of 1960 championship team. His 1965 season—66 catches, 1,190 yards, 10 TDs—is among the best ever for a tight end.

**28. Howard Porter.** Three-time All-American (1969–71) at Nova, where he averaged 22.8 points and 14.8 rebounds. Named NCAA Final Four MVP after Wildcats nearly toppled UCLA in 1971. Great combination of size and athleticism.

**27. Pete Rose.** His best years were spent elsewhere, but it's fair to say the Phillies never would have won a World Series without his contributions. Still had enough after arriving here (at age 37) to twice lead the NL in times-on-base. Four-time all-star as a Phil.

**26. Mike Quick.** Graceful, disciplined receiver made five straight Pro Bowls. Caught more TDs than anyone not named Jerry Rice from 1984–88—one of them a 99-yarder. Broken leg at age 29 stole his career. Among five Eagles receivers ranking between No. 21

and 35 on this list.

**25. Hal Greer.** Played entire 15-year career with the Sixers (nee Nationals), retiring as the sixth-leading scorer in NBA history (he is now 22nd). Top 10 in NBA in points and assists three separate seasons. Played in every all-star game from 1961–70.

**24. Pete Pihos.** "Golden Greek" named all-NFL first-teamer five times on offense, once as a defensive end. Led league in catches three straight seasons. Scored 63 TDs in just 107 games. Hall of Famer caught game-winning TD in 1949 Championship game.

**23. Kenny Durrett.** Best player in Big 5 since its 1955 inception. Had point-guard skills in a six-foot-eight body. La Salle star averaged 27.0 points as a senior, 23.7 for his career. Blew out knee as an All-American senior in 1971.

**22. Wilbert Montgomery.** Sixth-round pick became Eagles all-time rusher for season (1,512 yards in 1979) and career (6,538 yards). First player in team history to rush for more than 1,000 yards three different times. No one will forget his 42-yard TD sprint to open the 1980 NFC title game against Dallas.

**21. Tommy McDonald.** During his seven seasons here (1957–63), just one NFL player—Jim Brown—scored more than the 66 TDs he put up for the Birds. Deep threat averaged 19 yards per catch. Caught 35-yard TD in 1960 NFL title game. Smallest player (five-foot-nine) in Pro Football Hall of Fame.

**20. Bernard Hopkins.** "The Executioner" won 160-pound world title in 1992, held it for 13 years. Made 20 successful title defenses, destroying Trinidad and De La Hoya along the way. Career record: 46-4-1, with 31 KOs. A genuine Philadelphia guy. Outspoken and strategically brilliant.

**19. Moses Malone.** Arrived in 1982 to help a team that owed us one, and delivered NBA title. In 1982–83, he was league MVP for the regular season and Finals, all-NBA first-team, and all-defensive team. Played only five seasons in Philly, but what an impact—three times led league in rebounding, four times averaged more than 22 points per game. "Fo', fo', fo."

**18. Billy Cunningham.** The only guy who makes the lists of top players and top coaches here. The sixth man on the 1966–67 title team, he averaged 20.8 points and 10.1 rebounds over nine Sixers seasons. Three-time all-NBA first team. Named to league's 50th Anniversary All-Time Team.

**17. Bill Barber.** Hockey Hall of Famer was the left winger on Broad St. Bullies' high-scoring LCB Line. Ranks first in goals (420) in franchise history. Often overshadowed by more-colorful teammates, he was the hallmark of consistency—his nine 30-goal seasons are most of any Flyer. Scored 31 shorthanded goals and triggered Flyers power play from the point.

**16. Tom Gola.** Starred at La Salle High, La Salle College, and for the Warriors. Consensus All-American three straight years. Led La Salle to NIT title in 1951 (when it meant something) and NCAA title in 1954. His 2,201 career rebounds remain an NCAA record. Five-time all-star as a Warrior. Ranked in NBA top-10 in both assists and rebounds two separate years.

**15. Charles Barkley**. Tenacious, entertaining "Sir Charles" led NBA in rebounds in 1986–87, despite standing just under six-foot-five. Four-time first-team all-NBA and six-time all-star in his eight seasons here. Averaged 23.3 points and 11.6 rebounds as a Sixer. His .576 field goal percentage ranks second only to Wilt Chamberlain. A tremendous offensive force and maybe the most fun athlete ever to play in our city.

**14. Richie Ashburn.** Showed up from Nebraska and gave us 12 years as a great centerfielder, 30-plus as an even greater broadcaster. Won two batting titles for Phils and four times led NL in on-base percentage—before it was a trendy stat. Best career batting average (.311) of any post-World War II Phil. Deer-like outfielder and base runner, too often overshadowed by other great centerfielders of his era.

**13. Paul Arizin.** A high school, college, and pro star in Philadelphia. National college player of the year in 1950 at Nova, leading nation with 25.3-point average. Scored 85 points in a game, 1949. Made NBA all-star team each of his 10 seasons with the Warriors. Twice led NBA in scoring. Took Warriors to 1956 championship, averaging 28.9 points per game in playoffs.

**12. Allen Iverson.** Certainly the most controversial man on this list. First pick of 1996 draft won four scoring titles and the 2001 league MVP Award. Two-time All-Star Game MVP. Took Sixers to 2001 Finals, averaging 32.9 points in 22 playoff games. At under six-feet and 165 pounds, he regularly topped NBA charts in minutes, shots, steals, and tumbling to the hardwood. Only two players—Chamberlain and Jordan—top "The Answer's" career 28 per-game scoring average.

**11. Reggie White.** "Minister of Defense" was Birds' greatest lineman, registering 124 sacks in eight seasons. First game as Eagle: 10 tackles, 2-1/2 sacks. Had 21 sacks (one short of then-NFL record) in strike-shortened 1987. Cornerstone of "Gang Green" defense. At 295 pounds, he could outrun many running backs. His departure in 1993 started the downfall of the Braman-Kotite Eagles and led to a Packers Super Bowl victory. Died at age 43, made Hall of Fame 13 months later.

**10. Robin Roberts.** Six straight 20-win seasons for the Phils. Between 1950–55, this workhouse averaged 27 complete games, 323 innings, and 23 wins a season. Before the Cy Young Award existed, he won two "Sporting News Pitcher of the Year" awards. Backbone of the 1950 Whiz Kids at age 23. In his best season, 1952, he won 28 and finished second in MVP voting. His 234 Phils wins are second only to Steve Carlton. Gave up more homers (505) than any pitcher in history.

**9. Bernie Parent.** "Only God saves more." Top goalie of his era posted shutouts in both Cup-clinching games. Backbone of those title teams, winning back-to-back Vezina Trophies (top goalie) and Conn Smythes (playoff MVP) in 1974 and '75. His combined goals-against average those years—1.95 for regular season, 1.96 for playoffs. Fifty regular-season shutouts as a Flyer, plus six more in post-season. First Flyer in Hall of Fame. Eye injury ended his career at age 33.

**8. Steve Van Buren.** One of just seven running backs named to NFL's 75th anniversary team. A half-century after his retirement, he still holds many Eagles records, including 18 TDs in a season and 205 rush yards in a game. Ran for 196 yards in 1949 title game. Led NFL in rushing four times, and twice topped 1,000 yards in 12-game seasons. Nicknamed "Wham-Bam" for the sound it made when he hit the line. First Eagle elected to Pro Football Hall of Fame.

**7. Julius Erving.** Changed game of basketball before he got here and Sixers' fate after arriving in 1976. MVP in 1981, all-star each of his 11 seasons here. Five-time all-NBA first-teamer. "We owe you one." Despite highlight-film status, was an amazingly consistent player, averaging over 20 points per game nine straight seasons. "Doctor J's" gravity-defying, floating baseline scoop against the Lakers in the 1980 Finals may be most spectacular shot in NBA history.

**6. Joe Frazier.** "Smokin' Joe" won Olympic gold in 1964, the world heavyweight title four years later. His 1971 Madison Square Garden defense over Muhammad Ali established his status as a Hall of Famer; indeed, his trilogy of fights against Ali are regarded as boxing's greatest-ever spectacles. Career record of 32-4-1, losing twice each to Ali and George Foreman. His 27 KO victims include solid fighters Jimmy Ellis, Bob Foster, George Chuvalo, and Jerry Quarry.

**5. Chuck Bednarik.** Two-time All-American at Penn—at center and linebacker. Third in 1947 Heisman voting, heading a defense that gave up just 35 points in eight games. Listed by College Football News as the 42nd best player ever. Even better as a pro, giving Eagles 14 Hall of Fame seasons, most as a two-way player. "Concrete Charlie" is recalled for his shattering hit on Frank Gifford and game-ending tackle in 1960 NFL title game. Named to NFL's 75th Anniversary team.

**4. Bobby Clarke.** Did more to define his franchise than any player here, by instilling a work ethic and nastiness in the Flyers. Three-time MVP, two-time Stanley Cup champion. Twice led NHL in assists, three times topped 100 points. Overtime goal vs. Bruins in Game 2 of '74 Finals turned series to Flyers. Holds most franchise career scoring records. Great passer, face-off man, always came out of corner with puck. Plus/minus for career an amazing plus-506. Never booed (at least as a player).

**3. Steve Carlton.** Won four Cy Young Awards; no NL pitcher won more. "Lefty's" 1972 season—27 wins, 1.97 ERA for a 59-win team—is one of best in baseball history. A horse, he topped 250 innings 10 times for the Phils. Holds franchise records for wins (241), starts (499), and strikeouts (3,031). First-ballot Hall of Famer. Started and won two games—including clincher—in 1980 World Series. Said Willie Stargell: "Hitting him is like trying to drink coffee with a fork."

**2. Mike Schmidt.** Without question the best third baseman ever. Led NL in homers eight times. His 548 HRs rank seventh among pre-steroid players. A warehouse full of awards: Three-time MVP, 10 Gold Gloves, 12 All-Star appearances. Played 18 seasons in Philadelphia, most of any athlete. In best season, 1980, had 48 homers, 121 RBIs, won World Series MVP. Elected to Hall of Fame in 1995 with 96 percent of vote, fourth-highest ever. Cool, aloof, always professional.

**1. Wilt Chamberlain.** The numbers boggle: 30.1 points per game for a career, 50.4 for a season, 100 in a single night. The most dominant, revolutionary player in basketball history. Overbrook High grad only played seven pro seasons here, but what years they were, including the 1967 title year in which he won one of his four MVP awards (all in Philly). All-time NBA leader in rebounds, with 22.9 per game. At various times with Warriors and Sixers, he led league in scoring, rebounds, assists (!), shooting percentage, and women bedded. "The Dipper" would top this list even if we did it for the nation.

# Photography Credits:

Front cover photo: Pier Nicola D'Amico
Back cover photo: National Baseball Hall of Fame Library, Cooperstown, N.Y.

p. 13: © Jay Gorodetzer/Corbis
p. 21: Temple University Libraries, Urban Archives, Philadelphia, PA
p. 56: © Ray Stubblebine/Reuters/Landov
p. 59: AP Images
p. 63: © Michael Rougier/Time Life Pictures/Getty Images
p. 66: © Evan Agostini/Getty Images
p. 75: AP Images. Temple University Libraries, Urban Archives, Philadelphia, PA
p. 90: AP Images
p. 96: Temple University Libraries, Urban Archives, Philadelphia, PA
p. 113: © Jed Jacobsohn/Getty Images
p. 117: © Tom Mihalek/AFP/Getty Images
p. 127: Reprinted by permission from The Philadelphia Inquirer
p. 128: AP Images
p. 131: © Tom Mihalek/AFP/Getty Images
pp. 142, 149, 150, 155, 169 & 176: AP Images
p. 180: © Reuters/Corbis
p. 181: © Patrick Simione/Corbis
p. 183: AP Images
p. 197: © Ray Stubblebine/Reuters/Corbis
p. 246: © Bettmann/Corbis
p. 248: National Baseball Hall of Fame Library, Cooperstown, N.Y.
p. 261: AP Images
p. 272: © John W. McDonough/Sports Illustrated
p. 273: © Bruce Bennett Studios/Getty Images

# Index